BOOKS BY MARTHA ROSE SHULMAN

Supper Club Chez Martha Rose   1988
Gourmet Vegetarian Feasts   1987
Spicy Vegetarian Feasts   1986
Garlic Cookery   1984
Herbs and Honey Cookery   1984
Fast Vegetarian Feasts   1982, 1986
The Vegetarian Feast   1979

COLLABORATIONS
Dr. Lendon Smith's Teenage Diet   1986
with Lendon Smith, M.D.
Stress, Diet and Your Heart   1982
with Dean Ornish, M.D.

Supper Club Chez Martha Rose

Supper Club
Chez Martha Rose

MARTHA ROSE SHULMAN

Illustrations by Peters Day

ATHENEUM   *New York*   1988

Atheneum
Macmillan Publishing Company
866 Third Avenue, New York, N.Y. 10022

LOC 88-31701

Printed in the United States of America

DESIGN BY LAURA HOUGH

A ma chère Christine, sans laquelle tout cela n'aurait pas été
possible

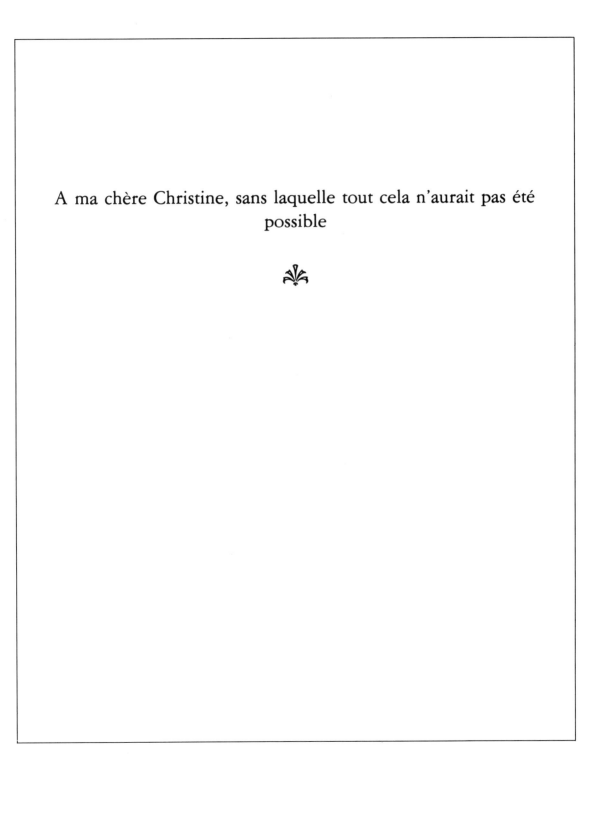

People ask me: why do you write about food, and eating and drinking? Why don't you write about the struggle for power and security, and about love, the way others do? . . .

The easiest answer is to say that, like most other humans, I am hungry. . . .

. . . We must eat. If, in the face of that dread fact, we can find other nourishment, and tolerance and compassion for it, we'll be no less full of human dignity.

There is a communion of more than our bodies when bread is broken and wine drunk. And that is my answer, when people ask me: Why do you write about hunger, and not wars or love?

M. F. K. FISHER,
Foreword to The Gastronomical Me

Contents

Author's Preface xiii

Acknowledgments xix

Introduction 1

SUPPER CLUB CHEZ MARTHA 1

ENTERTAINING ON A SMALL OR GRAND SCALE 6

INCREASING RECIPES FOR LARGE GROUPS 8

SEATING PLANS 8

ABOUT MY CUISINE 10

PART ONE: SUPPER CLUB MENUS 13

Some Basics: Breads, Pasta, and Piecrusts 15

September 47

October 61

November 77

November, continued: "Le Jour du Merci Donant," or More Thanksgiving Delights 91

December 101

January 111

February 125

March 135

April 145

May 155

June 163

Two July Menus 173

August 185

PART TWO: SPECIAL EVENTS 195

Tex-Mex in Paris 197
The Migathon 199
Tex-Mex Buffet for an International Herald Tribune Staff Party 200
New Year's Eve Chez Martha 209
A Picnic on the Seine 221

PART THREE: SPECIAL PEOPLE 231

Chez Christine 233
Recipes from Domaine Tempier 253

PART IV: FAVORITE DISHES FROM SMALL DINNER PARTIES 277

Author's Preface

Nothing has influenced and improved my cooking more than living in France. How could it not? France has lightened my touch, refined my palate, and broadened my repertoire. Over the years—I have lived in Paris since 1981—my dishes have become less complicated and my menus more imaginative. My cuisine has always been a low-fat, meatless one. It continues to be that, but now I cook a lot of fish, and I learned to do that here. My teachers were Lulu Peyraud, the wife of a winemaker in the south of France, and Gerard Alemandou, chef-proprietor of La Cagouille, one of the best fish restaurants in Paris, where I worked for three weeks in 1985.

My love affair with this country began in 1977, when I was living in Austin, Texas. I had been a professional cook for four years and had just gotten a contract for my first cookbook, *The Vegetarian Feast.* I was working at developing an elegant, low-fat meatless cuisine. At that point I was much more influenced by Mexican and Middle Eastern food than by European cooking, and all of my traveling had been to the south rather than across the Atlantic. Still, I had begun to teach myself the basics of French cuisine, and was experimenting with applying French techniques to more wholesome, lower-fat dishes.

At this time—the mid-seventies—great changes were taking place in France. Michel Guérard had appeared on the French gastronomic scene with his *cuisine minceur,* a very sophisticated low-calorie cuisine. He was one of a new breed of chefs, whose *nouvelle cuisine* was much lighter than the classical food of Escoffier. I first read about Guérard in *The New Yorker,* and a few years later, in 1977, I came across an inspiring cookbook by Roy Andries de Groot called *Revolutionizing French Cooking,* about the new chefs— people like Michel Guérard, Alain Chapel, Jacques Manière, Frédy Girardet. I was excited and curious about what these chefs were doing because they were incorporating a commitment to a healthier way of eating into haute cuisine. My goal was to create a meatless cuisine that didn't have a "brown rice and veggies" image, and although the French chefs weren't vegetarian, their principles were the same ones that had always guided me: good taste and health, with the idea that one should not be sacrificed for the other. But the sophistication of the French chefs was beyond anything I had ever come across, and as I studied and cooked from de Groot's book, I became convinced that it was time for me to go to France.

My brother was then studying medicine in Tours, so I wrote to him and his wife and told them I was coming, and hired a French tutor to help me brush up on the French I hadn't studied since high school, nine years earlier. I also wrote to all the chefs in de Groot's book. I described what I was doing, and asked them if they would prepare a vegetarian meal for me when I came to France, which I would then write about (this was a gamble, since I had never sold a magazine story in my life). Charles Barrier in Tours, Michel Guérard in Eugénie-les-Bains, Jacques Manière at Dodin Bouffant in Paris, and Roland Magne, at Au Pactole in Paris, agreed to do this; it made me feel I was coming to France with a definite purpose.

I felt at home in France from the moment I arrived, and everything I ate that summer inspired me. The meals prepared for me by two- and three-star chefs were revelations. The first great meal I had, at Au Pactole, began with a soft-boiled egg topped with the finest caviar, followed by ethereal vegetable mousses and a delicate *salade frisée,* with goat cheese and a mustardy vinaigrette, all of which I can still taste today. The wine I drank, a crisp Pouilly-Fumé, is also still vivid, and so is the memory of an elderly woman sitting at the next table. She was dining alone, and with such confidence. She drank a different wine with each course, knew exactly what she wanted to eat, and did not seem the least bit uncomfortable to be by herself. I watched her and saw that clearly the French knew not only something about the preparation of food, but also how to enjoy it.

But it wasn't just these fancy meals that inspired me. What really turned me on was that good food has a constant presence in France; gastronomy is part of everyday life. Everywhere I turned there was a bakery with enticing breads and pastries, a fromagerie with hundreds of beautiful cheeses, a charcuterie with a wide selection of sparkling salads and prepared vegetable and meat dishes. I enjoyed eating the salads I bought at a charcuterie and ate at a little café in Grenoble—*carottes rapées* and *celeri rémoulade*—and the pizza I ate at a roadside pizzeria above Nice, as much as the dishes I was served at fancy restaurants. I would spend entire mornings in open markets marveling at the lush produce that was all so young, fresh, and fragrant; inspired by vegetables like long, shiny eggplants, sweet-smelling red tomatoes, tiny string beans, and long braids of garlic, I would fill my baskets and go home and cook. I had come to France with a backpack full of cookbooks, among them Elizabeth David's *French Provincial Cooking* (Penguin, 1987) and *French Country Cooking* (Penguin, 1987), Richard Olney's *Simple French Food*

(Atheneum, 1984), and Mireille Johnston's *The Cuisine of the Sun* (Random House, 1977), and these became my bibles. I made ratatouilles, onion soups, warm chick-pea salads, *pommes dauphinoises*—simple but lusty French country food, much of it Provençal —that you could eat every day.

That summer I lived in Tours, a gentle city in the Loire Valley, and went to Paris for a few two- or three-day sojourns. The minute I arrived in Paris I seemed to know my way around. I never got lost, I never felt intimidated. Everything worked: the metro ran regularly and was safe, and you could walk everywhere if you had the time. Paris was in some ways like a big village; it was a city that never betrayed the eye—it was always beautiful, and life seemed to have a built-in balance. I decided that someday I would like to live here.

I came back to Paris for a week the following summer; it was one stop on a five-week whirlwind trip through Europe. We stayed with a woman who knew a lot about wine, and every night I chose a restaurant and she picked the wines. It was during this trip that I was introduced to truffles and had my first taste of a really great wine, both during the same meal, at a tiny restaurant called Le Petit Montmorency, which was then in the Marais section of Paris (now it is in the 8th arrondissement on the rue Rabelais). The slivered truffles were tossed with small new potatoes, fresh herbs, and olive oil in a subtle and luxurious warm salad. The wine was a Saint-Emilion.

The decisive trip was in 1980, when I rented a house for a month in the south of France with friends who were then living in London. It was a big stucco farmhouse, surrounded by lavender fields, called La Sara, just outside Bonnieux, an exquisite hill town in the Luberon Mountains east of Avignon. I had found it through the American restaurateur Alice Waters, proprietress of Chez Panisse in Berkeley, California, who is a good friend of the owner, Nathalie Waag. Nathalie loves good food, markets, and the south of France, and she was a marvelous guide (now she takes in groups of Americans and does gastronomic tours of the region). Ending up at La Sara turned out to be a tremendous stroke of luck; I met some wonderful people there and through Nathalie, among them Christine Ruiz Picasso, who would become my close friend and my Paris landlady, and Lulu and Lucien Peyraud, owners of Domaine Tempier, a winery just north of the Mediterranean town of Bandol, near Marseilles. I would spend weeks with the Peyrauds later on, learn much about winemaking, and be inspired by Lulu's delicious Provençal cooking.

At the end of that summer I went back to Austin, where I'd lived for nine years, but I kept dreaming of France. So I wrote to everybody I knew in Paris, asking them to keep their eyes open for an apartment big enough for three people: me and two close friends, Mary Collins and Maggie Megaw, who had grants for study and teaching in Paris the following year.

Christine was one of the people I wrote to. She had just moved to the south of France, but she still had her large apartment in Paris. One Saturday in February 1981, she phoned me in Austin to ask me if I wanted the apartment. Since I barely spoke French at that point I could hardly believe I was hearing correctly—sometimes I still think I'm dreaming—but in fact, it was true.

So in August 1981, I packed up my belongings, loaded my Volkswagen Dasher with as many suitcases and boxes filled with cooking utensils, Mexican food ingredients, and cookbooks as could fit, and drove to Montreal, stopping here and there along the way to visit friends. In Montreal I boarded the *Stefan Batory,* a Polish ocean liner, and sailed to Europe. I had bought a round-trip ticket.

Christine describes her apartment as banal and bourgeois, but to the eyes of an American there is nothing banal about it. It has ornate plaster moldings with cherubs, grape clusters, and floral designs, called *patisserie,* typical of turn-of-the-century Parisian apartments; it has many large rooms with French doors and balconies that face south. The carpets in the living room, entry hall, and library are a deep red to match the upholstery; the walls are white; and there is a large gilded mirror above the fireplace in the living room. It's warm and inviting, perfect for entertaining.

I knew within weeks that I wanted to stay in Paris much longer than the "open-ended year" I told everyone I was coming for, and traded in the return part of my boat ticket. I spent the first twelve months exploring the city, studying the French language and cuisine, and catering Mexican food. Just when I really began to panic about work, I answered a want ad in the *International Herald Tribune* and got a job as a private cook for the sculptress Niki de Saint-Phalle.

Niki is most well known for her large, amusing sculptures of women, called "Nanas," and for her architectural sculpture. She has a house in a small village about thirty miles south of Paris, and two or three days a week I'd drive out to her house, cook dishes that would keep, bake bread, and cater dinner parties for her and her friends. There were always interesting people around—artists like Jean Tinguely, curators, writers—and I loved the working environment. Niki and her assistant Ricardo would work in the studio while I cooked, and we would all sit down to meals together. In August I went to Saint Moritz for three weeks to cook for Niki and her entourage.

That job was another lucky break; it gave me the confidence to stay in France. Niki and her friends were enthusiastic about my cooking, and their positive response to my food led me to believe that I would find other willing eaters.

Niki moved to Italy to work on an ambitious sculpture garden late in the fall of 1982, but by then I was busy with my own cooking and writing projects. In the back of my mind I'd been thinking about starting a "supper club," serving regular paying dinners in my apartment to large groups of people. I had done this in Austin in the early seventies when I first started cooking. By the winter of 1983 I felt that I knew enough people in Paris to try out the idea, so I sent off invitations. It took, and now "Supper Club chez Martha" has become a kind of Paris institution.

I knew that eventually the Supper Club dinners, the recipes I have learned from Christine and Lulu, and the dishes I make for noteworthy events like New Year's Eve parties and picnics on the Seine would find their way into a cookbook. It is as much a book about my love affair with France, the last five years of my life, and a *way* of life, as it is a cookbook; and it's for you to enjoy.

Martha Rose Shulman
Paris, August 1988

Acknowledgments

Once I work out a recipe I test it, but I can't always be sure of my objectivity; I may be so familiar with the recipe that what may be confusing to my readers won't be confusing for me, or I may change something and not even be aware of it. The recipes in this book have also been tested by my assistant, Laurie Dill. Laurie not only cooked all the dishes, but made many comments and suggestions. I'm very grateful for her good palate and her diligence. Laurie was also been my chief Supper Club assistant for one and a half years. Thank you, La, for chopping all those onions, peeling all that garlic, chopping kilos of tomatoes, washing and drying heads and heads of lettuce, and much more. And also, for always making my tables look so beautiful.

I am very grateful to Jon Winroth for contributing wine suggestions for each menu in this book.

Supper Club would never run so smoothly if it weren't for my second assistants, Siena Herrera during the first three years and later Chase Kennedy and Ann Trager. They all have an eye for food, and it's such a pleasure to see their beautiful plates at each setting when we come to the table.

Thank you, Joyce Johnson, for your enthusiasm about this book. And thank you, Roger Friedman, for all of your support.

Thank you, Peters Day (La Mouche), for your wonderful illustrations.

Christine et Lulu, vous deux méritez bien un chapitre chacune, mais je tiens à vous témoigner dès maintenant ma gratitude.

Sabine, thanks for helping me with my French.

Finally, I want to thank all my Supper Club guests, and especially the "regulars." You know who you are. You always leave a little of your warmth and good will behind when you go, so it's there to welcome people the next time. Supper Club chez Martha is what it is because of you.

Supper Club Chez Martha Rose

Introduction

SUPPER CLUB CHEZ MARTHA

Once a month, on Thursday nights, twenty-five people come to my apartment for dinner. They begin to arrive around eight-thirty for aperitifs, which I serve in my large, friendly living room, and continue arriving until nine-thirty or ten, when I begin to lure them away from their cocktail conversations by asking them to find their places at the two long tables.

The tables, which are in different rooms, each seat twelve to thirteen people. They have been set with colorful Provençal tablecloths and napkins—red, green, blue, or yellow—white porcelain plates, low flower arrangements, and candles. There is a handwritten menu, which also serves as a placecard, at each setting. In winter a fire has been lit in the living room; in late spring and summer, when it stays light until ten, the French doors leading out onto the balcony are wide open. A tall, extravagant vase of flowers—gladiolas in the fall, tulips and irises in winter, daisies, roses, hollyhocks and lilies in the spring—decorates the mantle above the fireplace in the living room.

The group is an ever-changing one, although there are many "regulars." Some are French, more are American, and there is usually a smattering of other nationalities. But the mix is always interesting, and my guests all seem to have one thing in common: congeniality. They've heard about my Supper Club through friends who have come, or I've invited them, and they pay what is called here a "participation."

"Supper Club chez Martha" is unique; it isn't a dinner party—nobody is obligated to be there—and it isn't a restaurant; it's not open to the public, and the "participation" just

covers the cost of the food and wine. It is a soiree, and people choose to come and keep returning because it is a marvelous meeting ground, and because of the food, which is never the same from one dinner to the next. The French are fascinated by the concept of the supper club, and always tell me what an American phenomenon it is; yet it is not too different from the old-fashioned salon.

I first had the idea for a supper club in 1973, when I was living in Austin and had decided to make a career out of cooking. The two things I loved to do best were to give parties and to cook. I didn't want to open a restaurant—too risky—but I needed to cook for people and expand my repertoire. The supper club would allow me to do these things.

I called it Martha's Moon House Supper Club, because my house had a big crescent moon window in the wooden front door. In those days I did the dinners once a week, for

SUPPER CLUB
CHEZ MARTHA ROSE

thirty-five people, and they sat on the floor at long low tables. They paid $1.50 (some paid with food stamps); most of us were hippies and poor in those halcyon days. I operated this supper club for two years, and then had to move out of my house and into a smaller one. I didn't have the space for a large group anymore. At that point I began catering, and put the supper club concept away. But I always missed it, and hoped that I would be able to start another one.

The notion came alive again when I came to Paris. Supper Club chez Martha was small at first—only fourteen or fifteen people. But it caught on so quickly that I had a large table with benches built, and arranged my apartment so that the big dining room and the library could each accommodate tables for twelve to fourteen people (once I even did a sit-down Thanksgiving dinner for forty).

In September and in January I send out announcements for the opening of the "season" to everyone on my ever-expanding mailing list, with the dates of the dinners. I urge everyone to call for reservations as soon as possible, because the dinners fill up quickly.

I spend a week or two working on the menus and testing recipes. I walk around the city with the menu on my mind, scouting markets, composing plates in my imagination, thinking about combinations of courses. I consider colors, textures, and the balance of the meal, and always take into account time requirements; cooking for twenty-five people is not like cooking for four to six, and certain dishes just aren't feasible, even with an assistant. And because I am both hostess and cook, I can't choose dishes that require lots of last-minute preparation or supervision. Sometimes my meals have a seasonal or an ethnic theme (I am known for my Mexican food and always kick off the "season" with a Mexican or Tex-Mex meal); sometimes they are Provençal in character; sometimes I'll take a French idea and give the menu an American twist. One of my menus, for example, begins with a typically French salad with baked goat cheese, followed by my Provençal-style fish soup, called *"Chowder" à la Provençale,* which I serve with Texas cornbread. Dessert is a pear crisp, very American in character with pecans in the topping, but it is moistened with a crème anglaise. These are happy marriages. Always, my cuisine is healthy and seasonal, inspired by the best products the gorgeous Paris markets have to offer.

The weekend before my dinner I make lists. I have a notebook for shopping lists, and make up a preparation schedule, which I post in my kitchen so I can check things off as I get them done. I begin preparations on Monday, xeroxing menus and doing whatever supermarket shopping is necessary, but the real push begins on Tuesday. I go from market to market, searching out ingredients and good buys, and begin, with the help of Laurie Dill, any preparation that can be done this far in advance. Marketing and preparation continue on Wednesday; that's the day I order my fish if fish is on the menu, to be picked up early Thursday morning. In the evenings I work on the seating plan.

Thursday is a nonstop day for Laurie and me in the kitchen. If I am ahead in the morning, I'll work very slowly so I have to rush in the afternoon. I seem to thrive on a certain amount of tension; there is something inside of me that wants to rush toward the end.

But by seven or seven-fifteen I'm out of the kitchen. The next forty-five minutes is my quiet time, and it's essential. I take a hot bath and retreat to my bedroom, where I close the door and curtains, unplug the phone, turn off the lights, and lie on my back on the floor, my legs over my head. I close my eyes, breathe deeply, and let go of the day's tension. In a way, I forget that I was in the kitchen all day. Then I get dressed and go out and join my second assistant, who arrives at eight to help serve, wash dishes, and prepare the plates for the first course.

This last half hour is a bit crazed with final details. I set out the menu-placecards, making any necessary last-minute changes. My assistant sets out ashtrays, small bowls with radish roses and olives; I prepare the ice bucket and open the aperitif wine, or mix up the margaritas if it's a Mexican meal. I explain to my assistant how I want the plates to look for the first course, and he or she begins to uncork wine for the dinner and to cut bread, which goes into pretty, napkin-lined baskets.

Then the doorbell begins to ring (if anybody comes early, I make them work): it's showtime. I move into my hostess mode, and for the next hour I'm running track between the kitchen, front door, and living room, constantly putting on and taking off my apron, as if I were doing quick costume changes between scenes. Every time the doorbell rings I wonder, "Who will it be?" The guests bring me new energy; it really is as if somebody else had spent all day in the kitchen. During the cocktail hour, I am busy making introductions and filling glasses; but everybody makes it so easy by being curious and nice. Maybe it's because so many of my guests are foreigners living in Paris who share a passion for the city. "You spend your first year in Paris figuring out how to work it so you can spend the rest of your life here," I once overheard one of my guests say—she was a woman who has lived here for thirty years. People are always running into friends and acquaintances from other spheres of their lives, and even making professional connections. The rooms buzz with talk and fun.

By the time everybody has had a drink or two, they are so engaged in conversation that, hungry as they are, they refuse to be torn away from each other. But eventually they do find their seats at the table, and a new phase of the party —the dinner—begins. I always have as good a time as my guests. I sit at the head of the table in the dining room, only disappearing between courses to do last-minute tasks in the kitchen, while my assistant clears the plates. I warn my dinner partners that they will have to put up with my comings and goings, and while I'm in the kitchen I listen for the crescendo-ing sounds of table talk and laughter, signs that the dinner is a success.

The meals consist of three courses, and I serve a wine that will go with both the first and main dish. The first course is usually some kind of salad, attractively composed on individual plates, which are set at each place before we sit down. In most instances we serve the main course and dessert from the buffet in the dining room. After dessert I serve coffee and *infusion* (herb tea, verbena or mint) in the living room. This is phase three of the evening: more mingling. People stay until the last metro, at about twelve-thirty, although some soirees have gone on much later. Before they leave, many guests exchange telephone numbers and addresses. An ever-expanding network of friends is growing out of my Supper Club, and it's been heartwarming to see it begin around my tables.

ENTERTAINING ON A SMALL OR GRAND SCALE

Cooking and entertaining have gone hand in hand for me ever since I began cooking at the age of seventeen. I've never been attracted to restaurant work because it's too repetitive, and no matter how creative the cooking, it's too far behind the scenes. Catering is also behind-the-scenes work, but you do become involved with the party and the guests, even though they're somebody else's.

My Paris apartment has provided the setting for all sorts of events over the last five years, not just Supper Club chez Martha. There have been innumerable cocktail parties, small dinner parties, brunches, and New Year's Eve extravaganzas. Sometimes when I want to give a big party but don't have time to do a lot of cooking, I ask people to bring things to eat, but I always manage to pull off some kind of a buffet. Giving a party is a performance, with a curtain time, a stage set, and an audience. It's show biz, it's in my blood, and it's irresistible.

No matter how large or small your guest list, successful entertaining depends on a few simple rules. The most important one is *organization.* You can't be *too* organized. Make lists.

Try to do as much as possible in advance. Set tables or prepare the buffet the night before. Even if you fall behind in the kitchen, there is something very reassuring, even calming, about tables that are beautifully set and waiting. Before the guests arrive, set out bowls of radishes and olives, or an attractive platter of crudités, so they'll have something to nibble on even before the first course. Open a good bottle of wine.

Choose menus that don't involve too much last-minute preparation. Otherwise you'll be in the kitchen the whole time and your guests will never see you. You will notice that my Supper Club menus all include dishes that will hold and can be reheated at the last minute, or whose final cooking is unsupervised, like the baked fish fillets with salsa on page 56, the lasagne on page 105, and the cannelloni on page 150. During the summer months, many of my main dishes are cold, so all of the cooking is done in advance. I have noted throughout what can be done ahead of time. You will also find that for the most part, the Supper Club dishes are not too labor intensive. That's because I'm multiplying the recipes by three or four for my dinners, and certain dishes I love to serve for four or six aren't feasible for large groups. I've included these recipes in the "Favorite Dishes from Small Dinner Parties" section (page 277).

Once you've got these practical matters taken care of, what are the secrets of being the host or hostess with the mostest once the evening gets under way? I think the most important duty of a host or hostess is making introductions. I'm always annoyed when I go to a party and the person giving it doesn't fulfill this function. It doesn't take much, but people have to have a springboard from which to jump into conversation. Even if you don't know your guests well, you probably know at least one thing about each of them, like where they're from or what they do. Mention that one thing and let it be the hook.

If you're throwing a really big party, you need to think about how you're going to keep the place in order. Remember to set trashcans, or boxes with heavy garbage bags, tucked away under tables, so that empty bottles and paper plates can be quickly disposed of, and ashtrays emptied. If you can possibly hire somebody to help with this, do so. It's too depressing to see a beautiful setting strewn with empty bottles, used paper plates, glasses, and cigarette butts halfway into a party. All you need to do is make a few rounds every hour or so to keep it under control.

Finally, try to set aside at least half an hour for yourself before everybody arrives. This time is invaluable for me, even if I sometimes have to rush in the kitchen to get it. If you're rushing right up until the last minute, you'll have no time to regain your composure, and you'll need that once the party gets underway.

INCREASING RECIPES FOR LARGE GROUPS

With the exception of some of the dishes in the last section of this book, I have cooked all of these recipes for up to twenty-five people (and in the case of Mexican food, for a hundred and fifty). All of them can be easily increased for numbers up to thirty-five by multiplying the quantities in the recipe by the appropriate factor. Once you get beyond thirty-five, the factor changes, but it's not within the scope of this book to deal with that. For twenty-five people I use a factor of 3, 4, or 5, depending on whether the recipe feeds four, six, or eight. If a recipe feeds six to eight I would rather err on the side of more, and will multiply by 4 rather than 3; however, if I note that a recipe feeds six to eight "generously," multiplying by 3 suffices. The most important thing to take into consideration when you are feeding a crowd is that you will need more time for preparation of the ingredients: whatever you are multiplying the recipe by, figure on that much more time for cutting and chopping. Do as much ahead of time as possible and organize your refrigerator so you'll have enough storage space.

SEATING PLANS

I devote hours each month to my seating plans. It's always a challenge, mostly because I've got two long tables, each with twelve to thirteen people to deal with. If they were round it would be easier. I have to consider overall configurations as well as who sits next to whom.

First, I picture the whole group and try to imagine what the dynamic will be. Are they mostly high-energy, fun people? Are there (usually not) many shy people? Will there be a big crowd of journalists tonight, or photographers, or musicians? Sometimes there are a lot of newcomers on the list, but usually half the guests are old friends. I think about people who might enjoy each other's company. Then I make a diagram of the table, cut out strips of paper with guests' names on them, and start moving the strips around. Often there will be several people in the same profession or in overlapping professions, and I'll try to place them near each other. I try to make sure that each table has a few dynamic people, good conversationalists who can talk to anyone. Then there is the language consideration. Almost all the Americans who have lived here for a while speak French, but not all the French people who come to my dinners speak English. I have to make sure that nobody has a dinner partner he or she can't converse with.

If guests are coming for the first time and don't know anybody, I try to seat them near me. If a newcomer is being brought by friends, I'll usually seat the members of the party near each other. However, I often split couples up. For one thing, there is always a shortage of men at my dinners, and I try to sprinkle them somewhat evenly among the tables.

I have to think in terms of fours and sixes as well as twos and threes. Four people sit on each bench at my big wooden table, with two people at each end. Usually the guests at the ends of the table are engaged in conversation with one or two people at the end of the bench. But the inside two people on the bench stand a chance of being left out of the conversation, especially if one of the people at the end, or the person directly across from him, is the type who engages in conversation with one person all evening. So I try to put at least one gregarious person at each end of the table.

Inevitably I'll get a last-minute cancellation or two that will mess up my whole arrangement. Perhaps I've placed two people next to each other who have a lot in common, and one of them gets sick. It's usually not too difficult to find replacements, but I have to redo the seating plan. Once I got a last-minute reservation from two men on a night when we happened to have a larger than usual surplus of women. I changed the entire seating plan about an hour before the dinner, and then one of the men called me to ask if I was serving anything with cheese in it, as he was deathly allergic. Wouldn't you know that on this night I had made spinach lasagne! He cancelled. But faced with having to change the seating plan again (and wanting the extra man), I called him back and offered to make a special dish for him, since nothing but the lasagne contained cheese. Happily, he came after all. This kind of thing happens all the time.

ABOUT MY CUISINE

Because I'm living and cooking in France, most people I meet assume that I focus on French cuisine. But that isn't really the case. My first year here I sat in on some cooking classes at La Varenne and Le Cordon Bleu, but not for very long. The fact is, cooking with large quantities of butter, sugar, and meat just doesn't interest me. On the other hand, I am passionate about Provençal and other Mediterranean cuisines, which rely on a bounty of vegetables, grains and legumes, fish, and lots of herbs and garlic. My cuisine is a vegetarian one with fish, not because I'm against eating meat, but because I don't eat it myself. Over the years I've lost my taste for it; I've also found that meatless cooking is an easy way to maintain a low-fat diet. This isn't to say that you won't find some traditional French dishes here, but I always try to reduce the fat and sugar. You will see, as you work through the recipes in this book, that I am an eclectic cook who loves garlic and olive oil (kept at a minimum), vibrant flavors and bright colors—substantial food that will leave you feeling wholesome, healthy, and happy.

A Note on the Metric Equivalents in These Recipes

For the purposes of this book, 2 pounds corresponds to 1 kilo (kg), ½ pound to 250 grams and ¾ pound to 350 grams. In reality, 1 pound equals 455 grams, but when you are marketing in a European market you wouldn't ask for 455 grams of, say, apples, you'd ask for a half a kilo (in French, *une livre,* or a pound). Exact weights, rather than approximate ones, are given in some pastry recipes, where measures have to be exact.

A Note on Honey

Very few of my dishes are sweetened with sugar; I have always worked with honey. It's important, though, to find a mild-flavored honey, or the flavor of the honey will over-power the dish. Mild honeys are lighter in color than strong-flavored honeys. I recommend acacia or clover as the best all-around types. If you can't find a light honey, substitute sugar or brown sugar.

Wine Suggestions

With all of the menus I've noted the wines I served as aperitifs and with the meals. I've also listed Jon Winroth's suggestions. Jon is an American wine writer who has lived in Paris for over thirty years; he came here on a Fulbright to do research for a history dissertation, but found that he was more interested in wine than in modern Greek history and spent more time in wine bars than in libraries. Now he is one of France's most respected oenologists. He also happens to be my neighbor, a lucky break for me; I met him my first week here. He has taught me much of what I know about wine, and has introduced me to all of my favorite wine bistros in Paris. He started L'Académie du Vin with Steven Spurrier; is the author of *Wine As You Like It,* published in 1981 by the *International Herald Tribune*; is the wine columnist for the French magazines *Elle* and *Lui;* and contributes regularly to other publications.

Part I:
Supper Club
Menus

Some Basics:
Breads, Pasta, and Piecrusts

SOURDOUGH COUNTRY BREAD
Pain de Campagne

SOURDOUGH COUNTRY BREAD WITH CORNMEAL AND OATS OR BRAN
Pain de Campagne au Mais et à l'Avoíne

SOURDOUGH COUNTRY BREAD WITH RAISINS
Pain aux Raisins

COUNTRY RYE BREAD WITH RAISINS
Pain de Campagne au Seigle et aux Raisins Secs

MIXED GRAINS BREAD
Pain aux Céréales

MILLET AND CORNMEAL BREAD
Pain au Millet et au Mais

CUMIN AND CORNMEAL BREAD
Pain au Cumin

SOURDOUGH BAGUETTES
Baguettes de Campagne

HERBED WHOLE-WHEAT BREAD
Pain aux Herbes

COUNTRY BREAD WITH OLIVES
Pain de Campagne aux Olives

PESTO BREAD
Pain au Basilic

TEXAS CORNBREAD
Pain de Mais à l'Américaine

HOMEMADE PASTA
Pâtes Fraiches Maison

WHOLE-WHEAT PIECRUSTS
Pâtes Brisées Complètes

HOMEMADE TORTILLAS
Tortillas Maison

BLINIS

GARLIC CROUTONS
Croutons à l'Ail

These are the recipes that come up repeatedly—breads, pasta, piecrusts, croutons. They all involve basic techniques, so I've put them together in this chapter. Bread has always been my mainstay, and I never tire of making it. Even though I make the same kinds over and over again, the experience is never the same. I always have Sourdough Country Bread, the *pain de campagne,* and Mixed Grains Bread on hand. When I plan my Supper Club menus I choose a bread that will go with the spirit of the meal—thus Pesto Bread with the December lasagne dinner, Cumin and Cornmeal Bread with my Mexican food, Mixed Grains Bread for November and Thanksgiving dinners. You might want to try different breads than the ones I've suggested with these menus.

My whole-wheat piecrusts are crumbly and light, not like the cardboard crusts that got vegetarianism off to such a bad start in the early seventies. They aren't as easy to roll out as white-flour crusts, but the extra labor is worth the effort. The resulting crusts have a rich, nutty taste, which I prefer to their refined counterparts.

When I make pasta, I always use part whole-grain (whole wheat or buckwheat) flour. Like the piecrusts, pasta containing whole-grain flours has a deep, nutty taste. I love the deep green color of spinach pasta, and the delicate flecks of green in herb pastas. The more you make pasta, the easier it gets, so eventually you will think nothing of an impromptu dinner of homemade fettuccine or tagliarini and the sauce of your choice.

A Note on Freezing Bread

It's best to double-wrap bread before freezing. Allow it to cool completely. Wrap first in either plastic wrap or foil, then in foil or plastic bags.

SOURDOUGH COUNTRY BREAD

Pain De Campagne

T his bread has become a mainstay in my home, and you will see how versatile it is. It's the bread I most often serve at my Supper Club. It has a tart, earthy flavor and a very hard crust. The bread is chewy and dense, and has great staying power.

I have three people to thank for getting me going with this recipe. First Lionel Poilane, who supplies Paris with thousands of loaves of his *pain de campagne* every day; his is made with a more refined flour. The bread is somewhere between whole wheat and white, and I love it for its sour taste, hard crust, and moist, chewy texture. Then, Lionel's brother Max, who let me work in his bakery for a month during my first year here. It was there that I began to understand that the dough for *pain de campagne* should be quite wet. And finally, Patricia Wells, for working out a recipe for Poilane's *chef,* or sourdough leavener, which is the only leavener used in real French country bread. Unlike most sourdough starters, the *chef* isn't runny, but is more like a spongy dough. I have frozen the *chef,* carried it with me unfrozen from place to place—from Paris to America, from Paris to Yugoslavia in a car, and from Yugoslavia back to Italy, Provence, and finally home to Paris. Sometimes I use it alone to make authentic *pain de campagne,* which rises for eight to twelve hours, never gets airy, but has a marvelous sour taste. I've combined it with yeast in this version to make a faster rising, puffier bread that still has the denseness and the sour flavor.

Mix together the water and flour and knead into a smooth ball on a floured work surface. The dough should be soft and sticky. Flour your hands so you can work with it. Return it to the bowl, cover with a damp towel, and let sit at room temperature for 72 hours. The dough will form a crust on the top and turn a grayish color, which is normal. If you keep wetting the towel it will reduce the drying. The dough will rise slightly and take on an acidic aroma.

Add the water to the starter and blend together. If the crust on the top is like cardboard or wood, you will have to peel it off and discard it. Try blending it before you resort to this. Add the flour and stir to blend. Transfer the dough to a floured work surface and knead into a smooth ball.

Return it to the bowl, cover with a damp towel, and let sit in a warm place for 24 to 48 hours. Again, a crust may form on the top. If it is like cardboard or wood, peel it off and discard before proceeding with the recipe.

MIXING THE DOUGH BY HAND: Combine the sourdough starter, the water or the water and coffee, and the yeast. Whisk together until the starter and yeast are thoroughly dissolved. Whisk in the molasses and the salt.

Fold in the flour, 1 cup (115 g) at a time. By the time you have added 4 cups (455 g), you should be able to knead. I usually do this right in the bowl, as the dough is sticky and unwieldy. Using a pastry scraper instead of your hands to fold the dough for kneading will help. Knead for 10 minutes, adding flour as necessary.

MIXING THE DOUGH IN AN ELECTRIC MIXER: Combine the starter, the water or water and coffee, the yeast and the molasses in the bowl of your electric mixer. Use the mixer attachment (not the dough hook and not the wire whip) to combine these ingredients. When the starter and the yeast are thoroughly dissolved, add the salt and 4 cups (455 g) of the

FOR THE STARTER

THE FIRST DAY
1/3 cup (90 ml) water
1 cup (115 g) flour,
    whole-wheat or unbleached
    white

AFTER 72 HOURS
1/2 cup (120 ml) lukewarm
    water
1 1/2 cups (170 g)
    whole-wheat or unbleached
    white flour

FOR THE BREAD
All of the sourdough starter
2 cups (450 ml) lukewarm
    water or 1 cup (225 ml)
    lukewarm water plus 1 cup
    (225 ml) coffee
Scant 1 tablespoon (1
    envelope) active dry yeast
1 tablespoon blackstrap
    molasses (optional)
1 scant tablespoon salt
4 1/2 to 5 cups (515 to 575 g)
    whole-wheat flour
    cornmeal for the baking
    sheet

flour all at once. Mix together briefly, using the mixing attachment, until everything is amalgamated. Then scrape off the mixing attachment and replace it with the dough hook. Knead at a low speed for 10 minutes, adding up to a cup of flour if the dough seems very liquid (it should be sticky).

RISING, FORMING THE LOAF, BAKING: Cover the dough and let rise in a warm spot for 1 1/2 hours. Flour your hands and wrists and punch down the dough. Knead for 2 or 3 minutes on a lightly floured surface, using a pastry scraper to make it easier. Remove a cup of the dough and place in a bowl, to use as a starter for your next loaf of bread. Cover the starter and refrigerate after a few hours if not using again in a day's time.

Dust a clean, dry towel with flour and line a bowl or basket. Form the dough into a ball, dust the surface with flour, and place, rounded side down, in the towel-lined bowl or basket (called *banneton* in French). Cover with a towel and let rise in a warm spot for 1 1/2 to 2 hours, until almost doubled in bulk. You can also let the dough rise in the refrigerator for several hours or overnight.

Preheat the oven to 400° F (200° C, gas mark 6). Place an empty pan on the bottom shelf of the oven. When the oven is heated, pour 2 cups (450 ml) water into the pan; the steam will help give the bread a thick, hard crust. Turn the dough out onto an unoiled baking sheet (or preferably a baking stone) dusted with cornmeal, peel off the towel, and slash the dough with a sharp knife or a razor. Place it in the oven and bake 45 minutes, until brown and it responds to tapping with a hollow thumping sound. Remove from the oven and cool on a rack.

MAKES 1 LARGE LOAF

SOURDOUGH COUNTRY BREAD WITH CORNMEAL AND OATS OR BRAN

Pain de Campagne au Mais et à L'Avoine

This is the bread I most often made in Yugoslavia and Italy when I traveled to these countries during the summer of '85. I had brought my sourdough along, but not enough whole-wheat flour to make more than one big loaf, and as there were five of us, one loaf went quickly. The Yugoslavian white flour is quite good, with little flakes of grain still in it and a great texture. But I like a bread with a lot of texture and sustenance, so I used whatever grains I could find to make up for the absence of whole-wheat flour. These turned out to be polenta and oats. Later, staying at Christine's for a week on the way back, I got the idea of incorporating bran into the bread. She buys an excellent whole-wheat bread with bran at a bakery in Apt, and I liked it so much I began adding bran instead of oats to my bread.

Follow the preceding recipe for Sourdough Country Bread, using the same sourdough starter (the *chef*). Substitute 1 cup (115 g) bran or rolled oats and 1 cup (140 g) cornmeal for 2 cups (225 g) of the whole-wheat flour. Proceed with the recipe.

MAKES 1 LOAF

SOURDOUGH COUNTRY BREAD WITH RAISINS
Pain aux Raisins

The sweetness and abundance of the raisins make a great contrast with the sour bread. The bread was inspired by Lionel Poilane's dense rye raisin rolls. My frequent cravings for these rolls are easy to satisfy because his beautiful rue du Cherche-Midi bakery is a half a block from my apartment.

See recipe for Sourdough Country Bread (page 18). Substitute 1 ½ cups (170 g) rye flour for 1 ½ cups (170 g) of the whole-wheat flour.

When forming the loaf, knead in 2 cups (340 g) raisins. Proceed with the recipe.

MAKES 1 LARGE LOAF

COUNTRY RYE BREAD WITH RAISINS
Pain de Campagne au Seigle et aux Raisins Secs

This rye raisin bread is less acidic than the previous recipe. It takes two and a half or three days from start to finish. If you begin the starter in the afternoon or evening, you will mix up the sponge the following evening and finish the bread the following day. If you mix the starter in the morning, you will mix the sponge the following morning and finish the bread that night.

DAY 1: MAKING THE STARTER: In a small bowl, dissolve the yeast in the water and whisk in the flour. Combine well, cover with plastic wrap, and set in a draft-free spot to rise for 24 hours.

DAY 2: MIXING THE SPONGE: Stir down the starter and scrape it into a bread bowl. Whisk in the water, molasses, the unbleached flour, and the rye flour. Blend well, cover with plastic wrap, and set the bowl in a draft-free place for 12 hours.

DAY 3: MIXING UP THE DOUGH, FINAL RISING, AND BAKING: Fold the lukewarm water, the salt, the whole-wheat flour, and 1 cup (115 g) of the rye flour into the dough. Fold in the additional rye flour, 1/2 cup (55 g) at a time, until the dough can be turned out of the bowl in more or less one piece. Place 1/2 cup (55 g) unbleached white flour on your kneading surface and scrape out the dough. The dough will be very sticky. Flour your hands well. If the dough is too sticky to handle, use a pastry scraper instead of your hands to fold the dough for kneading. Knead for about 10 minutes, adding unbleached white flour by the handful, as necessary. After about 5 minutes the dough should give up some of its stickiness and become easier to work with.

Wash out and oil your bowl. Shape the dough into a ball and place in the oiled bowl, seam side up first, then seam side down. Cover with plastic wrap and set in a warm place to rise for 1 hour.

Punch down the dough and turn onto a well-floured work surface. Press out to a 1-inch thickness and spread the raisins or currants over the surface. Fold the dough over and knead several times until they are evenly distributed.

Divide the dough into 3 equal pieces (or see note, below, for rolls). Shape into round balls and place on a large, oiled baking sheet. Cover with wax paper or a towel and set in a warm place to rise for 30 minutes. Meanwhile, preheat the oven to 400° F (200° C, gas mark 6).

Uncover the loaves, and using a razor blade or a thin, sharp knife, make 2 intersecting Xs across the top of each loaf,

FOR THE STARTER

1 teaspoon active dry yeast
1 cup (225 ml) lukewarm water
1 cup (115 g) rye flour

FOR THE SPONGE

All of the starter
1 1/4 cups (285 ml) lukewarm water
2 tablespoons molasses
1 cup (115 g) unbleached white flour
1 1/2 cups (170 g) rye flour

FOR THE DOUGH

All of the sponge
1/2 cup (120 ml) lukewarm water
1 tablespoon salt
1 cup (115 g) whole-wheat flour
2 cups (225 g) rye flour
1 cup (115 g) unbleached white flour, as needed

FOR THE LOAVES

All of the dough
1 pound (450 g) raisins or currants
1 egg yolk, beaten with 1 tablespoon water or milk

so that 8 intersecting lines radiate out from the center like a star. Brush with the eggwash and place in the preheated oven. Bake 45 to 50 minutes, turning the baking sheet around and brushing once more with the eggwash halfway through the baking.

When the bottom crusts respond to tapping with a hollow thump, remove the loaves from the oven and cool on racks.

MAKES 2 LARGE LOAVES OR 3 SMALLER LOAVES

NOTE: For rolls: Divide the dough into 2-ounce (55 g) pieces and roll into balls. Place on oiled baking sheets, cover with wax paper, and let rise about 1 hour, until doubled in size. Preheat the oven about 20 minutes before baking.

Brush the rolls with eggwash and slash an X across the tops. Bake 25 to 30 minutes, turning the sheets around and brushing again halfway through the baking. Cool on racks or eat while still warm.

MIXED GRAINS BREAD
Pain Aux Cereales

Here we go again, the bread that is in my first two cookbooks must again be given here, because after all is said and done it is my favorite bread, and I still live on it—along with the other breads in this book. It is a dense, cakey, slightly sweet, grainy bread, chewy and wholesome. When you eat it you experience a range of textures and a sweet variation of flavors from the different grains. The only problem I sometimes have with this bread is that it can crumble; I haven't figured out why it crumbles sometimes and why it doesn't at other times. The only inconvenience this might pose is that sandwiches packed in a lunchbox might fall apart; and when you slice it up for a dinner party some of the pieces might not look too neat. But since it's a rather rustic bread anyway, this shouldn't matter. You can vary the grains in this bread, substituting one kind of flake for another, for example wheat or rye instead of oats, cornmeal for ground millet, chick-pea flour for soy flour.

This bread takes about 5 hours from start to finish, but the dough can be refrigerated after you knead it or punch it down, so you needn't feel tied to the house for all that time.

MIXING UP THE SPONGE: Dissolve the yeast in the warm water in a large bowl. Mix in the honey and molasses. Whisk in the flour, a cup at a time. When all the flour has been added, whisk a hundred times, changing directions every once in a while. This really won't take too long. The sponge should have the consistency of thick mud. Cover and set it in a warm place for 1 hour, until bubbly.

MIXING THE DOUGH, KNEADING, AND FIRST RISE: Fold the oil, then the salt, into the sponge, using a large wooden spoon and turning the bowl between folds. Fold in the grains, one at a time.

Now begin folding in the flour. After 2 cups the dough should hold together in a sticky mass. Place the third cup on your kneading surface and scrape out the dough. Flour your hands and begin kneading the dough. At first you will have to treat it gingerly, as it is sticky, and you'll have to keep flouring your hands. But after a few minutes the dough will begin to stiffen and will become easier to work with. Knead, adding more flour as necessary, for 10 minutes. The dough should be elastic and stiff, and the surface slightly tacky. Shape it into a ball. Oil the bowl, place the dough in the bowl, seam side up first, then seam side down. Cover and let rise in a warm spot for an hour.

PUNCHING DOWN, SHAPING LOAVES, BAKING: Punch down the dough. At this point you can cover it, set it in a warm place, and let it rise one more time, for 45 to 60 minutes, in the bowl. The extra rise will make a lighter loaf but is not absolutely necessary.

FOR THE SPONGE

- *1 scant tablespoon (1 envelope) active dry yeast*
- *3 cups (750 ml) lukewarm water*
- *2 tablespoons mild-flavored honey*
- *2 tablespoons blackstrap molasses*
- *2 cups (225 g) unbleached white flour*
- *2 cups (225 g) whole-wheat flour*

FOR THE DOUGH

- *¼ cup (60 ml) safflower oil*
- *1 tablespoon salt*
- *¾ cup (85 g) oat flakes (may substitute wheat or rye)*
- *¾ cup (130 g) bulgur or cracked wheat*
- *¾ cup (170 g) millet, ground to a flour in a blender, or ¾ cup (115 g) stoneground cornmeal*
- *¾ cup (85 g) soy flour or chick-pea flour*
- *3 cups (340 g) whole-wheat flour, as needed*

FOR THE LOAVES

- *1 egg, beaten with 2 tablespoons water*
- *2 tablespoons sesame seeds*

Either with or without the additional rising, turn the dough out onto a lightly floured work surface. Knead it a couple of times, and divide the dough in half. Form 2 loaves and place them in oiled 8×4×3-inch or 9×5×3-inch loaf pans, seam side up first, then seam side down. Brush the loaves lightly with the beaten egg and water; sprinkle with sesame seeds, and brush again. Cover and let rise until the tops of the loaves rise above the edge of the pans. This will take anywhere from 20 to 45 minutes, depending on the weather and the stage at which you shaped the loaves.

When the loaves have risen, preheat the oven to 350° F (180° C, gas mark 4). Using a razor blade or sharp knife, slash the loaves across the top in 3 places and bake on a middle rack for 50 to 60 minutes in the preheated oven. Halfway through the baking, brush again with the eggwash. The bread is done when it is golden brown and responds to tapping with a hollow thumping sound.

Remove from the pans and cool on a rack.

These loaves freeze very well.

MAKES 2 LOAVES

MILLET AND CORNMEAL BREAD
Pain au Millet et au Mais

This lovely, slightly golden colored bread is a lot like my Mixed Grains Bread, but more crumbly. It has a rich, grainy texture.

MAKING THE SPONGE: Dissolve the yeast in the warm water in a large bowl. Stir in the honey. Stir in the flour, a cup at a time, and whisk the mixture until smooth, about a hundred times. Cover with plastic wrap or a damp towel and set in a warm place to rise for 1 hour.

MIXING THE DOUGH AND KNEADING: Fold the oil or butter and the salt, then the oats, ground millet, and cornmeal into the sponge. Begin folding in the whole-wheat flour, a cup at a time, and as soon as you can turn out the dough, scrape it out onto a floured kneading surface. Knead the dough, adding flour as necessary, for 10 minutes, or until stiff and elastic. Wash out and oil your bowl, shape the dough into a ball, and place it in the bowl, seam side up first, then seam side down. Cover and let rise for 1½ hours.

PUNCHING DOWN, SHAPING LOAVES, BAKING: Punch down the dough and turn out onto a floured surface. Knead for a minute or two, then divide in half and form two loaves. Place the loaves in oiled loaf pans, seam side up first, then seam side down. Cover the loaves with a damp towel and let rise in a warm spot for 1 hour, or until the dough rises above the edges of the pans.

During the last 15 minutes of rising, preheat the oven to 350° F (180° C, gas mark 4).

Gently brush the loaves with the egg beaten with the water. Sprinkle with sesame seeds, brush again, and slash 3 times across the top with a razor blade or sharp knife. Bake in the preheated oven for 50 to 60 minutes, brushing again with eggwash halfway through the baking. When the loaves are golden brown and respond to tapping with a hollow thumping sound, remove them from the pans and cool on a rack.

MAKES 2 LOAVES

FOR THE SPONGE

1 scant tablespoon (1 envelope) active dry yeast

3 cups (750 ml) lukewarm water

3 tablespoons mild-flavored honey

2 cups (225 g) unbleached white flour

2 cups (225 g) whole-wheat flour

FOR THE DOUGH

¼ cup (60 ml) safflower oil or melted butter

Scant 1 tablespoon salt

¾ cup (85 g) rolled oats

1½ cups (225 g) ground millet

1 cup (140 g) stoneground cornmeal

2 to 3 cups (225 to 340 g) whole-wheat flour, as necessary

FOR THE LOAVES

1 egg, beaten with 1 tablespoon water

2 tablespoons sesame seeds

CUMIN AND CORNMEAL BREAD
Pain au Cumin

1 scant tablespoon (1 envelope) active dry yeast
1/2 cup (120 ml) lukewarm water
1 tablespoon mild-flavored honey
1 cup (225 ml) plain low-fat yogurt, at room temperature
2 large eggs
2 tablespoons safflower oil
1 1/2 teaspoons salt
2 tablespoons cumin seeds
1 cup (140 g) stoneground cornmeal
3 cups (340 g) whole-wheat flour
Unbleached flour as necessary, for kneading

I always try to serve a bread at my Supper Club that fits in with the spirit of the meal. For my Mexican dinners I've created this bread, which combines two ingredients that are essential to Mexican cuisine, cumin and corn. This recipe is adapted from one of my herb bread recipes; the dough is moist, and the cornmeal gives the loaf a marvelous grainy texture. The bread has a rich, buttery taste, although there is no butter in it. It's a convenient bread to make, because it doesn't require too much rising time.

Dissolve the yeast in the warm water in a large bowl. Stir in the honey and let sit 10 minutes. Add the yogurt, 1 egg, safflower oil, salt, and cumin seeds, and mix well. Fold in the cornmeal, then the whole-wheat flour, a cup at a time. The dough will be sticky, yet solid enough to turn out of the bowl after you have added 2 cups. Place the third cup on your board and turn out the dough. Knead, adding unbleached flour as necessary, for 10 minutes. The dough will be sticky.

Wash out and oil your bowl, return the dough to it, and let rise, covered, in a warm place for 1 1/2 hours, until doubled in bulk.

Punch down the dough, turn it out, and form into a loaf. Place in an oiled loaf pan and let rise again, covered, in a warm place for 1 hour, or until the dough rises above the edges of the pan.

Preheat the oven to 375° F (190° C, gas mark 5). Beat the remaining egg and use to brush the loaf lightly. Slash with a razor blade or a sharp knife, place in the oven, and bake for 50 minutes. When the loaf is golden brown and responds to tapping with a hollow thumping sound, remove from the pan and cool on a rack.

MAKES 2 LOAVES

SOURDOUGH BAGUETTES
Baguettes de Campagne

This is less dense than the round *pain de campagne* (Sourdough Country Bread, page 18). It also doesn't have as good staying power, perhaps because of the shape of the loaves. But it's so good that it isn't difficult to go through a loaf at one sitting. Use for *"Pain Bagnat"* (the Niçoise salad sandwiches on page 226).

1 envelope active dry yeast
1 cup (225 ml) lukewarm water
1 teaspoon mild-flavored honey
1 tablespoon safflower oil
2 teaspoons salt
½ cup (120 ml) sourdough starter (see page 19)
2 cups (225 g) whole-wheat flour
¾ to 1½ cups (85 to 170 g) unbleached white flour, as necessary

Dissolve the yeast in the lukewarm water in a large bowl. Stir in the honey, oil, and salt. Stir in the sourdough starter. Add the whole-wheat flour, 1 cup (115 g) at a time. The second cup should make the dough thick and almost ready to be turned out onto your kneading surface.

Place about ½ cup (55 g) unbleached white flour on your kneading surface and scrape out the dough. Begin to knead, adding flour as necessary. Knead for 10 minutes. The dough should be slightly sticky.

Wash out and oil your bowl. Shape the dough into a ball and place it in the bowl, seam side up first, then seam side down. Cover with a damp towel or plastic wrap and set in a warm spot to rise for 2 hours.

Punch down the dough and turn it out onto a lightly floured surface. Knead for a few minutes, then divide in half. Shape into 2 long, slender baguette-shaped loaves. To do this, flatten out the dough into a rectangle about ½ inch (1.5 cm) thick. Fold it lengthwise like a letter, pinch the ends, then roll the dough on the table like a sausage, moving your hands from the center to the ends, until the loaf is long and slender, about 2 inches (5 cm) in diameter. Oil baguette pans and dust with cornmeal. Place the loaves in the pans, cover, and let rise for 1½ to 2 hours, until doubled in bulk. Towards the end of the rising time, preheat the oven to 375° F (190° C, gas mark 5). Place an empty pan on a lower rack in the oven.

Just before putting the loaves in the oven, pour 2 cups (450 ml) water into the empty pan. Slash the loaves 3 or 4 times across on the diagonal, place in the oven, and bake 35 to 45 minutes, until they are brown and respond to tapping with a hollow thumping sound.

Remove from the pans and cool on a rack.

MAKES 2 LOAVES

NOTE: Baguette pans can be obtained in kitchenware stores. You could also use a long "banneton"—a long basket lined with towels or muslin, as for Pain de Campagne.

HERBED WHOLE-WHEAT BREAD
Pain Aux Herbes

1 scant tablespoon (1 envelope) active dry yeast

2 cups (450 ml) lukewarm water

1 tablespoon mild-flavored honey

5 tablespoons safflower oil

1 small onion, minced

1 clove garlic, minced or put through a press

1 cup (225 ml) plain low-fat yogurt, at room temperature

Scant 1 tablespoon salt

2 teaspoons dried thyme

2 tablespoons dried dill weed

2 teaspoons dried sage

Dissolve the yeast in the lukewarm water in a large bowl. Add the honey and let sit for 5 minutes. Meanwhile, heat 1 tablespoon of the safflower oil in a skillet and sauté the onion with the garlic, stirring over medium-low heat until the onion is tender. Remove from the heat.

Stir the yogurt into the yeast mixture, then add the remaining 4 tablespoons safflower oil, the salt, thyme, dill weed, and sage. Stir in the sautéed onion and garlic. Whisk in 3 cups (340 g) of the whole-wheat flour and fold in the rest, 1 cup (115 g) at a time. Fold in 1 cup (115 g) unbleached white flour and place the remaining 1 cup (115 g) on your kneading surface. Scrape the dough out onto your kneading surface (you can also knead in the bowl if the dough is too sticky). Knead for 10 minutes, flouring your hands often and using a pastry scraper to scrape up and fold over the dough if it is sticky and hard to work with. When the dough is stiff and elastic, knead it into a ball, oil your washed-out bowl and place the dough in it, seam side up first, then seam side down. Cover with a damp towel or plastic wrap and set in a warm spot to rise for 1½ hours, or until doubled in bulk.

Punch down the dough and turn it out onto a lightly floured kneading surface. Oil 2 loaf pans. Knead the dough for a minute or two, cut into 2 equal pieces, and form each piece into a ball. Then roll each ball into a loaf shape, and place the loaves in the oiled loaf pans, seam side up first, then seam side down. Cover with a damp towel and set in a warm place to rise until doubled in bulk, or until the dough rises above the edges of the pans, about 1 hour.

Twenty minutes before you wish to bake, preheat the oven to 375° F (190° C, gas mark 5). Brush the loaves gently with the egg beaten with the water, then sprinkle with the optional dill seeds. Brush again, slash the loaves and place in the preheated oven. Bake 45 to 50 minutes, or until they are golden brown and respond to tapping with a hollow thumping sound. Remove from the pans and cool on a rack.

MAKES 2 LOAVES

6 cups (680 g) whole-wheat flour
2 cups (225 g) unbleached white flour, plus additional for kneading
1 egg, beaten with 2 tablespoons water
Dill seeds (optional)

COUNTRY BREAD WITH OLIVES
Pain de Campagne aux Olives

This bread is slightly different from my other *pain de campagne* (Sourdough Country Bread, page 18), in that it is less acidic and a little lighter. You can also make olive bread using the other recipe. Just add the olives when you form the loaves, as instructed here.

This is a three-day bread. You mix the starter on the first day, the sponge on the second, and the dough on the third.

DAY 1: MIXING THE STARTER: Two days before you wish to bake, dissolve the yeast in the water in a bowl and stir in the flour. Mix thoroughly, cover with plastic wrap, and set in a draft-free place for 24 hours.

DAY 2: MIXING UP THE SPONGE: Stir the water into the starter. Whisk in the flour, a cup at a time. Mix well, cover again, and set in a draft-free place for another 24 hours.

DAY 3: MIXING THE DOUGH, KNEADING, RISING, SHAPING, BAKING: Fold the salt into the sponge, then the whole-wheat flour, 1 cup (115 g) at a time. By the time you add the third cup you should be able to turn the dough out onto a floured surface. Place ½ cup (55 g) unbleached white flour on your kneading surface and scrape the dough out of the bowl. Knead, flouring your hands often and adding unbleached flour to the kneading surface, for 10 minutes, or until the dough is elastic. It will be sticky, and it will help if you use a pastry scraper to turn the dough. Shape the dough into a ball, oil your washed-out bowl, and place the dough in it, seam side up first, then seam side down. Cover and let rise in a warm place for 1½ hours, until doubled in bulk.

FOR THE STARTER
1 scant tablespoon (1 envelope) active dry yeast
1 cup (225 ml) lukewarm water
1 cup (115 g) whole-wheat flour

FOR THE SPONGE
All of the starter
2 cups (450 ml) lukewarm water
3 cups (340 g) whole-wheat flour

FOR THE DOUGH
All of the sponge
Scant 1 tablespoon salt
3 cups (340 g) whole-wheat flour
Up to 2 cups (225 g) unbleached white flour, as necessary
½ pound (225 g) imported Provençal or Greek olives, pitted and halved or roughly chopped

Punch the dough down and turn it out onto a lightly floured board. Spread the olives over the surface of the dough, fold the dough in half, and knead for a couple of minutes, until the olives are evenly distributed through the dough. Divide the dough in half, if making two loaves, and shape into balls, or shape into one large ball. Place in baskets *(bannetons)* or bowls lined with generously floured dish towels, cover lightly with a dish towel, and let rise for about 2 hours, until doubled in bulk.

Thirty minutes before the end of the rising, preheat the oven to 400° F (200° C, gas mark 6) and heat baking stones in the oven if you are using them. Also heat an empty pan on a lower rack. Dust your baking stone or sheet with cornmeal and carefully reverse the loaf or loaves onto it. Slash the loaves across the top with a razor blade or sharp knife and slide them into the preheated oven. Pour 2 cups (450 ml) water into the hot pan, close the oven door, and bake for 50 to 60 minutes, until the bread is dark brown and responds to tapping with a hollow thumping sound. Remove from the oven and cool on a rack.

MAKES 1 LARGE OR 2 SMALL LOAVES

PESTO BREAD
Pain au Basilic

This is inspired by Carol Field's Pesto Bread, which I came across in her lovely book, *The Italian Baker* (Harper & Row, 1985). When I read her recipe my mouth began to water, as I imagined accompanying an Italian meal with this rich, heady bread. In principle I like to save my pesto for pasta; I make batches of it every summer, and freeze it for winter meals. So in a way I was a little reluctant to give up some of my precious basil paste for bread; yet I couldn't resist trying the recipe. I have changed Carol Field's version slightly, substituting whole-wheat flour for some of the unbleached white, and reducing the oil.

First make the pesto. Stir in the additional ¼ cup Parmesan.

Dissolve the yeast in the water and let sit for 10 minutes. Stir in the pesto and combine thoroughly. Add the safflower oil and salt, and fold in the whole-wheat flour. Fold in the unbleached white flour and turn the dough onto a lightly floured surface.

Knead for 10 minutes, or until the dough is smooth and elastic (can also be done in a mixer). Shape into a ball.

Wash out your bowl, lightly oil it, and place the dough in it, seam side up first, then seam side down. Cover and let rise in a warm place for about 1½ hours, or until doubled in bulk.

Punch down the dough and divide into 2 equal pieces. Knead each piece briefly and shape into a tight round loaf. If you are going to bake on baking stones, place the dough on a baking sheet sprinkled with cornmeal; otherwise place it on an oiled baking sheet. Cover and let rise in a warm place for 45 minutes to an hour, until doubled in bulk.

Preheat the oven to 450° F (230° C, gas mark 8). If using baking stones, heat the stones in the oven for 30 minutes and sprinkle with cornmeal just before you slide the loaves onto them. Slash the loaves with a razor blade or sharp knife and

½ cup (100 g) pesto (see page 293)

¼ cup (30 g) freshly grated Parmesan

1 package active dry yeast

1 cup (225 ml) plus 2 tablespoons lukewarm water

1 tablespoon safflower oil

2 teaspoons salt

2 cups (225 g) whole-wheat flour

2 cups (225 g) unbleached white flour, plus additional for kneading

Cornmeal (optional)

SUPPER CLUB
CHEZ MARTHA ROSE

slide them onto the hot stones, or if you are baking on the baking sheet that the loaves have risen on, place this in the oven. Turn down the heat to 400° F (200° C, gas mark 6) and spray the loaves with water three times in the first 10 minutes. Bake 40 minutes, until the loaves are a deep brown color and respond to tapping with a hollow thumping sound. Remove from the oven and cool on a rack.

MAKES 2 SMALL LOAVES

TEXAS CORNBREAD
Pain de Mais à l'Américaine

This is obviously a dish I brought with me to France, and it is one that I'm often inspired to make. The French love it and so do I. It goes very well with many of the soups and salads I serve. I usually serve it with my Chowder à la Provençale.

Preheat the oven to 450° F (230° C, gas mark 8).

Sift together the cornmeal, flour, baking powder, salt, and baking soda into a large bowl. Beat together the yogurt, milk, honey, and eggs in another bowl.

Place the butter in a 9 × 9-inch (22 × 22 cm) baking pan or a 9-inch (22 cm) cast-iron skillet and place the pan in the oven for 3 or 4 minutes, until the butter melts. Remove from the heat, brush the butter over the sides and bottom of the pan, and pour any remaining butter into the yogurt and egg mixture. Stir this together well, then fold the liquid mixture into the dry mixture. Do this quickly, with just a few strokes of a wooden spoon or plastic spatula. Don't worry about lumps. You don't want to overwork the batter.

1 cup (140 g) stoneground cornmeal

1/2 cup (55 g) whole-wheat flour

1 tablespoon baking powder

3/4 teaspoon salt

1/2 teaspoon baking soda

1 cup (225 ml) plain low-fat yogurt or buttermilk

1/2 cup (120 ml) milk

1 tablespoon mild-flavored honey

2 large eggs

Pour the batter into the warm greased pan, place in the oven, and bake 30 to 35 minutes, until the top is golden brown and a toothpick inserted in the center comes out clean. Let cool in the pan or serve hot.

SERVES 8 TO 10

HOMEMADE PASTA
Pâtes Fraiches Maison

Nothing compares to home-made pasta. I learned to make it in a cooking class with Ann Clark in Austin years ago, and I can still remember my feeling of discovery when I tasted the fresh, slippery, light noodles. I have worked with many recipes since then, for regular pasta, green pasta, whole-wheat pasta, and buckwheat pasta. I've found that, because of the nature of the flour, for each kind the proportions of flour and eggs are slightly different. But the method is always the same. Whole-wheat flour absorbs more moisture than refined flour, so you use slightly less flour in whole-grain pastas. Below are the proportions for regular, whole-wheat, herb, spinach and buckwheat pastas, with instructions that apply to all of them.

NOTE ON QUANTITIES: For each additional 2 portions, add an egg and increase unbleached flour quantities by 4 ounces where using unbleached white flour only, 3 1/2 ounces where using a combination of whole-wheat and other flours, and add 1/8 teaspoon salt.

For the spinach pasta, the spinach replaces one of the eggs, so the easiest way to increase quantities is to double the proportions given here, and freeze or dry any pasta you don't use.

REGULAR PASTA

8 ounces (225 g) unbleached white flour
Heaping 1/4 teaspoon salt
2 large eggs
Water, if necessary

HERB PASTA

Add 4 teaspoons finely chopped fresh herbs, such as parsley or basil, to the regular or whole-wheat pasta recipe. Mix with the flour. The dough will be beautifully speckled.

USING THE FOOD PROCESSOR: If you have one, by all means use it. Pasta-making will be a snap. Put the flours, herbs for herb pasta, and salt in the bowl of your food processor and mix together by turning on the machine for a few seconds. With the machine off, add the eggs, or the egg and spinach for spinach pasta, and the sesame oil for buckwheat pasta. Now turn on the machine, and in just a few seconds (or maybe half a minute), the dough should either come together on the blades or, instead of coming together, form many little balls in the bowl, which you can then gather together in a solid mass with your hands. In any case, the process shouldn't take more than a minute. If the mixture seems wet, it will dry a little as you knead it, and you can (and should) always dust the pasta with flour before you roll it out. If it seems too dry, add a teaspoon of water to the food processor and continue to process a few seconds longer.

Now remove from the food processor and knead the dough for 5 to 10 minutes, until stiff. You can knead it like bread, folding it over and leaning into it on a very lightly floured surface, or you can squeeze the dough from one end to the other, back and forth, or you can slam it down on the work surface, pick it up, and slam it down again. Whatever seems easiest. The dough is stiff and will be much more difficult to knead than bread. Wrap it in plastic wrap and allow it to rest for 30 minutes before rolling it out. Or refrigerate it for up to 2 days, wrapped in plastic. The dough can also be frozen.

MAKING THE DOUGH BY HAND: You should probably learn to do this, even if you do have a food processor, just so you know how it's done (and who knows, you may find yourself in a French farmhouse one summer with no food processor!). Sift together the flours and salt, stir in the herbs for herb pasta, and place on a large work surface or in a large bowl, in a mound. Make a depression in the center of the mound and break the eggs into this well. Add the sesame oil for buckwheat pasta. Using a fork, gently beat the eggs and oil together. When they are lightly beaten, begin brushing flour in from the top of the "walls" of the well and incorporating it into the eggs with your fork. Use your free hand to keep the walls of the well intact while you brush in flour, a little at a time. Don't worry if the egg breaks through the sides of the

WHOLE-WHEAT PASTA

3 ounces (85 g) whole-wheat flour
4 ounces (115 g) unbleached white flour
Heaping 1/4 teaspoon salt
2 large eggs
Water, if necessary

SPINACH PASTA

3 ounces (85 g) whole-wheat pastry flour plus 4 ounces (115 g) unbleached white flour, or 8 ounces (225 g) unbleached white flour
1/4 teaspoon salt
1 large egg
1 ounce (30 g) spinach, stemmed, washed, thoroughly dried, and very finely chopped (1/3 cup)

BUCKWHEAT PASTA

3 ounces (85 g) whole-wheat pastry flour
2 ounces (55 g) buckwheat flour
2 ounces (55 g) unbleached white flour
Heaping 1/4 teaspoon salt
1 teaspoon sesame oil
2 large eggs

well; just push the mixture back into the middle, incorporating flour as you do. As soon as it becomes impossible to incorporate any more flour into the mixture with your fork, brush in the remaining flour and incorporate as much as you can with your hands. Now brush away any hard bits of egg and flour that haven't been amalgamated, and gather the mixture into a ball. Knead and let rest as above.

ROLLING OUT THE DOUGH: I use a hand pasta machine to roll out my dough. It's a very satisfying, simple gadget. First cut the dough into quarters, to facilitate rolling. Flatten it down a little, and with the roller set on 1, roll it through. The edges will be very jagged. Fold these jagged edges in toward each other, press down, and roll the dough again through the first setting. Repeat this process at each setting, dusting with a little unbleached white flour if the dough seems damp. With whole-grain doughs, 4 is usually the thinnest setting you can use before the dough tears. If you can roll the dough through at 5 without tearing it, by all means do so, unless you are going to use the noodles for a salad (salad noodles need to be more substantial; they will become mushy if they're too thin). For noodles, once you've rolled them to the desired thickness, attach the noodle-cutting attachment and cut fettuccine or spaghetti. For ravioli, lasagne, and cannelloni, roll out wide sheets (see recipes for further instructions).

Let the pasta dry for 15 minutes before cooking it.

At this point you can either cook the pasta, or dry it further by laying it out on flour-dusted wax paper, over the back of a chair, or over a dowel for 24 to 48 hours (it takes longer in a humid climate). Once dry, store in a tightly covered container. You can also freeze fresh pasta. Once you have rolled it out and cut noodles, dust with unbleached white flour, wrap in plastic, then freeze in a plastic bag. Fresh pasta will keep, well dusted and wrapped in plastic or sealed in a plastic bag, for a day in the refrigerator.

TO COOK: Fresh pasta cooks, literally, in seconds. Bring a large pot of water to a rolling boil. Add a generous amount of salt and a tablespoon of cooking oil. Add the pasta. It will float to the surface at once. Remove immediately and toss with sauce. If serving cold, rinse with cold water. To cook frozen pasta, transfer it directly from the freezer to the boiling water.

SERVES 4 AS MAIN COURSE, 6 AS A SIDE DISH

WHOLE-WHEAT PIECRUSTS
Pâtés Brisées Complètes

I have always had a weakness for a good tart crust. Whole-wheat crusts have a reputation for tasting and feeling like cardboard; that's because in the sixties and seventies, when whole foods were finding their way into the American marketplace, a lot of people who didn't know much about cooking and baking were selling pies whose crusts were made entirely with coarsely ground whole-wheat flour, strong flavored oils like peanut or soybean oil, too much handling, and not enough taste and care. But there's no reason why a wholesome piecrust can't be delicate. You can avoid the heavy, cardboard texture by using a mixture of whole-wheat and unbleached white or light whole-wheat pastry flours, letting the dough rest for a sufficient amount of time, and handling it with a light touch.

These recipes call for unsalted butter. If you aren't using dairy products, a good-quality margarine will work, but it won't have the same rich flavor.

My dessert crusts contain honey instead of sugar. They aren't as easy to roll out as the more traditional kind, but I love the flavor, sweet but not cloying.

I must warn you again that these crusts won't roll out easily, like the ones your mother used to make. You won't be able to roll them around the pin and lift them easily into the pan. Crusts made with whole-wheat flour tend to break apart when you work with them, so you must work briskly and the dough must be cold. I roll them out between pieces of parchment or wax paper if they are really hard to handle. Then I peel off the top piece, reverse the dough into the pan, and peel off the bottom piece of paper. Wherever a traditional dough would normally ease into the edge of a pan, my crust is more likely to break. Then you must spend some time pressing the edges together. Sometimes you have to work the dough up the sides of the pan, pressing out with your hands, and patching pieces together. As I said, it takes patience. But the end result will be as beautiful as any crust you've ever seen, and will have a rich, full-bodied taste.

General Technique for My Piecrusts

1. Mix together dry ingredients (flours, ground nuts if called for, salt).

2. Cut in the butter, which should be very cold and cut into small pieces. You can do this in a food processor, using the pulse action, or in an electric mixer, or with forks or two knives, or with your hands. If you use your hands, work quickly; pick up handfuls of the flour and butter with both hands and roll them between your thumbs and first two fingers. Keep picking up handfuls until the butter is evenly distributed through the flour and the mixture resembles oatmeal. Then briskly rub the mixture between the palms of your hands, until you have a mixture resembling coarse cornmeal. Now add the liquids and gather the dough together in a ball. Press together, without working too much, so the dough is cohesive, and wrap in plastic wrap. Refrigerate several hours, preferably overnight. The dough can also be frozen at this point.

ROLLING OUT THE DOUGH: Remove from the refrigerator and let sit for about 45 minutes before rolling. It helps to have a heavy rolling pin. Place the dough on a piece of wax paper or parchment, lightly dust your rolling pin, and slam the pin down on the dough, *wham!* Don't be alarmed by the noise.

Turn the dough a quarter turn and continue to *wham* it until it is flattened out to about 1 inch (2.5 cm) thick. Lightly flour the top of the dough and roll, from the center out to the edge, turning the wax paper; you may need two pieces of paper underneath, side by side. If the dough is sticky, place a piece of paper on top, too, and roll out between the two pieces. When the dough is rolled out enough to fit your tart pan, peel off the top piece of wax paper or parchment, reverse the dough into the pan, and peel off the bottom piece.

The dough may have broken wherever it was supposed to ease into the bends of the pie pan. Not to worry. Use your fingers to press the edges toward each other, then to press them together. If the dough isn't lining the pan evenly, just cut and patch, pressing the edges.

To get a pretty edge around the top of the pan, gently press the dough up the edge from the bottom so that you have some extra at the top, then pinch little creases, using your thumb and index finger of one hand and index finger of the other, all around the edge of the pan. The crust can be refrigerated or frozen at this point.

Sweet Almond Piecrust

This is delicious with fruit tarts as well as American pies like pumpkin and apple. Because the almonds add oil to the mixture, I have never needed to add the additional tablespoon of water, but I've listed it just in case the crust seems dry to you.

Mix together the flours, ground almonds, and salt. Cut in the butter. Mix in the honey and almond extract. If the dough comes together, gather it up into a ball. If it seems dry, add the tablespoon of ice-cold water, then gather into a ball. Wrap in plastic wrap and refrigerate several hours, preferably overnight.

Roll out the dough and line a 12- to 14-inch (30 to 35 cm) tart pan. Proceed with the recipe.

MAKES ONE 12- TO 14-INCH (30 TO 35 CM) CRUST

1 cup (115 g) whole-wheat flour or whole-wheat pastry flour

1/2 cup (55 g) unbleached white flour

1/2 cup (55 g) finely ground almonds

1/4 teaspoon salt

4 ounces (115 g) unsalted butter

2 tablespoons mild-flavored honey

1/2 teaspoon almond extract (optional)

1 tablespoon ice-cold water, if necessary

Sweet Dessert Crust

1 cup (115 g) whole-wheat
flour
1 cup (115 g) unbleached
white flour
1/4 teaspoon salt
4 ounces (115 g) unsalted
butter
2 tablespoons mild-flavored
honey
1 tablespoon ice-cold water, if
necessary

Mix together the flours and salt. Cut in the butter. Mix in the honey. If the dough comes together, gather it into a ball. If it seems dry, add the tablespoon of ice-cold water, then gather into a ball. Wrap in plastic wrap and refrigerate for several hours, preferably overnight.

Roll out the crust between pieces of wax paper or parchment and line a 12- or 14-inch (30 to 35 cm) tart pan. Proceed with recipe.

MAKES ONE 12- TO 14-INCH (30 TO 35 CM) CRUST

Savory Whole-Wheat Crust

1 cup (115 g) whole-wheat
flour
1 cup (115 g) unbleached
white flour
1/4 teaspoon salt
4 ounces (115 g) unsalted
butter
2 to 3 tablespoons ice-cold
water, as necessary

Follow the above technique, omitting the honey.

MAKES ONE 12- TO 14-INCH (30 TO 35 CM) CRUST

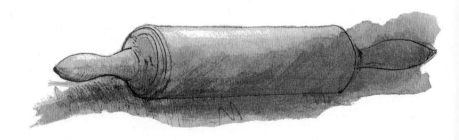

HOMEMADE TORTILLAS
Tortillas Maison

Before I found a reliable source for corn tortillas here in Paris, at a restaurant on the Montparnasse called the Café Pacifico, I used to make my own. That's why I'd brought all the masa, the *comal,* and the tortilla press, after all. What a labor of love! For nachos we made cute little round ones, which we fried for chips. For chalupas the tortillas were slightly larger. The first time we catered a *Herald Tribune* party, before Café Pacifico was around, six of us sat around one night until about two A.M. rolling out small chalupa crisps—four hundred of them. It was assembly-line work, although looking back on it reminds me more of a sewing bee; everyone except me (I was at the stove cooking the tortillas) was sitting around my kitchen table rolling, pressing, and jabbering. There was something very satisfying in knowing that we had made all those tortillas and chips from scratch; but it wasn't satisfying enough to keep us from buying them the next year.

Adding a small amount of flour to the masa harina is a trick I learned from Austin friends. It may not be authentic, but the resulting tortillas are moister and less crumbly than all-masa tortillas.

Mix together the masa harina, flour, and salt in a bowl. Pour in 1 cup of the water all at once and mix together quickly with your hands. The dough should not be in a big lump; it should be slightly crumbly but not too dry. If the dough seems too dry add a little more water, a tablespoon at a time. Let rest for 15 minutes.

Take up golf ball–sized pieces of the dough and form into balls.

Heat a *comal,* griddle, or heavy-bottomed frying pan over medium-high heat; have ready two zip-lock plastic bags. To

2 cups (225 g) masa harina

¼ cup (30 g) unbleached white flour

½ teaspoon salt

1 cup (225 ml) plus 2 to 3 tablespoons water, as necessary

press out the tortillas place one of the plastic bags on your tortilla press and a ball of dough on top of this. Press down a little with your thumb, and place the other plastic bag on top. Now press the tortilla, being careful not to press too hard or your tortilla might stick, and will be too thin. Lift the press and peel off the top bag. Flip the tortilla gently onto the peeled-off bag and peel off the bottom bag.

Transfer the tortilla to the hot *comal* or frying pan and cook about 1 minute, until it is just beginning to dry around the edges. Turn and cook another minute. Remove from the heat. Wrap loosely in foil or a dish towel to keep warm. Continue making tortillas, stacking and wrapping, until all the dough is used up. If the dough becomes dry, sprinkle on a little water.

Reheat the tortillas, if necessary, by wrapping them in foil and putting them in a low oven.

MAKES 12 CORN TORTILLAS

Tortilla Chips or Chalupa Crisps

For chips, either roll the dough into tiny pea-size balls and press and cook as for normal tortillas; or cut cooked tortillas into quarters or sixths. Heat 1 quart (1 L) safflower, vegetable, or corn oil to 360° F (180° C) and deep-fry the handmade or cut tortillas in batches until golden. Drain on paper towels in a colander.

Chips and chalupa crisps should be fried on the day you are planning to serve them, as they tend to get stale.

BLINIS

These earthy-tasting yeasted buckwheat pancakes are great for parties (see my New Years Eve Buffet, page 209); they've been both the focal point of several soirées at my house, or one dish among many on a buffet. They're easy to make and keep well, either in the refrigerator or freezer.

Dissolve the yeast in half the milk. Beat in the egg yolks and sugar.

Sift together the flours and salt. Stir half into the liquid mixture and whisk together until completely smooth. Cover and set in a warm place to rise for 1 hour.

Beat the remaining milk into the yeast mixture and add the remaining flour and melted butter. Combine well. Strain through a medium-fine sieve or a chinois, cover, and let rise for another hour in a warm place. At this point the batter can be refrigerated for several hours, or overnight.

Just before cooking, beat the egg whites to stiff peaks and fold them into the batter.

Heat a crêpe pan or nonstick skillet over medium-high heat. Brush with butter (it should sizzle). Cook the blini, using about 1/4 to 1/3 cup (60 to 80 ml) batter per pancake for large blini, and 2 tablespoons for finger-food size. Cook 30 seconds to a minute on the first side, until bubbles break through, then turn and cook 30 seconds on the other side. Stack and keep warm in a low oven. If not using them right away, wrap the blini tightly in foil. Reheat in a medium oven.

MAKES 12 LARGE OR 24 TO 36 SMALL BLINI

2 tablespoons active dry yeast

4 cups (1 L) warm milk

4 large eggs, separated

2 teaspoons sugar

1 cup (115 g) whole-wheat flour

1 cup (115 g) unbleached white flour

1/2 cup (55 g) buckwheat flour

1 teaspoon salt

2 teaspoons unsalted butter, melted

NOTE: These freeze well. Separate between pieces of wax paper, wrap in foil, and place in plastic bags. They can be transferred immediately from the freezer, wrapped in the foil, to a 350° F (180° C, gas mark 4) oven. They will take about 40 minutes to thaw.

GARLIC CROUTONS
Croutons à l'Ail

*Thin slices of Sourdough
    Country Bread (page 18)
    or baguette*
*1 or 2 cloves garlic, cut in
    half lengthwise*
Olive oil (optional)

These are great with Tapenade (page 67), with melted goat cheese in a salad, or cut into cubes and added to a salad or soup.

Toast the bread in a toaster or under a broiler until lightly browned. Remove from the heat and immediately rub one or both sides (depending on your taste for garlic) with the cut side of a garlic clove. Brush lightly with olive oil, if you wish.

September
Grand Overture de la Saison

SOIRÉE MEXICAINE

MARGARITAS

BLACK BEAN NACHOS
Nachos aux Haricots Noírs

TOMATO HALVES STUFFED WITH GUACAMOLE
Tomates à la Purée d'Avocat

BAKED FISH FILLETS WITH SALSA
Filets de Poisson à la Salsa

MEXICAN RICE
Riz à la Mexicaine

PAN-FRIED CUCUMBERS
Concombres Poêlés

CUMIN AND CORNMEAL BREAD (PAGE 28)
Pain au Cumin

PEACH SHERBET WITH PEACH GARNISH
Sorbet aux Pêches avec son Garniture de Pêches

HONEY-LEMON REFRIGERATOR COOKIES
Galettes au Miel et au Citron

Côtes Ventoux
JON WINROTH'S WINE SUGGESTIONS: BEAUJOLAIS, BROUILLY

The September Supper Club is the first one of the fall "season." Paris is upbeat. During the first week of the month, called *la rentrée* because so many Parisians are away during July and August, the calm of the summer gives way to a back-to-school, back-to-work bustle.

I always serve Mexican food on "opening night." It ensures (or perhaps the tequila ensures) a lively evening. Guests loosen up quickly with a zesty margarita, and the colorful, vibrant food is a welcome change from French cuisine.

When I first served this menu, in September 1985, we had been having a beautiful Indian summer. It was warm enough to stand on the balcony and drink margaritas while we watched the almost full moon come up.

For this meal I wanted to do fish fillets with salsa. At first I thought I might do the fish *en papillote,* but when Laurie Dill and I tested different versions of the recipe, we ended up liking the one given here, and it was a relief not to have to do twenty-four papillotes. We marinated the fillets in lemon juice and olive oil with garlic and coriander, then baked them in a tightly covered baking dish. We ran the glistening red salsa along the side of the fish on the plate, and served bright saffron-tinted Spanish rice and sautéed cucumbers on the side. The crunchy cucumbers made a perfect garnish; I wanted a green vegetable, but didn't want to complicate the course or confuse the palate. These had a nice, clean taste.

For this dish you need a fish with a firm texture. Cod would have done, but even better was what my fishmonger called *rascasse du nord.* It's much like redfish or red snapper. I picked up three kilos of very nice, firm, pink-white fillets in the morning and had them all laid out in their lemon–olive oil marinade in the baking dishes by the afternoon.

The colorful first course was something I'd visualized for a while, five generous black bean nachos around a portion of guacamole, in a tomato half, in the center of the plate. By the time we sat down at the table, the nachos had cooled off considerably, but everyone enjoyed them just the same.

I'd always been reluctant to serve sherbet for my supper clubs, since I don't have a large sorbetière and my freezer capacity is limited. But finally, after reading all the ice cream and sherbet recipes in Alice B. Toklas's cookbook—and I know *she* didn't use newfangled gadgets—I decided to try it the good old-fashioned way, letting the sherbet freeze in baking dishes, and breaking up the ice crystals once or twice. I used a beautiful adaptation of a recipe from *Cooking from an Italian Garden* (Harcourt, Brace, Jovanovich, 1985), by Paola Scaravelli and Jon Cohen, and was very pleased with the results. I tested the recipe a few weeks before the dinner and discovered that the sherbet held very well in the freezer, so I knew it was one of those desserts I could make a few days in advance. After Mexican food, sherbet is delightfully refreshing. I froze the sherbets in small ramekins, then unmolded them into small soup bowls and garnished them with sliced peaches and mint. The honey-lemon cookies were passed on plates.

The 1983 Caves de Sylla Côtes du Ventoux, which I always buy by the case in Apt when I visit Christine Picasso in Provence, was an excellent accompaniment to the meal. The light, fruity wine should be served chilled.

MARGARITAS

There is only one secret to a great margarita: fresh lime juice, squeezed, if possible, just before serving time. The juice will hold, if necessary, for a couple of hours, but then the taste begins to sour.

A margarita is a very congenial drink, perhaps because of all that lime juice consumed with the alcohol. Of course you don't want people to drink too much, but one before dinner has always contributed to a very animated table.

FOR EACH DRINK

1 ½ ounces (45 ml) tequila
1 ounce (30 ml) fresh lime juice
⅔ to ¾ ounces (20 to 25 ml) Triple Sec or Cointreau, to taste (I use the larger amount, as people seem to prefer the slightly sweeter version)

Mix together the tequila, lime juice, and Triple Sec. For a margarita that is less potent but still delicious, though obviously a bit more diluted, you can blend up the mixture with ice. Or you can shake the margaritas with ice and pour them off, or serve them on the rocks. For Supper Club I blend them with ice; it makes the tequila go further, and keeps the guests from getting too "animated."

For a large batch, just remember:

1 part lime juice
1 ½ parts tequila

⅔ to ¾ part Triple Sec or Cointreau, depending on how sweet you like it

BLACK BEAN NACHOS
Nachos aux Haricots Noirs

The beans for these nachos have a rich, earthy flavor, redolent of garlic, cumin, and chili, and that's the reason they are so popular.

1 cup Black Bean Frijoles (see recipe below; freeze leftovers)

1 pound (500 g) ripe tomatoes, diced small

1 to 2 fresh jalapeño or serrano peppers, to taste, seeded and minced

3 tablespoons minced fresh coriander

2 tablespoons minced red onion

1 to 2 tablespoons red wine vinegar, to taste

Salt to taste

30 corn tortilla chips (see note)

3 ounces (85 g) Cheddar cheese, grated (3/4 cup)

1/2 cup (120 ml) crème fraîche or plain low-fat yogurt

Additional fresh coriander leaves for garnish

First make the refried beans.

Make a *salsa fresca* by combining the tomatoes, hot peppers, minced coriander, red onion, vinegar and salt to taste. Set aside.

Sprinkle the tortilla chips with the grated cheese and melt the cheese under the broiler or in a hot oven.

Spread frijoles over each chip and heat through under the broiler. Remove from the heat, place on a serving platter or plates, and top with small dabs of crème fraîche or plain low-fat yogurt, then a small spoonful of the *salsa fresca* (you may substitute a commercial brand of bottled "salsa" or Mexican-style hot sauce, but it's not as good or as pretty). Garnish with fresh coriander leaves and serve.

MAKES 30 NACHOS

NOTE: You can make your own chips by quartering prepared corn tortillas and deep frying, then draining them on paper towels.

TO PREPARE AHEAD OF TIME: If you are making your own tortilla chips, prepare them on the day of the dinner so they will be fresh.

The beans can be prepared well in advance, and to make things easier for you, should be. They will hold for up to 3 days in the refrigerator, and they freeze well. Save some of the cooking liquid—refrigerate it in a jar—so you can moisten them, as they tend to dry out. Reheat them, covered, for 20 to 30 minutes, in a 325° F (170° C, gas mark 3) oven. The remaining ingredients can be prepared early in the day and held in the refrigerator in covered bowls or containers.

Assemble the nachos close to serving time, or the chips will become soggy.

SALSA FRESCA

This vibrant fresh tomato salsa, *picante* with fresh hot peppers and pungent with coriander, comes up in virtually all of my Tex-Mex menus. It will hold for a few hours in the refrigerator.

Combine all the ingredients in a bowl and chill until ready to serve.

MAKES ABOUT 2 CUPS

1 1/2 pounds (750 g) ripe tomatoes, chopped
1/2 small yellow or bermuda onion, finely minced
1 to 3 jalapeño or serrano peppers, to taste, minced
4 tablespoons chopped fresh coriander
1 tablespoon red wine vinegar (or more, to taste)
Salt to taste

BLACK BEAN FRIJOLES REFRITOS

1 pound (500 g) black beans

16 cups (4 L) water

3 tablespoons safflower or
vegetable oil

1 large onion, chopped

4 to 6 large cloves garlic, to
taste, minced or put
through a press

Salt to taste

3 tablespoons chopped fresh
coriander

2 to 3 teaspoons ground cumin

2 to 3 teaspoons mild chili
powder

Wash and pick over the beans and soak them overnight or for several hours in 8 cups (2 L) water. *Use bottled water if your water is very hard.* Drain.

Heat 1 tablespoon of the oil in a large, heavy-bottomed saucepan or Dutch oven and sauté the onion with 2 cloves of the garlic until the onion is tender. Add the beans and 8 cups (2 L) fresh water and bring to a boil. Add the remaining garlic, reduce the heat, cover, and simmer 1 hour. Add salt to taste and more garlic, if you wish, and the coriander, and continue to simmer until the beans are soft and the liquid thick and aromatic, about 1 more hour. Adjust seasonings and remove from the heat.

Allow the beans to cool a while, then drain off about two-thirds of the liquid, retaining it in a separate bowl (use some of it later to moisten the beans). Mash the beans coarsely, in batches, in a food processor or blender or with a potato masher. Make sure not to puree them; you want texture.

Heat the remaining 2 tablespoons oil in a large, heavy-bottomed frying pan and add the cumin and chili powder. Sauté for a minute and add the mashed beans (this can be done in batches, depending on the size of your skillet). Fry the beans, stirring often, until they begin to get crusty and aromatic. If they seem too dry, add some of the reserved cooking liquid. Mash and stir the beans as they cook. There should be enough liquid so they bubble as they cook, while at the same time a thin crust forms on the bottom. Cook for about 15 to 20 minutes, then, if you are serving the beans on their own, transfer to an oiled serving dish.

SERVES 6 TO 8

NOTE: This recipe makes twice as much as you need for the nachos. Freeze what you don't use.

TOMATO HALVES STUFFED WITH GUACAMOLE
Tomates à la Purée d'Avocat

Guacamole is one of those dishes that should be made close to serving time. The color will fade a little no matter what, but lemon juice will keep the guacamole from becoming brown. If the color does change too much for your liking, stir in a small amount of crème fraîche. It's important to use the right kind of avocado—the knobby, dark-skinned California Haas variety. The thin-skinned Florida type is too watery for a good guacamole.

These are lovely in the center of a plate, surrounded by Black Bean Nachos (page 52).

Cut the avocados in half, pit, and scoop out the flesh. Mash, using a pestle or a heavy wooden spoon. Add the chopped tomatoes and lemon juice and continue to mash. Stir in the onion, garlic, cumin, chili powder, and salt to taste. Correct the seasoning and refrigerate.

Scoop out the pulp from the halved tomatoes. Correct the guacamole seasonings once again and fill the tomatoes. Place on a plate. Garnish with coriander and a few corn tortilla chips.

If serving with the Black Bean Nachos (page 52) place the nachos around the tomatoes and use some of the salsa from that recipe to garnish the tomatoes.

SERVES 6

3 ripe medium-size or large
   Haas avocados (the knobby,
   dark-skinned kind)
5 ripe tomatoes (2 chopped, 3
   fairly large ones sliced in
   half)
Juice of 1 to 2 lemons, to taste
½ small red onion, very finely
   minced
1 small clove garlic, minced or
   put through a press
¼ teaspoon ground cumin, or
   more to taste
¼ teaspoon ground chili
   powder, or more to taste
Salt to taste
Fresh coriander and tortilla
   chips (see page 43 for
   homemade) for garnish

BAKED FISH FILLETS WITH SALSA
Filets de Poisson à la Salsa

This is a good dish for a dinner party, because all of the ingredients can be prepared well in advance. The fish bakes in 12 minutes, so it's just a question of watching it carefully once you put it in the oven. This dish has a very clean taste; the lemony fish fillets go nicely with the vibrant salsa. It's light, lovely to look at, and would be appropriate during any season, as long as you can find good fresh tomatoes.

FOR THE FISH

*Salt and freshly ground
  pepper to taste*

*6 fish fillets (about 1 1/2
  pounds), either cod,
  snapper, whiting, bream, or
  a more delicate fish like sole
  or plaice*

*1/4 cup (60 ml) fresh lemon
  juice*

2 tablespoons olive oil

*1 to 2 cloves garlic, to taste,
  minced or put through a
  press*

*1 tablespoon minced fresh
  coriander*

FOR THE SALSA

1 recipe Salsa Fresca, page 53.

Salt and pepper the fish fillets. Mix together the lemon juice, olive oil, garlic, and coriander in a shallow ovenproof casserole. Marinate the fish in this mixture while you prepare the salsa.

Combine all the ingredients for the salsa in a bowl. Correct seasonings. Chill until 30 minutes before you are ready to bake the fish.

Preheat the oven to 400° F (200° C, gas mark 6). Cover the casserole tightly with foil or a lid and bake for 12 minutes, or until the fish flakes. Remove from the heat and transfer to warm plates with a slotted spatula. Place a generous helping of salsa along the side of the fish and serve.

TO PREPARE AHEAD OF TIME: The fish can marinate for several hours. Prepare the marinade, add the fish, and cover the casserole tightly with aluminum foil. Refrigerate until 30 minutes before baking, turning the fillets once or twice. The salsa will hold for several hours; refrigerate in a covered bowl.

SERVES 6

Variation: Use small whole whitings, deboned.

MEXICAN RICE
Riz à la Mexicaine

Have the stock simmering in a saucepan.

Heat the butter or oil over medium heat in a large, heavy-bottomed, lidded frying pan or flameproof casserole and add the onion and garlic. Cook, stirring, until the onion is tender. Add the rice and cook, stirring, for 1 minute. Add the pepper and tomatoes and stir together for a couple of minutes.

Add the wine and cook, stirring with a wooden spoon, until the liquid has just about evaporated. Begin adding the simmering stock, a ladleful at a time. Add the saffron with the first ladleful. Cook, stirring all the while, until each ladleful of stock is almost completely absorbed. Continue adding and stirring until the rice is cooked al dente, which should take 20 to 30 minutes. Add the peas halfway through the cooking, so that they cook 10 to 15 minutes in all. Add salt and freshly ground pepper to taste.

TO PREPARE AHEAD OF TIME: The rice will hold for several hours. You can transfer it to an oiled casserole, cover, and reheat for 30 minutes in a moderate oven, or you can hold it in the frying pan, covered with foil so it won't dry out. Shortly before serving, uncover, add a little oil to the pan, and reheat, stirring, on top of the stove.

SERVES 6

1 quart (1 L) chicken or vegetable stock

1 tablespoon unsalted butter or safflower oil

½ medium-size onion, minced

2 large cloves garlic, minced or put through a press

1 ½ cups (340 g) long-grain rice

1 sweet green or red pepper, seeded and cut in thin strips

¾ pound ripe tomatoes, seeded and chopped

¼ cup (60 ml) dry white wine

½ teaspoon saffron threads

1 cup (170 g) fresh or thawed frozen peas

Salt and freshly ground pepper to taste

PAN-FRIED CUCUMBERS
Concombres Poêlés

1 to 2 tablespoons butter, as
   necessary
1 clove garlic, minced or put
   through a press (optional)
2 long European-style
   cucumbers, peeled and sliced
   ¼ inch (.5 cm) thick
Salt and freshly ground
   pepper to taste
1 tablespoon minced fresh
   parsley

These delicate sautéed cucumbers go nicely with spicy main dishes. Be careful not to overcook them.

Heat the butter in a large skillet and add the garlic. Sauté over medium heat for 1 minute, then add the cucumbers and increase the heat to medium-high. Sauté, stirring, for 5 minutes. The cucumbers should become translucent but should not brown. Add salt and freshly ground pepper to taste and transfer to a warm serving dish. Sprinkle with chopped fresh parsley and serve.

SERVES 4 TO 6

PEACH SHERBET WITH PEACH GARNISH
Sorbet aux Pêches avec son Garniture de Pêches

In September the Paris markets are still bounteous with the last of the summer fruit, including ripe, juicy peaches from Provence, Italy, and Spain. The touch of almond in this luscious sherbet enhances the sweet flavor of the peaches.

MAKING THE SHERBET: Bring a large pot of water to a boil and blanch the peaches for 20 seconds. Drain, run them under cold water, and remove the skins. Pit and place in a blender or food processor, along with the almond extract and lemon juice. Blend to a puree and set aside in the refrigerator.

Combine the water and the honey in a large saucepan, at least twice their volume (honey bubbles up dramatically) and bring to a boil. Reduce the heat and simmer 10 minutes. Remove from the heat and allow to cool.

Blend together the syrup and the peach puree. Transfer to a sorbetière or ice cream maker and freeze according to instructions (see note). Transfer the sherbet to individual molds or an attractive bowl, cover with plastic, then tightly with foil (if the foil is in direct contact with the sherbet, the aluminum will react with the acid in the fruit). Work quickly to cover and return to the freezer before the mixture melts to a liquid, or ice crystals will form again when it freezes.

MAKING THE GARNISH: Mix together the orange juice, lemon juice and honey. Toss with the peaches and marinate for at least 1 hour in the refrigerator.

About 30 minutes before serving, place the sherbet in the refrigerator to soften. Unmold or scoop out and serve in individual bowls, garnished with the fresh peaches and mint leaves.

NOTE: You can also transfer the mixture to a shallow baking dish or ice-cube trays, cover with foil, and place in the freezer for 2 hours, or until almost frozen. Remove from the freezer and blend in a food processor or electric mixer to break up the ice crystals. Return to the bowl or ice trays, cover and freeze for another 2 hours, or until solid. Break up the ice crystals once more, then mold and freeze the sherbet as directed in the recipe.

TO PREPARE AHEAD OF TIME: The nice thing about this sherbet is that it will hold for weeks in the freezer. You could even make it in September and surprise guests with it later in the fall, although you will have to use frozen peaches for garnish if you can't find fresh. The garnish will hold for several hours in a covered bowl in the refrigerator.

SERVES 6

FOR THE SHERBET

2 pounds (1 kg) fresh, ripe peaches

¼ teaspoon almond extract

⅓ cup (90 ml) fresh-squeezed lemon juice

1 cup (225 ml) water

⅓ cup (90 ml) mild-flavored honey

FOR THE GARNISH

Juice of ½ orange

Juice of ½ lemon

1 tablespoon mild-flavored honey (optional)

3 fresh, ripe peaches, pitted

HONEY-LEMON
REFRIGERATOR COOKIES
Galettes au Miel et au Citron

These cookies are great for entertaining because you can make up the dough days in advance. They are tangy and not too sweet.

6 ounces (170 g) unsalted butter

⅔ cup (140 ml) mild-flavored honey

2 teaspoons vanilla

1 large egg

Pinch of salt

2 tablespoons fresh lemon juice

2 tablespoons grated lemon zest

1 cup (115 g) whole-wheat pastry flour

1½ cups (170 g) unbleached white flour

¼ to ½ teaspoon ground cloves, to taste

In a food processor or electric mixer cream the butter and honey. Beat in the vanilla, egg, salt, lemon juice, and lemon zest. Gradually add the flours and cloves. The dough will be very soft and sticky.

Divide the dough in half and, using a spatula, spread it on two long pieces of wax paper or plastic wrap. Don't be intimidated by how wet the dough is; use the spatula to spread the dough on the paper, then carefully shape it into a cylinder about 2 inches (5 cm) in diameter and roll it up in the paper. Don't worry if your "cylinder" isn't perfectly round; these cookies usually have very irregular shapes. Place the dough in the freezer for 2 hours, or refrigerate it overnight.

About 45 minutes before baking time, put the dough, if refrigerated, in the freezer to facilitate cutting. Preheat the oven to 350° F (180° C, gas mark 4). Butter 4 baking sheets.

Unwrap the chilled dough, cut off a quarter of the log, and return the rest of the dough to the freezer so it doesn't soften. Cut the dough in very thin slices, about ¼ inch (.75 cm) thick or even thinner, if possible. Place the slices on the baking sheets, about ½ inch (1.5 cm) apart. Bake for 10 to 15 minutes, until golden brown around the edges and crisp. While the first batch is baking, slice more cookies and place them on the remaining baking sheets. When the cookies are done, transfer them to a rack and allow to cool. Store in a tightly sealed tin.

MAKES 4 DOZEN COOKIES

October

DINER PROVENÇAL

Bandol Rosé or Vin Gris de Cadenne, olives, radis

MIXED PROVENÇAL HORS D'OEUVRES
Assiette d'Hors d'Oeuvres Provençaux

ZUCCHINI AND RICE MOLD
Tian de Courgettes

SALAD OF LAMB'S LETTUCE
Salade de Mâche

VEGETABLES AND EGGS WITH OLIVE PASTE
Tapenade en Barquettes

ROASTED SWEET RED PEPPERS
Poivrons Rôtis

PROVENÇAL VEGETABLE SOUP WITH PESTO (PAGE 282)
La Soupe au Pistou

SOURDOUGH COUNTRY BREAD (PAGE 18)
Pain de Campagne

BAKED FRESH FIGS WITH CRÈME ANGLAISE
Figues au Four à la Crème Anglaise
or

FIG TART WITH GREEN GRAPES
Tarte aux Figues et aux Raisins

Côteaux de Tricastin
JON WINROTH'S WINE SUGGESTIONS: CÔTES DE PROVENCE ROSÉ, TAVEL

Gorgeous fall weather persisted through September and October of 1985, and the night I served this meal everybody was in a marvelous mood. I hadn't even been too hassled that morning when the French union that controls the electric company called a strike. I just called my guests and told them to bring candles.

Often in Paris you wake up and there is no electricity. You check all the fuses, you know you've paid your bill, then you find out that the CGT has called a strike. This always seems to happen on a day that I'm giving a dinner party. Once I changed my menu completely because I thought that the gas would be off too, and the meal would have to be a cold one. Luckily by noon I had my power back and didn't have to scrape my knuckles grating cheese. But I did have to rearrange my cooking schedule, because I'd planned to use my Cuisinart and Kitchenaid in the morning for the *tians* and the crème anglaise.

I'd been thinking Provençal since the beginning of the month, when Laurie and I had gone down to the Provençal winery Domaine Tempier, for the end of the harvest. We had eaten Lulu Peyraud's marvelous food, had helped make bouillabaisse for 35 people, had breakfasted on figs which we picked ourselves, and had visited inspiring, colorful Mediterranean markets. With all of the lusty Mediterranean flavors still fresh in my mouth, I wanted to create a meal with lots of garlic, herbs, olive oil, olives, basil and figs. In anticipation of the pistou, I'd been freezing basil for months.

The Assiette d'Hors d'Oeuvres Provençaux is my version of an entree served at a Niçoise restaurant on the rue du Cherche-Midi called La Porte Fausse. I especially love their *tian de courgettes,* a mold of zucchini, rice, Parmesan, and egg, and found I could replicate it, or nearly, with my recipe. I also adore roasted red peppers with lots of garlic. Laurie arranged all the plates, and they looked gorgeous with the colorful combination of *tian,* roasted red peppers, dark green mâche (lamb's lettuce) tossed with a mild vinaigrette, pungent, glistening tapenade spread on tomato halves, raw red pepper slices, and hard-boiled eggs.

The soup was hot, hot, heady with basil, garlic and Parmesan, and comforting. Unfortunately the green beans and sliced zucchini cooked a little too long. I learned my lesson: now when I serve this soup in quantity I steam the green vegetables separately and add them to the bowls as I serve them. The soup needs that bright green color.

Figs are one of my great weaknesses, and have been ever since I lived in Austin, where fig trees grow in everybody's back yard. They do in Provence as well. My first year in France I went to Domaine Tempier during the harvest and stayed for three weeks; I would walk up to the hillside village of Le Castellet every morning and stop for a snack at a fig tree on the way there and back. I have made both the fig tart and the baked figs to go with this meal. The baked figs with crème anglaise was inspired many years ago by a heavenly dessert of roasted figs, just beginning to caramelize, that I ate at l'Archestrate, then a three-star restaurant owned by chef Alain Senderens, who is now at Lucas Carton.

MIXED PROVENÇAL HORS D'OEUVRES
Assiette d'Hors d'Oeuvres Provençaux

On each plate, arrange a slice of the Zucchini and Rice Mold; a portion of Roasted Red Peppers; a tomato, one or two wide slices of red pepper, a zucchini slice, a half egg and a crouton, each with the tapenade; and a small portion of the Salad of Lamb's Lettuce tossed with its mild vinaigrette.

ZUCCHINI AND RICE MOLD
Tian de Courgettes

This is a simple but extraordinary vegetable terrine called a *tian* after the name of the casserole it is traditionally cooked in. It is one of my favorite Provençal dishes. The satisfying, chewy texture of the rice contrasts nicely with the zucchini.

Preheat the oven to 375° F (190° C, gas mark 5) and butter a 9 × 5 × 3-inch (22 × 12 × 8 cm) loaf pan or a 1 ½ quart (1 ½ L) casserole.

Heat 2 tablespoons of the olive oil in a large, heavy-bottomed skillet and sauté the onion until tender over medium-low heat. Add the zucchini and the garlic, and sauté, stirring often, for 10 minutes over a low flame. Remove from the heat.

Beat the eggs in a large bowl and stir in the cheeses, parsley, rice, thyme, and sautéed vegetables. Add salt and freshly ground pepper to taste. Turn into the prepared baking dish. Sprinkle the breadcrumbs over the top and drizzle with the remaining tablespoon of olive oil. Bake 40 to 60 minutes, until firm. The dish will take a little longer, maybe up to an hour, in a loaf pan, because it is deeper and takes longer to cook through the center. Remove from the heat and cool for at least 20 minutes before serving. Serve warm or cold, cut into slices or squares.

3 tablespoons olive oil
1 onion, minced
2 pounds (1 kg) zucchini, finely chopped
1 to 2 cloves garlic, to taste, minced or put through a press
2 large eggs
2 ounces (55 g) Gruyère cheese, grated (½ cup)
2 tablespoons freshly grated Parmesan cheese
½ cup (15 g) chopped fresh parsley
½ cup (115 g) raw short-grain brown or Italian Arborio rice, cooked in 1 ½ cups water according to directions on page 81
¼ to ½ teaspoon dried thyme, to taste
Salt and freshly ground pepper to taste
2 heaping tablespoons homemade breadcrumbs

TO PREPARE AHEAD OF TIME: The ingredients for this can be prepared the day before you make it. Store them in plastic bags or covered containers in the refrigerator. The baked terrine will hold for up to a day in the refrigerator, tightly covered. It does not freeze well.

SERVES 6 TO 8

ROASTED SWEET RED PEPPERS
Poivrons Rôtis

I don't know of anybody who doesn't love this dish, although some like it more garlicky than others. My Yugoslavian friend Zoran Mojsilov is used to lots of garlic and a fair amount of vinegar, whereas Christine Picasso uses no vinegar or garlic at all, just olive oil and salt. My version is toned-down Yugoslavian style, with a hint of Provence if I have fresh basil on hand.

There are several ways to roast the peppers. You can place them directly over a gas flame or below a broiler. Or you can put them in a dry skillet over an electric or gas burner, or in a baking dish in a hot oven. You want all the skin to blister and blacken. Keep turning the peppers until they are uniformly charred, then place them in a paper bag or wrap in a dishtowel until cool enough to handle.

Peel off the blackened skin, split the peppers in half, and remove the seeds and inner membranes. Rinse them quickly under cool water and pat dry. Cut the halved peppers in half lengthwise, or in wide strips. Place them in a bowl or serving dish and toss with the garlic, olive oil, vinegar and salt to taste. Cover and refrigerate until ready to serve. Toss with the basil shortly before serving.

TO PREPARE AHEAD OF TIME: These will hold for several days in the refrigerator in a covered bowl. But don't add the basil until shortly before you serve.

SERVES 6 TO 8

6 to 8 medium-size sweet red peppers

2 large cloves garlic, minced or put through a press (more to taste)

8 tablespoons olive oil

3 tablespoons red wine vinegar, or more to taste

Salt to taste

1 to 2 tablespoons fresh chopped basil, to taste

TAPENADE

X good

❦

This is an intense Provençal olive paste, heady with garlic, capers, and anchovies. It will keep for weeks in the refrigerator and makes a marvelous hors d'oeuvre, spread thinly on garlic croutons (page 46) or on raw vegetables.

Pit the olives and puree them, along with the garlic, capers, anchovies, thyme, and rosemary in a mortar and pestle or in a food processor. Add the remaining ingredients and continue to process until you have a smooth paste. Place in a bowl, cover, and refrigerate until ready to use.

Spread on croutons or raw vegetables and serve as an hors d'oeuvre, with a Provençal rosé, a dry white wine, or champagne.

TO PREPARE AHEAD OF TIME: This will hold for weeks in the refrigerator. Keep it in a jar or covered container, and pour a thin film of olive oil over the surface to keep it from drying out.

SERVES 10 AS AN HORS D'OEUVRE

½ pound (250 g) imported black Provençal olives (use Greek if these cannot be found)

2 cloves garlic, minced or put through a press

1 ½ tablespoons capers

4 to 6 anchovy fillets, to taste

¼ to ½ teaspoon dried thyme, to taste

¼ to ½ teaspoon dried rosemary, to taste, crumbled

4 tablespoons olive oil

2 tablespoons fresh-squeezed lemon juice

1 to 2 tablespoons Cognac (optional)

1 teaspoon Dijon mustard

Lots of freshly ground black pepper

VEGETABLES AND EGGS WITH OLIVE PASTE
Tapenade en Barquettes

The *tapenade* is stretched with the yolks of the hard-boiled eggs, which results in a slightly milder tasting version. This makes a wonderful first course as well as a beautiful hors d'oeuvre platter. I also recommend it for picnics (see the menu for "A Picnic on the Seine," page 221).

6 large eggs, hard-boiled
1 recipe Tapenade (recipe above)
6 small or medium tomatoes, cut in half
3 small zucchini, cut in half lengthwise, then into 3-inch (8 cm) lengths
2 sweet red peppers, seeded and cut in wide strips

FOR GARNISH
Chopped fresh parsley
Lemon rounds or wedges,
Radishes

Peel the hard-boiled eggs and cut them in half lengthwise. Carefully remove the yolks and reserve the whites. Mash the yolks with the tapenade and blend together thoroughly.

Turn the tomatoes upside down on a rack and let them drain 15 minutes.

Blanch the zucchini pieces in a large pot of boiling water, refresh them under cold water, and scoop out the seeds.

Spread a generous portion of tapenade over the tomatoes, zucchini pieces, and red pepper slices. Fill the reserved egg whites. Place the barquettes on a large platter or on individual plates and garnish with chopped fresh parsley, lemon, and radishes.

TO PREPARE AHEAD OF TIME: The egg yolks make this dish more perishable than tapenade made without them, but it will still hold for 4 or 5 days in the refrigerator, in a covered container. You can prepare the eggs and vegetables several hours before you wish to serve them, and hold them in the refrigerator on a platter, in covered containers, or in plastic bags.

SERVES 6 TO 8

SALAD OF LAMB'S LETTUCE
Salade de Mâche

Mache, which is called "lamb's lettuce" in the States, are small, delicate, soft-textured dark-green leaves, which should not be overpowered by a sharp vinaigrette. This simple salad, with its clean, uncomplicated taste, was a welcome compliment to the other heady items on my Provençal hors d'oeuvres plate.

Make sure you wash the lamb's lettuce thoroughly, as a lot of sand tends to get trapped at the bottom of the stems.

Wash and dry the salad greens.

Mix together the vinegar, mustard, salt and pepper. Whisk in the olive oil. Toss with the lamb's lettuce just before serving.

TO PREPARE AHEAD OF TIME: The dressing will hold for several hours, in or out of the refrigerator, and if the lamb's lettuce is carefully dried it will also hold in the refrigerator for several hours.

SERVES 6 TO 8

3/4 pound (340 g) baby lamb's lettuce, carefully washed and dried

2 to 3 tablespoons red wine vinegar, to taste

1/2 teaspoon Dijon mustard

Salt and freshly ground pepper to taste

6 to 8 tablespoons good-quality olive oil, to taste

wonderful

PROVENÇAL VEGETABLE SOUP WITH PESTO
La Soupe au Pistou

This is a Provençal minestrone, with the special addition of the *pistou,* a kind of pesto without the nuts, enriched with tomato and more cheese than Italian pesto. It's a heady, marvelous meal in itself.

FOR THE SOUP

1 cup (250 g) white or navy beans, washed and picked over

4 quarts (4 L) water

2 tablespoons olive oil

2 medium-size onions, chopped

4 cloves garlic, minced or put through a press

1 bouquet garni (made with 1 stalk celery, 1 bay leaf, 2 sprigs fresh parsley and 2 sprigs fresh thyme, tied together)

2 Parmesan rinds (optional)

3/4 pound (340 g) new or russet potatoes, scrubbed and diced

1 leek, white part only, cleaned and sliced

3/4 pound carrots, thinly sliced

1 pound (500 g) tomatoes, peeled and quartered

3/4 pound (340 g) zucchini, half chopped, half thinly sliced

SUPPER CLUB
CHEZ MARTHA ROSE

MAKING THE SOUP

Soak the beans overnight or for several hours in 1 quart (1 L) of the water (use bottled if your water is hard). Drain.

Heat the 2 tablespoons olive oil in a heavy-bottomed soup pot and add the onions and half the garlic. Sauté over medium heat until the onions are tender and add the beans, the bouquet garni, and 2 quarts (2 L) water. Bring to a boil, reduce the heat, cover, and cook 1 hour. The beans should be almost tender and the broth aromatic.

Add the remaining 1 quart (1 L) water and 2 cloves garlic, the Parmesan rinds, leek, carrots, potatoes, tomatoes and the diced, but not the sliced, zucchini, and salt to taste. Cover and simmer 1 hour. Adjust seasonings.

MAKING THE PISTOU

While the soup is simmering, pound together the garlic and basil in a mortar, or puree in a food processor. Drizzle in the oil, continuing to pound or process until you have a smooth paste. Work in the tomato and the cheese. Taste and add salt and freshly ground pepper to taste. Set aside.

COMPLETING THE SOUP

Ten to 15 minutes before you wish to serve the soup, add the sliced zucchini, green beans, and pasta. Simmer until the vegetables are tender but still bright green and the pasta is cooked al dente. Taste the soup, adjust the salt, and add freshly ground pepper to taste. Remove the parmesan rind and the bouquet garni.

The *pistou* is added to the soup at the last minute. It can either be stirred into the soup pot or added to each individual serving. Another alternative is to serve the soup and pass the *pistou* in its mortar, allowing your guests to stir in their own. Serve with a crusty country-style bread, such as Country Bread with Olives (page 32) and a crisp green salad.

TO PREPARE AHEAD OF TIME: This soup will hold for several days in the refrigerator. It's actually best if made the day before you serve it (see note below). Allow it to cool, then cover and refrigerate. The *pistou* enrichment can be made several days in advance, just up to the adding of the cheese and tomato, and held in a covered container in the refrigerator. Without the cheese and tomato it freezes well.

SERVES 6 TO 8

NOTE: If the soup is made the day before, proceed up to the adding of the sliced zucchini, green beans, and pasta. Reheat the soup before serving and adjust seasonings. Ten to 15 minutes before serving, add the sliced zucchini, green beans, and pasta and proceed as above, adding the pistou *at the last minute. If you are making this soup in quantity, steam the zucchini and green beans separately and add them to the soup when you serve it.*

½ pound (250 g) green beans, trimmed, cut in 1-inch (2.5 cm) lengths

1 cup (55 g) broken spaghetti or elbow macaroni

Salt and freshly ground pepper to taste

FOR THE PISTOU

2 to 4 cloves garlic, or more, to taste

2 cups (85 g), tightly packed, fresh basil

½ cup (120 ml) fruity olive oil

1 small tomato, peeled, seeded, and chopped

1 cup (100 g) freshly grated Parmesan, or a mixture of Gruyère and Parmesan

Salt and freshly ground pepper to taste

BAKED FRESH FIGS WITH CRÈME ANGLAISE
Figues au Four à la Crème Anglaise

I first developed this dish to go with a Moroccan meal. The figs are poached in a mixture of red wine, honey, and cinnamon. They are then removed from the wine, and the wine is strained and reduced by about a third. The poached figs can sit all day, until, shortly before serving, they are baked in a moderate oven for about 15 minutes.

Meanwhile you will have made a crème anglaise, seasoned with vanilla and nutmeg. To serve, first the wine syrup goes on a plate or in a bowl, then the hot figs, then the crème anglaise, which you can also dot around the edges of the syrup. The crème anglaise melts into the syrup, and it is beautiful and insanely delicious.

It really doesn't matter what order you do this in. The crème anglaise can be made before or after you poach the figs.

FOR THE FIGS

3 cups (700 ml—½ liter) red wine, not too full-bodied

½ cup (120 ml) mild-flavored honey

½ teaspoon ground cinnamon (or more, to taste)

½ teaspoon vanilla

1½ to 2 pounds (750 g to 1 kg) fresh ripe figs

POACHING THE FIGS: Combine the wine, honey, cinnamon, and vanilla and bring to a boil in a large, heavy-bottomed saucepan. Meanwhile make a lengthwise incision in each fig, but do not cut them in half all the way. The inside as well as the outside will now become infused with the heady, spicy wine and honey mixture.

Turn the wine to a simmer and drop in the figs. If they are very ripe, turn off the heat immediately and infuse for 5 to 10 minutes. If they are slightly hard, poach over heat for 15 minutes. Carefully remove the figs from the wine with a slotted spoon and place in a buttered flat baking dish. Strain the wine through a fine sieve and return it to the pot. Bring to a boil and reduce by about a third. Set aside. Set the dish aside and cover after the figs have cooled.

MAKING THE CRÈME ANGLAISE: With an electric mixer, beat together the egg yolks and honey at high speed until they are thick, lemon colored, and ribbony. At the same time, heat the milk to a simmer. Remove the milk from the heat and beat slowly into the egg yolks. Turn this mixture into a heavy-bottomed saucepan or top of a double boiler, or a saucepan set over a flame tamer, and stir over low heat until it thickens. By no means allow it to come to a simmer, or the egg yolks will curdle. When the mixture coats the front and back of your spoon like thick cream, remove it from the heat and continue to stir for a minute to cool. Stir in the vanilla and nutmeg and set aside. You can serve this on the figs at room temperature, chilled, or warm.

About 25 minutes before you wish to serve, preheat the oven to 375° F (190° C, gas mark 5). Place the figs in the oven and heat through for 10 to 15 minutes, until they are just beginning to dry. Remove them from the oven and pour on the wine.

TO SERVE: Spoon the wine into serving bowls, then add the figs and top with the crème anglaise.

TO PREPARE AHEAD OF TIME: Each part of this dish—the poached figs, the wine syrup, and the crème anglaise—will hold for several hours, in or out of the refrigerator. The crème anglaise can be made a day ahead of time. Allow it to cool, cover tightly, and refrigerate.

SERVES 6 TO 8

FOR THE CRÈME ANGLAISE

4 large egg yolks
1/2 cup (120 ml) mild-flavored honey
1 1/2 cups (350 ml) milk
1 teaspoon vanilla
Pinch of freshly grated nutmeg

FIG TART WITH GREEN GRAPES
Tarte aux Figues et aux Raisins

The light green grapes are beautiful alongside the figs in this tart. If you can find the big sweet Muscat grapes—they are often imported from Italy and France in the fall—use them. Otherwise use California seedless.

Sweet Almond Piecrust (page 41) or Sweet Dessert Crust (page 42)

FOR THE FIGS

1 pound (500 g) fresh ripe figs,

2 cups (1/2 liter) red wine, not too full bodied

1/2 cup (120 ml) mild-flavored honey

1/2 teaspoon ground cinnamon (or more to taste)

1/2 teaspoon vanilla extract

Crème anglaise prepared as directed on page 73

1 egg, beaten

1/2 pound (250 g) large green grapes, preferably Muscat

First make the crust. Refrigerate or freeze it until ready to prebake and assemble the tart.

The crème anglaise can be made before or after you prepare the figs. You can serve it on the tart at room temperature, chilled, or warm.

For the figs, combine the wine, honey, cinnamon, and 1/2 teaspoon vanilla and bring to a boil in a large, heavy-bottomed saucepan. Meanwhile cut the figs in half lengthwise. Turn the wine to a simmer and drop in the figs. Poach them for 5 minutes, and carefully remove from the wine with a slotted spoon and place in a flat baking dish. Strain the wine through a fine sieve and return it to the pot. Bring to a boil and reduce by half. Set aside.

If you object to leaving the seeds in the grapes, cut the grapes in half and remove the seeds. Otherwise leave whole.

Preheat the oven to 375° F (190° C, mark 5). Brush the crust with beaten egg and prebake it for 15 to 20 minutes, until golden brown. Arrange the figs, cut side up, and grapes, cut side down if you've removed the seeds, on the baked tart shell in an attractive pattern. Brush with the reduced wine.

Preheat the broiler. Place the tart under the broiler for 10 minutes, until the figs begin to caramelize. Remove from the heat and serve hot, or cool and serve, passing the crème anglaise or spooning a little over or alongside the tart.

TO PREPARE AHEAD OF TIME: The crust can be made days in advance, covered with foil, and frozen. The crème anglaise will hold for a day in the refrigerator, and the figs will hold for several hours. For best results, don't let the tart sit too long once it is assembled, as the crust will become soggy.

SERVES 8

November

SALUT AU BEAUJOLAIS NOUVEAU

Beaujolais Nouveau

SALAD OF WILD AND ITALIAN RICE WITH GREEN BEANS
Salade aux Deux Riz et aux Haricots Verts

MIXED GRAINS BREAD (PAGE 64)
Pain aux Céréales

BROCCOLI PUREE
Purée de Brocolis

MUSHROOM TART
Tarte aux Champignons

PUMPKIN, SWEET POTATO AND APPLE PUREE
Purée de Potiron, Patates, et Pommes

PUCKER-UP CRANBERRY RELISH
Délice d'Airelles

CRISP ALMOND COOKIES
My Biscotti di Prato

PEARS POACHED IN BEAUJOLAIS
Poires Pochées au Beaujolais

Gamay Primeur Château de Charmoise (Marionet)
JON WINROTH'S WINE SUGGESTION: ZINFANDEL

This meal was a kind of pre-Thanksgiving dinner without the turkey. It also happened to fall on the Beaujolais *nouveau* day in 1985. Beaujolais *nouveau* is the first wine made from the year's harvest that is ready to drink, and the government sets a date upon which it can legally be sold, which is usually the third Thursday in November. All the cafés post signs that say *"Le Beaujolais Nouveau est arrivé!"* and all over Paris people stop at watering holes to taste it. Cafés and wine bars that normally close at eight P.M. are packed with people and stay open until nine or ten. During the day business people—executives, shopkeepers, secretaries, and beauticians—open bottles at work so they and their employees can taste the year's wine. Some years the Beaujolais is smooth, fruity, and promising, other times it has tasted rough and unfinished to my palate. But whatever the quality of the wine, I love the way all of Paris gets involved.

Naturally, Beaujolais *nouveau* was the aperitif at this Supper Club. It should be drunk slightly chilled, and on this unseasonably cold, snowy evening I kept the wine on the balcony, which often serves as a refrigerator for me in the winter. My guests sat around the fireplace drinking the Beaujolais, and at dinner they tasted another *primeur,* or early wine, a gentle, fruity Gamay from the Touraine region.

I was pleased that my Supper Club would serve as a tasting ground that year, and it certainly did; more wine was consumed than at any dinner before or since. (More, as well, was spilled on the table than ever before, thanks to an exuberant Yugoslavian sculptor named Zoran Mojsilov.)

This was a fall/winter meal with earth tones and flavors, and delicious combinations of savory and sweet. The pale green broccoli puree, bright yellow-orange sweet potato and pumpkin puree, and red cranberry relish looked exquisite side by side on the plate, next to the fragrant mushroom tart. The shimmering pears poached in Beaujolais with the hard, almondy *biscotti*, meant to be dipped into the wine, completed the Beaujolais nouveau theme and provided a refreshing finish to the meal. Many of the American guests commented that the dinner had all the elements of Thanksgiving without the stuffed feeling you have at the end.

SALAD OF WILD AND ITALIAN RICE WITH GREEN BEANS
Salade aux Deux Riz et aux Haricots Verts

I always have wild rice on hand in Paris because my relatives and friends from Minneapolis send it to me regularly. I consider the grain a luxury, but I've seen some French people turn up their noses because it looks funny, even ugly, to them. This salad combines wild with brown or Italian Arborio rice; each rice is cooked separately in vegetable stock, and then they are tossed together with walnut oil. Shortly before serving, the grains are tossed in a vinaigrette with walnuts or pecans and mushrooms, bright green beans, and herbs, then spooned over a bed of lettuce. What an exciting contrast of textures, flavors and colors! Sweet red peppers garnish and set off the dish and add one more complementary taste.

The dressing for the rice is not very acidic, because the grains themselves taste so good and the mushrooms are tossed separately in lemon juice. But if you prefer a sharper vinaigrette, feel free to add more vinegar and/or mustard. Also, you can vary the herbs. Sometimes I use the rosemary and thyme, at other times I go for sweeter herbs like chervil, tarragon, or chives.

PREPARING THE WILD RICE: Bring 2 1/2 cups (550 ml) of the vegetable stock or bouillon to a boil in a large saucepan and add the wild rice and a little salt. When the liquid comes back to a boil, reduce the heat, cover, and simmer 35 minutes. If the grains are tender but not mushy, remove from the heat and drain off the excess stock. If still not tender, cook another 10 minutes, adding more water if necessary. Remove from the heat and pour off the excess stock.

PREPARING THE BROWN OR ITALIAN RICE: Meanwhile, in another saucepan, bring the remaining 1 1/2 cups (350 ml) stock or bouillon to a boil and add the brown or Italian rice and a little salt. Bring to a second boil, cover, reduce the heat, and simmer 35 to 40 minutes, until the rice is tender but not mushy (pour off any liquid that remains). Toss the two rices together in a large bowl with the walnut oil and set aside.

PREPARING THE SALAD: Slice the mushrooms and toss with the lemon juice. Set aside.

Blanch the green beans in boiling water for 1 or 2 minutes, drain, and rinse with cold water.

Mix together the vinegar, mustard, optional garlic, and the olive or safflower oil for the vinaigrette. Add salt and freshly ground pepper to taste and blend well. Just before serving, toss with the beans, then toss this mixture, along with the nuts, mushrooms, and all the chopped herbs, with the rice. Taste and correct seasonings, adding salt, pepper, garlic, or vinegar to taste.

TO SERVE: Line individual plates with lettuce leaves, top with the salad, and place the chervil sprigs on the top. Garnish with the strips of sweet red pepper. Or line a salad bowl or platter with the lettuce leaves, top with the salad, and decorate with the chervil and red peppers.

TO PREPARE AHEAD OF TIME: The rices can be cooked a day ahead and tossed with the walnut oil. Place in a bowl, cover, and refrigerate.

FOR THE SALAD

4 cups (1 L) vegetable stock or bouillon

1 cup (175 g) wild rice

1/2 cup (115 g) short-grain brown rice or Italian Arborio rice

Salt

1/2 cup (120 ml) walnut oil

1/2 pound (250 g) mushrooms, cleaned and sliced

Juice of 2 large lemons

1/2 pound (250 g) green beans, ends trimmed

1/2 cup (55 g) shelled walnuts or pecans

1/4 cup (10 g) chopped fresh parsley

FOR THE VINAIGRETTE

3 tablespoons red wine vinegar

1 teaspoon Dijon mustard

1 small clove garlic, minced or put through a press (optional)

6 tablespoons olive or safflower oil

1 to 2 teaspoons finely minced fresh rosemary, if available

1 teaspoon fresh thyme leaves, if available, or 1/4 teaspoon dried

Salt and freshly ground pepper to taste

1 small sweet red pepper, sliced in thin strips

1 bunch fresh chervil, if available

Lettuce leaves, either leaf or red-tip

The green beans can be blanched up to a day ahead and stored in a plastic bag in the refrigerator.

The herbs can be chopped up to a day ahead of time. Make sure they are dry before you chop them. Place in a bowl or plastic container, cover tightly, and refrigerate.

You can make the dressing several hours ahead of time. Hold it in or out of the refrigerator.

The mushrooms can be sliced several hours ahead and held in the refrigerator in a covered bowl. Do not add the lemon juice until close to serving, as the flavor changes after about a half hour.

SERVES 6

BROCCOLI PUREE
Purée de Brocolis

This bright green puree is an adaptation of a Silver Palate recipe for pureed broccoli with crème fraîche. I've reduced the amount of crème fraîche and substituted plain low-fat yogurt for their sour cream. This is a light, subtle dish; so subtle, in fact, that people often ask me what the vegetable is.

Preheat the oven to 350° F (180° C, gas mark 4). Butter an ovenproof serving dish.

Steam the broccoli until tender, about 8 to 10 minutes. Drain and refresh under cold water, then puree in a food processor or through a food mill. Add the crème fraîche and continue to puree until smooth. Stir in the yogurt, Parmesan, nutmeg, salt, and pepper. Taste and adjust seasonings.

Transfer the puree to the prepared serving dish and dot the top with butter. Bake for 25 minutes in the preheated oven, or until steaming hot. Serve at once.

TO PREPARE AHEAD OF TIME: The broccoli can be trimmed and steamed a day in advance. Drain it thoroughly and hold in the refrigerator in a plastic bag or covered bowl. The puree can be made several hours before baking and held in the refrigerator.

SERVES 6

3 pounds (1.5 kg) broccoli, stems peeled and chopped, tops separated into florets

½ cup (120 ml) crème fraîche

¾ cup (180 ml) plain low-fat yogurt

2 ounces (55 g) Parmesan cheese, freshly grated (½ cup)

¼ teaspoon freshly grated nutmeg

Salt and freshly ground pepper to taste

2 tablespoons unsalted butter

MUSHROOM TART
Tarte Aux Champignons

This is a hearty and heartwarming combination of sweet browned onions and savory, earthy mushrooms. The mushrooms are chunky and meaty. The night after I served this at Supper Club I was at a French dinner party where the conversation inevitably led to food, and a woman asked me if it wasn't terribly difficult to produce a satisfying meal without meat. I found myself using this tart to illustrate how certain vegetable dishes can satisfy in the same way that meat satisfies. In this case you get a meaty effect because of the flavor of the mushrooms and the way the liquid they release when they cook is reduced to a glaze. Not that I think that's necessary or even desirable in most cases, but here it just works that way.

I have cut the tart into small pieces and used it as an hors d'oeuvre as well as a main course. Try to make up the crust the day before. Or do it several days before, and freeze it.

If fresh wild mushrooms are available, use an assortment. If not, use dried cèpes and cultivated mushrooms.

Make the crust. Refrigerate until ready to prebake.

MAKING THE FILLING: Heat 2 tablespoons of the butter and 1 tablespoon of the oil in a large, heavy-bottomed skillet and sauté the onions, stirring occasionally, over medium-low heat for 30 to 40 minutes, or until browned and caramelized.

While the onions are browning, prepare the mushrooms. Place the dried cèpes, if using, in a bowl and pour on boiling water to cover. Let them sit for about 20 minutes, or until softened; drain and rinse thoroughly. Squeeze dry. Save the soaking liquid for vegetable stock.

Trim the fresh mushrooms, wash them quickly, and wipe dry. Cut into quarters if large, in half if small.

When the onions are ready, transfer to a bowl and set aside. Add the remaining tablespoon of butter and 1 tablespoon oil to the skillet and heat over medium heat. Add the mushrooms and sauté, stirring, for about 5 minutes, until they begin to release their liquid. Add the garlic, dried mushrooms, and more oil if necessary. After about 10 minutes add the wine and soy sauce and continue to sauté, stirring from time to time, for another 5 to 10 minutes. Stir in the thyme and rosemary and add salt and freshly ground pepper to taste. Raise the heat and cook, stirring, until the liquid is reduced by about three fourths, so the mushrooms are glazed and a little liquid remains in the pan. Taste and adjust the seasonings, adding a little salt, pepper, soy sauce or garlic if you wish, and transfer to the bowl with the browned onions.

BAKING THE TART: Preheat the oven to 375° F (190° C, gas mark 5). Beat the eggs in a bowl. Prick the tart crust with a fork and brush with some of the beaten egg; this will prevent the crust from becoming soggy. Place it in the preheated oven for about 8 minutes, or until just crisp on the bottom, and remove from the heat.

Stir the milk or crème fraîche into the beaten eggs, along with the cheese and parsley. Add the mushrooms and onions and combine thoroughly. Adjust seasonings.

Turn the mushroom mixture into the crust and bake in the preheated oven for 30 to 40 minutes, until firm. Remove from the heat. Serve hot or at room temperature.

TO PREPARE AHEAD OF TIME: The unbaked crust can be made several days in advance and stored, covered with foil, in the refrigerator or freezer.

The mushroom and onion filling, without the eggs and milk or crème fraîche, can be made a day in advance. Allow it to cool, transfer to a bowl, cover and refrigerate. Allow to come to room temperature before baking.

The tart can be cooked an hour or so before you wish to serve it and reheated at the last minute.

SERVES 6 TO 8

*Savory Whole-Wheat Crust
(page 42)*

3 tablespoons butter

4 medium or large onions, chopped

2 to 3 tablespoons safflower or olive oil, as necessary

2 ounces (55 g) dried cèpes

Boiling water to cover (optional)

2 pounds (1 kg) fresh wild mushrooms, such as cèpes, shiitaki, oyster mushrooms, or girolles, or 2 pounds (1 kg) fresh cultivated mushrooms

1 to 2 tablespoons olive oil, as necessary

3 to 4 cloves garlic, to taste, minced or put through a press

¼ cup (60 ml) dry white wine

1 to 2 tablespoons soy sauce, or more to taste

½ teaspoon dried thyme

½ to 1 teaspoon dried rosemary, to taste, crumbled

Salt and freshly ground pepper to taste

4 large eggs

½ cup (120 ml) low-fat milk or (for a richer version) crème fraîche

3 ounces (85 g) grated Gruyère cheese (⅔ cup)

3 tablespoons chopped fresh parsley

PUMPKIN, SWEET POTATO, AND APPLE PUREE
Purée de Potiron, Patates, et Pommes

1 pound (500 g) sweet
  potatoes
2 tart apples
1 pound (500 g) pumpkin,
  seeds and strings removed
Unsalted butter
Juice of 1 lime
1/4 cup (60 ml) plain low-fat
  yogurt or crème fraîche
2 tablespoons melted unsalted
  butter
1 tablespoon mild-flavored
  honey
Salt to taste (optional)

Of all the dishes I serve for my Thanksgiving or Thanksgiving-type meals, this one gets the biggest raves. The contrast of tart and sweet is sublime, the texture is smooth and light, and the color is gorgeous. It's a beguiling combination; my guests always ask me what's in it (and it's so simple!). The puree contrasts nicely with savory dishes.

Preheat the oven to 425° F (220° C, gas mark 7). Rub the skins of the sweet potatoes and apples and the surface of the pumpkin with butter, and pierce the sweet potatoes and apples in a few places with a knife. Place the vegetables, with the pumpkin cut side down, on an oiled baking sheet or baking sheets and bake until they are all tender. The apples will be done first, after about 30 minutes, then the pumpkin, after about 45 minutes, and finally the sweet potatoes, after about 50 minutes. Remove them from the oven as they are done; then, when cool enough to handle, remove the skins from the potatoes and pumpkin, and the skins and cores from the apples.

Cut the sweet potatoes, pumpkin, and apples into chunks and puree in a food processor or through the fine blade of a food mill. Add the remaining ingredients and blend together well. Place in a buttered serving dish and warm in a 350° F (180° C, gas mark 4) oven until steaming. Serve hot.

TO PREPARE AHEAD OF TIME: The sweet potatoes, pumpkin, and apples can all be baked, skinned and pureed a day in advance and held in the refrigerator.

SERVES 6

SUPPER CLUB
CHEZ MARTHA ROSE

PUCKER-UP CRANBERRY RELISH
Délices d'Airelles

My friend Stewart McBride, a journalist who lives in Paris, gave this tart mixture of cranberries, oranges, nuts, and honey its name. In my local St.-Germain market there is one woman who sells Ocean Spray cranberries. I don't know where she gets them, but in the fall I'm one of her best customers.

This cranberry sauce is so much more refreshing than the usual sweet, cooked variety. It makes a great leftover. Eat it in the morning with yogurt.

Place all the ingredients in a food processor and blend until you have a uniform, very finely chopped mixture. The texture will be crunchy. Chill until ready to serve.

TO PREPARE AHEAD OF TIME: This can be made a day in advance, although it's best made the day you are going to serve it.

SERVES 8

1 pound (500 g), or 1 bag, fresh cranberries

1 whole navel orange, skin included, washed and cut in eighths

1/2 cup (55 g) shelled fresh walnuts or pecans

1/4 cup (60 ml) mild-flavored honey

CRISP ALMOND COOKIES
My Biscotti Di Prato

An Italian might be scandalized by my version of this well-known Tuscan almond cookie, for mine are half as sweet, made with honey, not sugar, and with whole-wheat flour. I cut them much thinner than the traditional biscotti, and they aren't heavy. But like Italian biscotti, they are very hard and crunchy, with a deep roasted-almond flavor. They are perfect for dipping in sweet red wine, the way the Italians do, and for this reason I usually serve them with wine-poached or marinated fruit.

This dough becomes very stiff when you are incorporating the almonds, but with persistence you can work them all in. The cookies should be made a few days before you wish to serve them. They will keep in a well-sealed container for weeks.

4 ounces (115 g) almonds
2 large eggs plus 1 egg white
½ cup (120 ml) mild-flavored honey
2¾ cups (310 g) whole-wheat pastry flour or unbleached white flour
½ teaspoon baking soda
¼ teaspoon salt

Preheat the oven to 375° F (190° C, gas mark 5). Place the almonds on a baking sheet and roast them for about 10 minutes, until lightly golden and toasty-smelling. Remove from the oven. Grind 1 ounce (30 g) of the almonds fine and chop the rest into coarse pieces. Set aside.

In a mixer or a large bowl blend together the whole eggs and honey. Mix in 2½ cups (280 g) of the flour, the baking soda, and salt. When all the ingredients are mixed together, place the remaining ¼ cup (30 g) flour on a work surface, place the dough on the flour, and knead for 10 to 15 minutes. The dough will be stiff. (The ingredients can also be mixed together like pasta. Place 2½ cups (280 g) of flour in a mound on a board and make a well in the center. Break in the eggs, add baking soda and salt, and add the honey. Beat together with a fork, then mix in the remaining ¼ cup (30 g) flour, as needed. Gather into a ball and knead as above.

Now incorporate the ground and chopped almonds into

the dough. This will seem difficult at first because the dough is so stiff. The easiest way to do it is to press the dough out flat, add a handful of almonds, fold and knead a few minutes, then press out again and continue with this procedure until all the almonds have been added. You will get a good workout.

Divide the dough in half and shape into two long logs, about 2 inches (5 cm) wide. Place them on a buttered and flour-dusted baking sheet, not too close to each other. Beat the egg white until foamy and brush it over the logs. Bake in the preheated oven for 20 minutes, until golden brown and shiny. Remove from the oven and turn the oven heat down to 275° F (140° C, gas mark 1).

Cut the logs into thin slices, about ¼ to ½ inch (.75 to 1.5 cm) thick, at a 45-degree angle. Use a bread knife or a sharp chef's knife. Place the cookies on the baking sheet (or two baking sheets) and bake again for about 40 minutes in the slow oven, until dry and hard. Remove from the heat and cool. Keep in a covered container. These last a long time.

MAKES ABOUT 5 DOZEN COOKIES

PEARS POACHED IN BEAUJOLAIS
Poires Pochées au Beaujolais

This dish doesn't taste as strange as it may sound. Despite the quantity of peppercorns, their flavor is subtle, giving the wine, which has been sweetened with honey, a unique spicy taste that is altogether different from the usual sweet spice flavorings like cinnamon and nutmeg. The one thing that may annoy you is that many of the peppercorns will lodge in the sides of the pears. I love the way this makes the pears look, and don't mind picking them out. Should you chomp down on one it won't ruin your palate, because they are much milder after being poached. You can put the peppercorns in a cheesecloth bag if you want to remove them after cooking. The dessert is perfect after a rich meal. It is served chilled, so you must make it a few hours ahead of time. It looks beautiful when served from a cut-glass or white porcelain bowl.

6 Comice pears, firm but ripe
Water acidulated with the
 juice of a lemon
1 bottle (750 ml) Beaujolais
½ cup (120 ml) mild-flavored
 honey
2 tablespoons peppercorns

Peel the pears with a sharp knife, making sure to leave the stem intact. Drop them into a bowl of acidulated water. This will keep the pears from turning brown.

Combine the wine, honey, and peppercorns in a large saucepan and bring to a simmer. Simmer 10 minutes and carefully drop in the pears. Simmer, never letting the wine boil, for 10 minutes, and remove from the heat. Chill the pears in their liquid for several hours. Place the pears in a serving dish and strain in the wine. Discard the peppercorns.

Serve in wide bowls or sherbet dishes, with some of the wine ladled over the top.

SERVES 6

November, continued: "Le Jour du Merci Donnant," or More Thanksgiving Delights

CHAMPAGNE

CROUTONS WITH CAVIAR
Canapés au Caviar

CROUTONS WITH TAPENADE (PAGE 67)
Canapés à la Tapenade

SWEET AND SOUR CHERRY PICKLES
Cerises Aigres-Douces

RADISHES, OLIVES
Radis, Olives

SALAD OF WILD AND ITALIAN RICE WITH GREEN BEANS (PAGE 80)
Salade aux Deux Riz et aux Haricots Verts

MIXED GRAINS BREAD (PAGE 24)
Pain aux Céréales

ROAST TURKEY
Dinde Rotie

CORNBREAD STUFFING
Farce au Pain de Mais

MUSHROOM RAGOUT GRAVY
Sauce Ragoût de Champignons

BROCCOLI PUREE (PAGE 72)
Purée de Brocolis

PUMPKIN, SWEET POTATO, AND APPLE PUREE (PAGE 86)
Purée de Potiron, Patates, et Pommes

PUCKER-UP CRANBERRY RELISH (PAGE 87)
Délice d'Airelles

PECAN PIE
Tarte aux Pecans

PUMPKIN PIE
Tarte au Potiron

GAMAY PRIMEUR OR ZINFANDEL

"Le Fanksgeeving," which is what Art Buchwald calls *le jour du merci donnant* in his famous column run faithfully by the *International Herald Tribune* every turkey day, is always a special feast in Paris. My French friends, mystified as some of them may be by pumpkin pie, seem to love the holiday as much as the Americans, although they don't stuff themselves the way Americans do. Right up to feast time you see Americans scouring the markets and crowding Fauchon, the Paris equivalent of New York's Balducci's, in search of cranberries, sweet potatoes, and mincemeat. If you are alone in Paris and want to find someone to share the meal with, just go to the market, listen for English, and strike up a conversation; somebody will invite you.

Of course I always serve turkey; I'm not such a fanatic vegetarian, and tradition prevails. But being a bit nervous about my skill at roasting the bird—it's been a long time, after all—I leave that task up to my poultry purveyor in the St.-Germain market, Madame Decots. According to Jon Winroth and his wife, Doreen, who never seem to be wrong when it comes to gastronomy, Madame Decots sells the best poultry and eggs in Paris. Every November she puts up a big sign for the Americans; I don't know who writes it for her, but it says: "Order Your Thanksgiving Turkey Now." She was mighty pleased the year I ordered five big ones for Supper Club—and also perplexed when I brought her my cornbread stuffing. When I ran into the Winroths a little later that day at a neighborhood wine bar, they told me that Madame Decots, looking confused and worried, had taken them aside, shown them the "farce," and asked them, confidentially, if all this bread was indeed a stuffing. Was it typically American? In France they stuff their birds with livers, veal, and sausage (not exactly my style). Doreen reassured Madame Decots that not only was it typically American, but quite delicious. Madame was skeptical; nonetheless, every year she has dutifully stuffed and roasted my birds. I accompany the meat with a thick, savory mushroom ragout instead of a fatty gravy. The ragout is fabulous with the stuffing as well as the turkey, and is even great all by itself.

My desserts are traditional, pecan and pumpkin pies (I ask every American friend coming to Paris to bring me pecans). Although there are sweet pumpkin pies to be found in France, particularly in the Soulogne region, many French people scorn pumpkin served as dessert, and some refuse to eat it. To them pumpkin is strictly soup material, and to taste it sweet and spicy is as unacceptable to them as Brazilian sweet avocado pudding was to me when I encountered it in Rio. But pumpkin pie is one of my favorites, and the fresh pumpkin here is so good.

In France my Thanksgiving dinners have ranged from a small family affair with a couple of guests in my kitchen dining room to a Supper Club for forty (which I'll never do again).

My first Thanksgiving was a spontaneous one financed by a rich friend, who bought us vintage Champagne, caviar, oysters, and truffled goose. My two roommates, Maggie Megaw and Mary Collins, and I invited a couple of French friends, and the dinner was cozy and elegant.

Three years later Patricia and Walter Wells invited me to their beautiful house in Provence. Walter is the managing editor of the *International Herald Tribune,* and Patricia is a food writer/journalist, the author of *The Food Lover's Guide to Paris* and *The Food Lover's Guide to France.* Their house is named Chanteduc, and it is one of those places that both takes your breath away and feels like home from the moment you arrive. It is situated above the village of Vaison la Romaine, northeast of Avignon, in the department of the Vaucluse. Like all the old farmhouses in the Vaucluse, Chanteduc is stucco, with a red tile roof. It has a charming inner courtyard, where Pat has had a traditional stone baker's oven built, beautiful gardens, cherry trees and linden trees, a large vineyard, and a clear view of Mont Ventoux, the highest peak in the region. Every bedroom has a captivating view, and Patricia has decorated each one with great attention to detail; wherever you turn your head, your eye rests on something beautiful: a charming antique French vase filled with pink and yellow roses from the garden; a vintage American quilt, tucked over bright, crisp, lacy linens; a handsomely framed *belle epoque* Paris poster. Five days with the Wellses in this paradise was not long enough, and yet I have spent two-day weekends at their home and returned to Paris feeling as if I'd had a week-long vacation.

On that Thanksgiving we did leisurely cooking throughout the day, then took a long walk through the vineyards. Pat found seven chanterelles growing along a stone wall, and we raced to the pharmacy to have them analyzed, just to make sure we weren't going to poison ourselves. There was one mushroom for each person at the table, and Pat grilled them with a little olive oil and garlic; what a great way to kick off a memorable dinner. It was during that Thanksgiving that my journalist friend Stewart McBride christened my cranberry relish "Pucker-Up Cranberry Sauce."

We roasted sweet potatoes in the fireplace, which was fueled over the four-day holiday by one immense log. Along with the pumpkin pie, a recipe Pat had acquired in the Soulogne, Pat made a delicious chocolate cake, which kept reappearing at meals (and between them) throughout our stay.

Unfortunately Stewart and I had to leave Chanteduc a day earlier than the rest of the house guests. It was the opening day of the truffle season, and Stewart, who was doing a story, had to meet with a truffle mogul in another part of Provence. I had to get back to Paris to prepare for my Supper Club the following Thursday. I had mistakenly thought that Thanksgiving was the last Thursday in November, which it usually is, but that year there were five Thursdays and I got the day wrong. *Tant mieux,* I thought, I'll celebrate twice. Cooking for forty people hardly resembled the relaxing day I'd spent in the Vaucluse a week before, but the dinner was festive, with as many French as Americans.

SWEET AND SOUR CHERRY PICKLES

Cerises Aigres-Douces

I make these pickles in June or early July, when the markets abound with Bing cherries, black cherries, and Queen Annes. They can be stored for a year in a cool pantry, so they make a perfect hors d'oeuvre with drinks at fall and winter dinners.

1 pound (500 g) firm, ripe sweet or sour cherries

5 to 6 sprigs fresh tarragon, if available, rinsed and dried

2 cups (450 ml) good-quality white wine, sherry, or champagne vinegar

1/3 cup (90 ml) mild-flavored honey

1 teaspoon salt

Pick over the cherries, discarding any with blemishes or soft spots. Rinse, drain, and gently roll them in a towel. Cut the stems with scissors to 1/2 inch (1.5 cm).

Place the tarragon in a dry, sterilized quart canning jar and fill with the cherries.

Heat the vinegar, honey, and salt together in a saucepan to simmering. Stir together to mix the honey with the vinegar. Remove from the heat and cool completely.

Pour the cooled vinegar solution over the cherries, covering them completely (add more vinegar and a little honey if not completely covered). There should be 1/2 inch (1.5 cm) of headspace. Remove any bubbles by running a knife or chopstick around the inside edge of the jar. Seal the jar with a new sterilized canning lid, according to the manufacturer's directions. Store in a cool dark place for at least one month before serving.

MAKES 1 QUART

CORNBREAD STUFFING
Farce au Pain de Mais

Whether it's baked inside or outside a bird, this is my favorite stuffing, especially when it's served with the Mushroom Ragout Gravy (pg 98). This is the stuffing that the poultry lady, Madame Decots, thought so bizarre. But over the years she has gotten used to my strange "farce."

Heat the oil or butter in a wide, heavy-bottomed skillet and sauté the garlic and onion until the onion begins to soften. Add the celery and continue to sauté another minute or two. Add the cornbread, sage, thyme, rosemary, and freshly ground pepper and stir together thoroughly. Remove from the heat and stir in the red peppercorns and chopped parsley. Adjust the seasonings. Moisten with a little milk and use as a stuffing, or place in a buttered casserole, dot with butter, cover with foil, and heat through in a 325° F (170° C, gas mark 3) oven.

TO PREPARE AHEAD OF TIME: The cornbread can be made a day or two before you make the stuffing, and the stuffing can be made a day before you wish to serve it and held in the refrigerator in a covered bowl or container. I always bring it to Madame Decots the day before she roasts the turkey.
SERVES 8 TO 10, OR STUFFS AN 8-POUND (4 KG) TURKEY

NOTE: This stuffing is even tastier if the sage is added to the cornbread when you make the bread. It becomes infused with this earthy-flavored herb.

2 tablespoons safflower oil or butter

2 cloves garlic, minced or put through a press

1 onion, minced

2 to 3 medium-sized stalks celery, to taste, chopped

4 cups (340 g) crumbled cornbread (see recipe, page 35)

1 teaspoon rubbed sage (see note)

1 1/2 teaspoons dried thyme

1/2 teaspoon dried rosemary, crumbled

Freshly ground pepper to taste

1 tablespoon pink peppercorns (optional)

1/2 cup (15 g) chopped fresh parsley

3 tablespoons milk, as necessary, to moisten

MUSHROOM RAGOUT GRAVY
Sauce Ragoût de Champignons

This makes a savory, rich sauce for meat, stuffings, or grains, as well as a delicious ragout on its own. If you can get fresh wild mushrooms it will be truly special, but it is marvelous with regular mushrooms as well, as long as you can get hold of dried mushrooms, which are necessary for the strong, "meaty" broth.

Place the dried mushrooms in a bowl and cover with boiling water. Let sit for 30 minutes while you prepare the remaining ingredients.

Heat the butter in a large, heavy-bottomed skillet and add the shallots or onions. Cook over medium-low heat, stirring often, for about 20 minutes, or until golden brown. Add the olive or safflower oil and the sliced fresh mushrooms. Stir together and sauté for 5 to 10 minutes, until the mushrooms begin to release their liquid.

Meanwhile, drain the dried mushrooms and reserve the liquid. Rinse the mushrooms thoroughly to remove sand, squeeze dry, and add to the skillet, along with the garlic. Stir together and sauté a few minutes, adding oil if necessary. Add the wine and soy sauce and bring to a simmer.

Strain the soaking liquid from the mushrooms through a strainer lined with cheesecloth or through a coffee filter. Measure out 1 cup (225 ml) and add it to the mushrooms, along with the stock, thyme, and rosemary. Bring to a simmer, cover, and simmer 20 minutes. Uncover and raise the heat to high. Reduce the liquid by half. Taste and adjust seasonings, adding salt, pepper, garlic, or herbs to taste.

Remove a cupful of the mushrooms and puree them in a blender or food processor, then stir them back into the ragout. For a creamier mixture, add 2 tablespoons cream or crème fraîche.

1 cup (55 g) dried imported wild mushrooms, such as cèpes, porcini, or chanterelles

Boiling water to cover

2 tablespoons unsalted butter

2 large shallots or 1 medium onion, minced

1 tablespoon olive or safflower oil, or more as needed

1/2 pound (250 g) fresh wild mushrooms, such as porcini, shiitaki or chanterelles, if available, plus 1/2 pound (250 g) fresh regular mushrooms, or 1 pound (500 g) regular mushrooms in all if wild mushrooms are unavailable, cleaned, trimmed, and thickly sliced

3 to 4 cloves garlic, minced or put through a press

1/2 cup (120 ml) dry red wine

1 to 2 tablespoons soy sauce, to taste

2 cups (450 ml) vegetable stock or bouillon

1 teaspoon dried thyme

1/2 teaspoon dried rosemary, crumbled

SUPPER CLUB
CHEZ MARTHA ROSE

TO PREPARE AHEAD OF TIME: This dish holds well and can be made up to 2 days in advance and kept in the refrigerator in a covered bowl. Reheat before serving.

SERVES 8

Salt and freshly ground
* pepper to taste*
2 tablespoons heavy cream or
* crème fraîche (optional)*

PECAN PIE
Tarte Aux Pecans

This is different from the cloyingly sweet traditional pecan pie. Sweet it is, but there's no corn syrup or brown sugar, just mild-flavored honey and a hint of molasses.

Preheat the oven to 375° F (190° C, gas mark 5). Beat the eggs, then brush the crust with some of the beaten egg, prick, and prebake 8 minutes. Remove from the oven, leaving the oven on.

Cream together the butter, honey, and molasses. Beat in the eggs and add the rum, vanilla, nutmeg, and salt. Combine well. Fold in the pecans.

Turn the filling into the prebaked pie shell. Bake for 35 to 45 minutes, until a knife comes out clean when inserted in the center. The pie will puff up almost like a soufflé, but then, alas, it will fall.

Remove from the oven and cool on a rack. Serve with whipped cream flavored with nutmeg.

SERVES 8

Sweet Dessert Crust (page 42)
4 eggs
4 tablespoons unsalted butter
½ cup (120 ml) mild-flavored
* honey*
1 tablespoon molasses
1 tablespoon rum
1½ teaspoons vanilla
¼ teaspoon freshly grated
* nutmeg*
¼ teaspoon salt
2 cups (225 g) shelled pecans
Nutmeg-flavored whipped
* cream for topping*

PUMPKIN PIE
Tarte au Potiron

This is a spicy pumpkin pie with a touch of molasses.

Sweet Almond Piecrust (page 41) omitting almond extract

3 eggs

2 cups pumpkin puree, canned or fresh (see note)

1 cup (225 ml) milk

2 tablespoons unsalted butter, softened

1/2 cup (120 ml) mild-flavored honey

1 1/2 tablespoons molasses

1 to 2 tablespoons rum, to taste

1 1/2 teaspoons vanilla extract

2 teaspoons ground cinnamon

1 teaspoon grated fresh ginger or 1/2 teaspoon ground ginger

1/2 teaspoon freshly grated nutmeg

1/4 teaspoon ground mace

1/4 teaspoon ground cloves

1/4 teaspoon salt

Vanilla-flavored whipped cream or plain low-fat yogurt for topping

Preheat the oven to 375° F (190° C, gas mark 5). Beat the eggs and brush the piecrust with some of the beaten egg. Prebake the crust for 5 minutes, or until the bottom is just beginning to be crisp, and remove from the oven. Turn up the oven heat to 450° F (230° C, gas mark 8).

Blend together the remaining beaten eggs, pumpkin puree, milk, butter, honey, molasses, rum, vanilla, spices, and salt. Pour into the prebaked pie shell. Place in the preheated oven. After 10 minutes turn the heat down to 350° F (180° C, gas mark 4). Bake 45 to 50 minutes, or until firm to the touch. If the crust begins to burn on the edges, cover lightly with aluminum foil. Cool completely and serve with whipped cream flavored with vanilla or plain low-fat yogurt.

SERVES 8

NOTE: To make fresh pumpkin puree, preheat the oven to 425° F (220° C, gas mark 7). Remove the seeds and strings from a 2-pound pumpkin, place it, cut side down, on an oiled baking sheet, and bake until thoroughly soft, about 45 minutes. Peel away the skin, scraping off any pumpkin that adheres, and puree all the pumpkin in a food processor or blender until smooth. Measure 2 cups for the recipe; freeze any left over.

December

Crémant de Bourgogne Blue Fox

SALAD WITH WARM GREEN BEANS AND WALNUTS
Salade Tiède aux Haricots Verts et aux Noix

PESTO BREAD (PAGE 34)
Pain au Basilic

SOURDOUGH COUNTRY BREAD (PAGE 5)
Pain de Campagne

GREEN LASAGNE WITH SPINACH FILLING
Lasagne aux Epinards

SAUTÉED FENNEL AND RED PEPPERS
Fenouil et Poivrons Poêlés

TANGERINE SHERBET
Sorbet aux Clémentines

CORNMEAL AND ALMOND SHORTBREAD
Petits Gateaux aux Amandes et au Mais

Coteaux de Tricastin
JON WINROTH'S WINE SUGGESTION: SAINT-JOSEPH

My December Supper Club often feels like one of the first in a long string of holiday fêtes. That's one of the reasons I serve a sparkling wine as aperitif —that and the fact that in December the sun goes down at around four-thirty in the afternoon. By eight-thirty or nine a glass of Crémant de Bourgogne or Champagne is just what one needs to lift one's spirits.

A sensuous Italian meal might also do the trick. Every few months I like to serve an Italian dinner, but for twenty-five people I can't choose a pasta dish that is cooked and served at the last minute. So I serve dishes like the lasagne in this menu, the Deep-Dish Eggplant Torte on page 129, and the Springtime Cannelloni on page 150. Good Italian food isn't easy to come by in Paris, and these dishes fulfill my cravings for garlicky, savory tomato sauces, pasta, and Parmesan cheese.

This meal is beautifully balanced. The main dish is rich and filling—perfect for a cold, wet December night. It needs to be preceded and followed by a light first course and dessert. The salad is an elegant combination of mixed winter greens and tangy warm green beans and walnuts. The lasagne is set off by the lightly sautéed vegetables served on the side; the fennel, with its anisy taste, is especially refreshing. After the lasagne, the Tangerine Sherbet, garnished with marinated tangerines and served with small squares of the almond-scented Cornmeal and Almond Shortbread, is exquisite. When you follow a delicious meal with an ineffable, light dessert, everybody remembers the dinner.

SALAD WITH WARM GREEN BEANS AND WALNUTS
Salade Tiède aux Haricots Verts et aux Noix

Wash, dry, and toss together the lettuces, chervil and chives.

To make the dressing, stir together the vinegar, mustard, garlic, tarragon, salt, and freshly ground pepper. Whisk in the oils and mix well.

Bring a large pot of water to a rolling boil. Add a teaspoon of salt and blanch the beans for a minute or two. Drain the beans and rinse briefly with cold water. Place in a bowl.

Just before serving, toss the lettuce mixture with a third of the dressing. Heat the remaining dressing in a saucepan and add the nuts. Stir together, and when the nuts are heated through, toss with the green beans. Place the dressed greens on individual plates and top with the warm dressed beans and walnuts. Garnish with radishes and serve at once.

TO PREPARE AHEAD OF TIME: The lettuces can be washed and dried thoroughly a day in advance, and refrigerated in plastic bags.

The beans can be trimmed and blanched a day in advance. Reheat at the last minute by dumping them into boiling water for a couple of seconds. Drain and toss in the hot salad dressing with the nuts, as instructed in the recipe.

The dressing can be made a few hours before serving and held in or out of the refrigerator.

SERVES 4 TO 6

FOR THE SALAD
½ pound (250 g) mixed winter lettuces, such as red chicory, curly endive, arugula, and watercress
12 sprigs fresh chervil
2 tablespoons chopped fresh chives
½ pound (250 g) green beans, trimmed
1 teaspoon salt
½ cup (55 g) broken shelled walnuts
Radishes for garnish

FOR THE DRESSING
3 tablespoons balsamic vinegar
1 ½ teaspoons Dijon mustard
1 small clove garlic, minced or put through a press
¼ teaspoon dried tarragon
Salt and freshly ground pepper to taste
6 tablespoons safflower or olive oil, or a combination of the two
3 tablespoons walnut oil

GREEN LASAGNE WITH SPINACH FILLING
Lasagne aux Epinards

I don't know anybody who doesn't like a lasagne, especially this one. I have fond memories of making this lasagne for a late-night party on a Saturday afternoon in Austin while listening to *Madame Butterfly* on the radio; it was the first time I'd ever listened to an opera in its entirety—which gives you an idea of how long it takes to make this lasagne if you're making it for a crowd. The music was perfect for the sensual activity—for sensual it is, handling the light, slippery pasta and the rich spinach–ricotta–goat cheese filling, sprinkling the soft, freshly grated Parmesan, and watching the layers of green, red, and milky white pile up on top of one another.

Lasagne can often be heavy and too rich, but this one isn't. For one thing, there is so much spinach and parsley in it that you are eating a garden of greens along with the tomato sauce, pasta, and cheese. And the pasta itself is rolled very thin, unlike the thick, commercial variety. However, I wouldn't exactly call this dish "light," which is why I accompany it with a very simple salad and vegetable side dish, and an ethereal fruit sherbet.

The cheese filling here calls for goat cheese, and it's very important to find one that isn't too salty. St. Christophe Maure and very fresh local goat cheeses, if available to you, are your best bet.

MAKING THE TOMATO SAUCE: Heat the olive oil in a heavy-bottomed saucepan or Dutch oven and sauté the onion with half the garlic over medium heat until the onion is tender, about 5 minutes. Add the tomatoes, tomato paste, and sugar and bring to a simmer. Simmer, uncovered, for 30 minutes. Add the remaining garlic, the herbs and salt and freshly

FOR THE TOMATO SAUCE

1 tablespoon olive oil
1 small onion, chopped
4 to 5 cloves garlic, minced or
  put through a press
4 pounds (2 kg) fresh
  tomatoes, seeded and
  chopped, or four 28-ounce
  (780 g) cans, drained,
  seeded and chopped
2 tablespoons tomato paste
pinch of sugar
1 tablespoon chopped fresh
  basil or 1 teaspoon dried
1 teaspoon dried oregano, or
  more to taste
1/2 teaspoon dried thyme, or
  more to taste
Salt and freshly ground
  pepper to taste
Pinch of ground cinnamon

FOR THE PASTA

Spinach Pasta (page 37; see
  note)
Salt
Vegetable or olive oil

FOR THE FILLING

1 1/2 pounds (750 g) spinach
2 eggs
1 pound (500 g) ricotta cheese
1/2 pound (250 g) fresh goat
  cheese, not too salty
1/2 cup (15 g) plus 2
  tablespoons chopped fresh
  parsley, preferably
  flat-leafed

SUPPER CLUB
CHEZ MARTHA ROSE
106

ground pepper to taste and continue to simmer another 30 minutes. Add the cinnamon, then taste and adjust seasonings, adding more garlic, salt, pepper or herbs to taste. Set aside.

MAKING THE PASTA: Mix up the pasta dough according to the directions on page 37. Knead, wrap in plastic, and set aside to rest for 30 minutes.

MAKING THE FILLING: Stem and wash the spinach, but do not dry it. Wilt it in the water remaining on its leaves in a large, heavy-bottomed skillet over medium-high heat. Remove from the heat and squeeze dry in a towel. Chop fine.

Beat the eggs in a large bowl and beat in the ricotta, goat cheese, parsley, basil and garlic, 1/2 cup of the Parmesan, and the spinach. Add the nutmeg and combine thoroughly. Taste and add a little salt and pepper, if you wish. Set aside.

ROLLING OUT THE PASTA: For lasagne you will roll out the pasta and cook a few strips at a time, assembling the casserole as you go along. You have to work quickly once you drain the pasta, because the lasagne strips become sticky and difficult to work with.

Oil a large baking dish and bring a large pot of water to a boil.

Meanwhile, roll out the pasta according to the instructions on page 37, into as thin strips as possible, 4 to 5 inches (10 to 12 cm) wide and a few inches longer than the pan. Allow to dry for 15 minutes or longer before cooking.

COOKING THE PASTA, ASSEMBLING THE LASAGNE: Have all your ingredients lined up in this order: pasta, tomato sauce, ricotta-spinach mixture, mozzarella, remaining 1 cup Parmesan, and breadcrumbs.

Cook three or four strips of pasta at a time as follows: When the water reaches a boil, add a teaspoon of salt and a teaspoon of vegetable or olive oil. Add the fresh pasta, and after about 10 seconds, remove it from the water with a slotted spoon or deep-fry skimmer, transfer to a bowl of cold water, then drain at once on kitchen towels.

Depending on the amount of pasta you have, you will be making three or four layers. Spoon a very small amount of tomato sauce over the bottom of the baking dish. Lay three sheets of lasagne across the bottom of the dish so the edges overlap the sides of the pan. Spread a layer of the tomato sauce over the pasta. Top with a layer of the ricotta-spinach mixture, then a layer of mozzarella, and finally a layer of Parmesan. Continue cooking the pasta and layering the lasagne like this, ending with an added layer of pasta, tomato sauce and Parmesan. Take the overlapping edges of the pasta and fold them over the top like a package. Sprinkle the breadcrumbs over the top and dot with butter or drizzle on the olive oil. Cover with foil and set aside or refrigerate until shortly before baking time.

Preheat the oven to 350 degrees F (180 C, gas mark 4). Remove the foil and bake the lasagne 40 minutes, or until it is bubbling and starting to brown on the top. Remove from the oven, sprinkle with the additional parsley and serve.

TO PREPARE AHEAD OF TIME: The tomato sauce can be made up to 2 days in advance. Refrigerate in a covered bowl or container.

The pasta dough can be made a day in advance, wrapped tightly in plastic, and held in the refrigerator overnight. Don't roll it out, however, until you are ready to assemble the lasagne.

The ricotta-spinach filling can be made a day in advance and held in the refrigerator in a covered bowl or container.

The entire lasagne can be assembled up to a day in advance, covered with plastic wrap, then aluminum foil, and held in the refrigerator. Uncover and allow to come to room temperature before baking.

SERVES 6 TO 8

NOTE: You can also use packaged dried lasagne noodles for this. The lasagne will be heavier. Cook them al dente, according to the instructions on the box. This will take longer than fresh pasta, and you can cook six to eight noodles at a time.

¼ cup (70 g) chopped fresh basil, if available
2 cloves garlic, minced or put through a press
6 ounces (170 g) freshly grated Parmesan cheese (1 ½ cups)
⅛ teaspoon freshly grated nutmeg
Salt and freshly ground pepper to taste (optional)
¾ pound (340 g) skim-milk or fresh mozzarella cheese, thinly sliced
¼ cup (30 g) fresh or dry breadcrumbs, fine or coarse
2 tablespoons unsalted butter or olive oil

SAUTEED FENNEL AND RED PEPPERS

Fenouil et Poivrons Poêlés

This light, crunchy sauté is a great accompaniment for rich, complicated dishes. The night I served it with lasagne, one of my guests was allergic to cheese, so I tossed a large portion with homemade spinach fettucine noodles, and he was delighted. It looked as beautiful as it tasted.

2 tablespoons olive oil

3 sweet red peppers, cut in thin strips

1 pound (500 g) fennel, thinly sliced

1 large clove garlic, minced or put through a press

Salt and freshly ground pepper to taste

Heat the oil in a large, heavy-bottomed skillet and sauté the peppers with the fennel and garlic for 10 to 15 minutes over medium-high heat, stirring often. The vegetables should retain their crunch. Add salt and pepper to taste, and serve as a side dish.

SERVES 6

TO PREPARE AHEAD OF TIME: The vegetables can be prepared and held in the refrigerator several hours ahead of time. They should be cooked just before serving.

TANGERINE SHERBET
Sorbet Aux Clémentines

excellent

This popular dessert is very easy to prepare, but it will work only if you can find good, juicy tangerines.

MAKING THE SHERBET: Combine the honey and water in a large saucepan and bring to a boil. Reduce the heat and simmer 10 minutes. Remove from the heat and cool.

Stir the juices and orange zest into the cooled syrup. Either freeze in an ice cream freezer or sorbetière, or still-freeze according to the instructions in the note on page 59.

Spoon the frozen mixture into individual molds and cover each one with plastic wrap, then foil. Or oil a loaf pan and line it with plastic wrap. Spoon in the sherbet mixture and cover tightly with plastic and then foil. Freeze at least 8 hours. Work quickly so the frozen mixture doesn't melt to a liquid, or ice crystals will form again when it freezes.

MAKING THE GARNISH: Toss together the tangerine sections and the liqueur or Cointreau. Add the fresh mint leaves. Set aside or refrigerate until ready to serve.

Twenty minutes before serving, place the sherbet in the refrigerator to soften. If you froze the sherbet in the loaf pan, unmold it onto a platter. Cut slices with a sharp knife. If you froze it in individual molds, unmold into bowls. Top each serving with the tangerine garnish.

TO PREPARE AHEAD OF TIME: The sherbet can be made several days or even weeks before you wish to serve it. The garnish can be made several hours ahead of serving time and held in the refrigerator in a covered bowl.

SERVES 6

FOR THE SHERBET
½ cup (120 ml) mild-flavored honey
1 cup (225 ml) water
2 cups (450 ml) strained fresh tangerine juice (juice of about 2 pounds, 1 kg, tangerines)
Juice of 1 orange, strained
½ cup (120 ml) strained fresh lemon juice
Finely minced grated zest of 1 orange (optional)

FOR THE TANGERINE GARNISH
6 tangerines, peeled and sectioned
¼ cup (60 ml) tangerine or mandarin liqueur, or Cointreau
2 tablespoons chopped fresh mint leaves

CORNMEAL AND ALMOND SHORTBREAD

Petits Gateaux aux Amandes et au Mais

1 1/4 cups (125 g) raw almonds

3 tablespoons raw brown sugar

1 stick (115 g) unsalted butter, melted and cooled

1/4 cup (60 ml) mild-flavored honey

1 tablespoon malt syrup

2 large egg yolks

1 tablespoon fresh-squeezed lemon juice

Grated zest of 1 lemon

1 teaspoon vanilla

1/4 teaspoon almond extract

Scant 1 cup (100 g) either light whole-wheat pastry flour or unbleached white flour

7/8 cup (100 g) fine yellow cornmeal

Pinch of salt

This is based on Carol Field's recipe for *fregolata veneziana,* a sort of crumbly shortbread made in Venice. It's another terrific recipe that I came across in *The Italian Baker* and have modified, substituting honey for most of the sugar and unbleached white or whole-wheat pastry flour for all-purpose flour. Mine is a denser cookie/cake than the traditional version, and for this reason I cut it into tiny squares, which I serve with sherbets or marinated fruit.

Preheat the oven to 350° F (180° C, gas mark 4). Butter a 9 × 9-inch (22 × 22 cm) cake pan or a 9- or 10-inch (22 to 25 cm) pie plate.

Grind scant 1 cup (100 g) almonds to a fine powder, along with 2 tablespoons of the sugar, in a nut grinder or a food processor fitted with the steel blade. Transfer to a mixing bowl and beat in the butter. Add the honey and malt syrup and cream together until well blended. Beat in the egg yolks, lemon juice and zest, and the vanilla and almond extracts.

Sift together the flour, cornmeal, and salt. Stir this into the liquid mixture, and mix just until the dough comes together. It will be sticky. Do not overwork.

Spoon the dough into the prepared baking dish and spread it out in an even layer with your hands. Chop the remaining 1/4 cup (25 g) almonds and sprinkle over the dough along with the remaining tablespoon of sugar.

Bake 20 minutes in the preheated oven. Turn down the heat to 300° F (150° C, gas mark 2) and bake another 20 minutes, or until the top is beginning to brown and a tester comes out clean. Cool completely on a rack and cut into squares. These will keep for several days if well covered.

MAKES 12 TO 24 SQUARES

January

VIVA MEXICO!

MARGARITAS (PAGE 51)

GUACAMOLE NACHOS
Nachos aux Avocats

SOPA DE TORTILLA
Soupe aux Tortillas

CUMIN AND CORNMEAL BREAD (PAGE 28)
Pain au Cumin

MARINATED COD IN ESCABECHE
Cabillaud en Escabeche

BLUE CORN MASA CRÊPES
Galettes au Maïs Bleu

BLACK BEAN FRIJOLES (PAGE 54)
SALSA FRESCA (PAGE 53)
Frijoles aux Haricots Noir

TEXAS TEA CAKES
Galettes Texanes

PINEAPPLE-ORANGE-BANANA SHERBET WITH MINT
Sorbet aux Trois Fruits à la Menthe

Coteaux de Tricastin
JON WINROTH'S WINE SUGGESTIONS: HERMITAGE BLANC; CROZES-HERMITAGE
BLANC

With the exception of the dessert, most of this menu was inspired by a two-week vacation in the Yucatán. I made the meal just after the trip, when all the flavors of southern Mexico were still vivid. A friend and I had spent our Christmas holiday in a small hotel south of Cancún. Our bungalow was right on the beach, and we ate our meals in an open-air dining room with a thatched roof. I particularly enjoyed the soups I ate every night under the stars: a tangy lime soup with bits of chicken and chile peppers in a light broth seasoned with fresh coriander and lime juice; a tomatoey tortilla soup; and marvelous black beans. This course preceded fish or enchiladas, the fish most often grilled red snapper with a spicy tomato sauce. Dessert was always fresh fruit—sweet, juicy pineapple, luxurious mango, subtle papaya. When I got back to Paris that dull, gray January I couldn't wait to liven things up with a Mexican dinner party. The dining room was bright and cheery with colorful new tablecloths, napkins, baskets, and pottery I'd bought in Mexico.

When I serve Mexican food at my dinners, there are certain dishes I feel I must include, and it is always a challenge to come up with an original menu while not leaving out the traditional favorites: guacamole, tortillas, *frijoles, salsa fresca,* and of course, margaritas. For this meal I include an extra course, the Guacamole Nachos, which are easy to assemble while the guests are drinking their margaritas, and which look beautiful on the plate, garnished with radish roses or thin strips of red pepper. They are followed by the soup, which isn't a heavy one, so that people won't be too full for the main course, the marinated cod with zucchini, served on a soft masa crêpe. Here's where I fit in the salsa, a colorful garnish, and the savory, shiny black *frijoles*; they go perfectly with the light, pungent fish. The crêpes are delicate and delicious, whether made with regular masa harina or blue masa from New Mexico, which has a coarser texture. One of the reasons I serve them, one to a plate, gently folded over the fish, is that the fish often falls apart in the marinade. The crêpes serve as a kind of container and make a neater-looking dish. You can leave them out, however, if you feel that there is too much starch in the meal.

Dessert should be light. The zingy pineapple-orange-banana-mint sherbet is a refreshing, tasty palate cleanser. It's also convenient, like all my sherbets, because you can make it days in advance. Each ramekin is served on a plate, with two Texas Tea Cakes. The lemony cookies are fun; everybody sits around determining where Dallas, Houston, El Paso, and Austin are before they take their first bite.

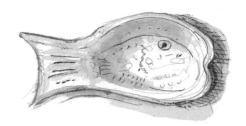

GUACAMOLE NACHOS
Nachos aux Avocats

I have served these on my own homemade small, round tortilla chips, as well as on quartered, deep-fried commercially made corn tortillas. The round ones are cute but time consuming.

Heat the oil in a wide saucepan, wok or deep fryer to 360° F (185° C). Deep-fry the tortilla chips until golden brown; remove with a deep-fry skimmer or slotted spoon and drain on paper towels. This should take a few seconds for each batch; allow the oil to come back up to 360° F (190° C) between batches.

Preheat the broiler. Sprinkle the cheese on the nacho chips and heat under the broiler just until the cheese melts. The melted cheese forms a kind of barrier between the chip and the guacamole so the chips won't get soggy as quickly.

Shortly before serving, arrange the chips on a platter, if serving as an appetizer, or arrange 5 to 6 to a plate, if serving as an entree, and top with the guacamole, a dab of yogurt or crème fraîche, and a spoonful of the salsa.

Garnish with the radishes or red pepper strips, tomato slices, and lime and serve, with more hot sauce on the side.

TO PREPARE AHEAD OF TIME: You can make the chips hours in advance. The chips with the cheese melted on them will hold for a couple of hours. The salsa can be made several hours ahead and held in a covered bowl in the refrigerator. Make the guacamole as close as possible to serving time and hold in a covered bowl in the refrigerator.

SERVES 4 TO 6

1 quart (1 L) safflower oil for deep frying

30 to 36 small, round Homemade Tortillas (page 43), or 8 to 10 large corn tortillas, quartered

2 ounces (55 g) Cheddar cheese, grated (½ cup)

Guacamole (page 55)

½ cup (120 ml) plain low-fat yogurt or crème fraîche

Salsa Fresca (page 53)

Radish roses or thin slices of sweet red pepper, sliced tomato, and sliced lime for garnish

SOPA DE TORTILLA
Soupe aux Tortillas

1 tablespoon olive oil

1 small onion, minced

4 cloves garlic, minced or put through a press

6 cups (1 1/2 L) Garlic Broth (page 117)

one 14 oz. (425 g) can tomatoes, with their liquid, pureed

3 tablespoons tomato paste

1 small dried cayenne pepper or 1/4 to 1/2 teaspoon hot chili powder

1 bay leaf

1/4 teaspoon dried oregano

1/4 teaspoon dried thyme

Salt and freshly ground pepper to taste

1 to 2 tablespoons fresh-squeezed lime juice

10 slightly stale tortillas, cut in narrow strips

1 quart (1 L) safflower or peanut oil for deep frying

1/4 cup (10 g) fresh coriander leaves

2 eggs

3 ounces (85 g) Gruyère cheese, grated (3/4 cup)

This dish brings me right back to the Yucatán, even if I can't get *chiles pasillas* in Paris. But with the savory broth, the spicy cayenne, and the rich flavor of fried tortillas and coriander, I don't miss them.

It's important to take the time to make Garlic Broth for this soup; the flavor depends on it.

Heat the olive oil in a heavy-bottomed soup pot or Dutch oven and sauté the onion with half the garlic until the onion is tender. Add the tomato puree and bring to a simmer. Cook, stirring occasionally, for about 10 minutes. Add the broth, the remaining minced garlic, the tomato paste, the cayenne pepper or chili powder, bay leaf, oregano, and thyme and bring to a simmer. Cover and simmer for 30 minutes. Season to taste with salt and freshly ground pepper. Add the lime juice.

Puree the soup through the medium blade of a food mill and return it to the pot.

While the soup is simmering (or you can do this well in advance), heat the safflower or peanut oil in a wide saucepan, wok, or deep fryer to 360° F (185° C), and deep-fry the tortilla strips just until crisp. Drain on paper towels and set aside.

Just before serving, heat the soup to a simmer, correct the seasonings and add the fresh coriander. Beat the eggs in a bowl and stir in some of the soup, then stir this back into the soup pot. Do not boil.

Place a generous handful of the crisp-fried tortilla strips in each soup bowl, ladle in the soup, top with a handful of grated Gruyère, and serve at once.

TO PREPARE AHEAD OF TIME: The Garlic Broth can be made a day or two in advance and refrigerated.

The soup will hold for a day in the refrigerator, without the coriander or eggs.

The tortilla strips can be fried several hours in advance.

SERVES 6

GARLIC BROTH

This makes a marvelous stock. It can also serve as a soup in its own right, with the addition of toasted croutons, a little grated cheese, and beaten or poached eggs.

Combine all the ingredients in a large, heavy-bottomed soup pot or Dutch oven and bring to a simmer. Cover and simmer 2 hours. Strain. This will keep in the refrigerator for a few days and freezes well.

MAKES 2 QUARTS (2 L)

2 quarts (2 L) water
2 large heads garlic, cloves
separated and peeled
1 bouquet garni (made with 2
sprigs parsley, 1 bay leaf,
and a sprig or two of
thyme)
Salt to taste

MARINATED COD IN ESCABECHE

Cabillaud en Escabeche

6 large cod fillets (1 1/2 to 2
 pounds, or 750 g to 1 kg)
2 1/4 cups (510 ml) water
1/4 cup (60 ml) fresh lime
 juice
Salt
1/2 teaspoon peppercorns
1/2 teaspoon coriander seeds
1/2 teaspoon cumin seeds
2 cloves
1/8 teaspoon ground cinnamon
2 cloves garlic, peeled
10 cloves garlic, toasted and
 peeled (see note)
1 1/4 cups (285 ml) wine
 vinegar
1/4 teaspoon dried oregano
2 bay leaves
Salt to taste
1/3 cup (90 ml) olive oil
4 shallots or 1 red onion,
 thinly sliced
1 medium-size zucchini, thinly
 sliced
Salsa Fresca (page 53)
12 Blue Corn Masa Crêpes
 (page 120) or hot corn
 tortillas (page 43)

This is based on a recipe by Diana Kennedy. Hers is more authentic, and calls for sierra or striped bass. I couldn't get either of those fish in Paris, and sea bass was too expensive, so I experimented with other fish, and found that cod did perfectly well for this dish. Kennedy has you fry the fish slices or fillets before you marinate them, but when I did that they fell apart too easily, so I tried baking the fillets. They fell apart anyway in the marinade, but I prefer baking them, as it requires less fat and is less time consuming.

The dish was quite a hit at Supper Club; the marinade is pungent with spices and tangy with vinegar. It's great for a dinner party because you make it in advance, and you can serve it hot or cold. If you're serving it hot, you just reheat it at the last minute on top of the stove. The combination of the fish on the masa crêpes, with the crunchy zucchini and salsa, and with refried black beans on the side, is sensational.

Place the fish in a baking dish. Combine 1 cup (225 ml) of the water with the lime juice and 1 teaspoon salt and pour over the fish. Marinate for 1 hour, turning once. Drain, leaving the fish with some of the liquid in the baking dish, and cover the baking dish tightly with foil.

Preheat the oven to 400° F (200° C, gas mark 6). Bake the fish 10 to 15 minutes, or until it is just baked through and flakes easily with a fork. Remove from the oven.

Meanwhile grind the spices together in a spice mill. Mash the peeled raw and roasted garlic together in a mortar and pestle. Add the ground spices and work with the pestle until you have a smooth paste. Combine with 1/2 cup (120 ml) each of vinegar, water, oregano, bay leaves, and salt to taste and bring to a boil. Add the remaining 1/4 cup (60 ml) each vinegar and water and the olive oil and bring to a second boil. Boil 1 minute and remove from the heat.

Pour the hot marinade over the baked fish. Add the onion or shallots and the zucchini, toss together gently and marinate 2 hours (or longer), turning, gently and carefully, once or twice. Adjust salt before serving.

If serving hot, heat just to a simmer on the stove right before serving; don't let the liquid boil or the fish will cook more and become tough and dry. Dish out with a slotted spoon and serve over the crêpes or hot corn tortillas. Garnish with the salsa.

TO PREPARE AHEAD OF TIME: The entire dish needs to be started at least 3 hours in advance, and can be done the morning of the evening you wish to serve it.

The crêpes can be made days in advance and frozen, stacked between squares of wax paper or parchment and sealed in a plastic bag. They will thaw in 3 hours, or thaw them overnight in the refrigerator.

SERVES 6

NOTE: To toast garlic, place the unpeeled cloves in a hot, dry skillet and cook, stirring with a wooden spoon, until the skin is uniformly charred and the flesh slightly transparent on the outside. Remove from the heat, and when cool enough to handle, remove the skins.

BLUE CORN MASA CRÊPES
Galettes au Mais Bleu

A friend of mine found this recipe in an issue of *Sunset Magazine* years ago. They are a delightful change from corn tortillas, and are excellent served on the side with any Mexican-style fish dish. I think they're best of all with the Cod en Escabeche (page 118), which is served right over the crêpes. I have made these both with blue corn masa from New Mexico and with regular *masa harina*. The blue corn masa has a much coarser texture than *masa harina*, so the crêpe has a different texture and taste (and color—slightly bluish, with intriguing blue specks). Both versions are good.

2 large eggs
¾ cup (180 ml) milk
1 tablespoon safflower oil
½ cup (55 g) blue corn masa
   or masa harina (see note)
2 tablespoons whole-wheat
   pastry flour
¼ teaspoon salt
Unsalted butter for cooking

Beat together the eggs, milk, and safflower oil. Beat in the masa, the whole-wheat flour, and the salt and blend well (this can be done in a blender). Let the batter rest in the refrigerator for about 30 minutes, to allow the flour to swell and soften.

Heat a crêpe pan or nonstick omelet pan over medium-high heat and brush with butter. Spoon in approximately 2 tablespoons batter for each crêpe, and swirl the pan to distribute the batter evenly. Cook for about one minute, or until the crêpe can be turned without breaking. Flip and brown for about half a minute on the other side. Turn onto a plate and continue until all the batter is used up, stacking crêpes as they are done.

TO PREPARE AHEAD OF TIME: The crêpes will hold for a day in the refrigerator and can be frozen (see page 45).
MAKES 10 TO 12 CRÊPES

NOTE: Masa harina, which is much more readily available than the blue corn masa, is specially processed cornmeal used specifically for corn tortillas. Do not substitute cornmeal. You can find the

Quaker brand wherever Mexican ingredients are sold, and if you live in the Southwest, you can often buy masa harina from tortilla factories.

TEXAS TEA CAKES
Galettes Texanes

These are honey lemon cookies, much like the ones on page 60, but a little crisper, and shaped like Texas. To be "authentic," you will need a Texas cookie cutter, which you can find in some kitchen supply stores. You can, of course, use any shape cutter you want.

In an electric mixer, cream the butter and honey. Beat in the egg, lemon juice, lemon zest, vanilla, baking powder, and salt. Add the flours. The dough will be soft and sticky.

Scrape the dough onto a piece of plastic wrap, wrap well, and refrigerate overnight, or freeze for 2 hours.

Preheat the oven to 350° F (180° C, gas mark 4). Cut the dough into small pieces and roll out each piece on a floured board or between pieces of wax paper. Keep the dough that you aren't working with in the freezer so it doesn't become too soft. The dough should be 1/8 to 1/4 inch (.25 to .75 cm) thick, depending on whether you like your cookies thin or fairly thick. Because the dough is wet, you must work quickly and briskly so it doesn't stick. It helps if you keep brushing the top of the dough and the board with flour. Cut in Texas shapes with a Texas cookie cutter. Using a spatula, transfer to buttered cookie sheets.

Bake the cookies 8 to 12 minutes, until beginning to brown on the edges. Cool on a rack. These will keep several days in tightly sealed containers.

MAKES 4 DOZEN COOKIES

1 1/2 sticks (6 ounces, 170 g) unsalted butter
2/3 cup (140 ml) mild-flavored honey
1 large egg
2 teaspoons vanilla
3 tablespoons fresh lemon juice
2 tablespoons finely chopped lemon zest
1 teaspoon baking powder
Pinch of salt
2 cups plus 2 tablespoons (280 g) sifted unbleached white flour
1 cup (115 g) sifted whole-wheat pastry flour

PINEAPPLE-ORANGE-BANANA MINT SHERBET

Sorbet aux Trois Fruits à la Menthe

The predominant flavors in this refreshing sherbet are pineapple, mint, and orange. There's just a little bit of banana, which adds sweetness and body. The mint is what makes this dish sing.

FOR THE SHERBET

⅓ cup (90 ml) mild-flavored
   honey

1 cup (225 ml) water

2 cups (450 ml) strained fresh
   orange juice (juice of about
   2 pounds, or 1 kg, oranges)

Juice of 1 large lime, strained

1 ripe pineapple, peeled, cored,
   and coarsely chopped

3 tablespoons chopped fresh
   mint leaves

½ small ripe banana

FOR THE ORANGE-MINT OR PINEAPPLE-MINT GARNISH

6 oranges, peeled and
   sectioned, or ½ ripe
   pineapple, peeled, trimmed,
   and chopped

¼ cup (60 ml) Grand
   Marnier or Cointreau

2 tablespoons chopped fresh
   mint leaves

MAKING THE SHERBET: Combine the honey and water in a large saucepan and bring to a boil. Reduce the heat and simmer 10 minutes. Remove from the heat and cool.

Puree the pineapple, mint leaves, and banana in a food processor or blender, using some of the orange juice to moisten it. Combine with the remaining juices.

Stir the pineapple mixture into the cooled syrup. Either freeze in an ice cream freezer or sorbetière, or still-freeze in a covered bowl according to the directions in the note on page 59.

After freezing by any method, spoon into individual molds, cover with plastic, then foil, and freeze. Or oil a loaf pan and line it with plastic wrap. Pour in the sherbet mixture, cover tightly with plastic wrap, then foil, and freeze. Work quickly so that the sherbet doesn't melt, or ice crystals will form again when it freezes.

MAKING THE GARNISH: Toss together the orange sections or chopped pineapple and the Grand Marnier or Cointreau. Add the fresh mint leaves. Set aside or refrigerate until ready to serve.

Twenty minutes before serving, place the sherbet in the refrigerator to soften. If you froze it in the loaf pan, unmold it onto a platter. Cut slices with a sharp knife. If you froze it in individual molds, unmold into bowls. Serve, topping each serving with the orange or pineapple garnish.

TO PREPARE AHEAD OF TIME: This sherbet, like all the others in the book, will hold, covered tightly, for weeks in the freezer. The garnish can be made several hours ahead and held in a covered bowl in the refrigerator.

SERVES 6

February

Vouvray Pétillant

RAVIOLI AND BROCCOLI SALAD
Salade de Raviolis et de Brocolis

SOURDOUGH COUNTRY BREAD (PAGE 18)
Pain de Campagne

DEEP-DISH EGGPLANT TORTE
Torte aux Aubergines

SAUTEED RED AND YELLOW PEPPERS
Poivrons Rouges et Jaunes Poêlés

CITRUS AND DATE GRATIN
Gratin de Fruits d'Hiver

Côtes du Rhône
JON WINROTH'S WINE SUGGESTION: BANDOL ROUGE

Everything in this menu is showy—the lovely ravioli tossed with bright green broccoli florets and little wild mushrooms; the extravagant eggplant torte, which is like an eggplant Parmesan in a crust; the colorful red and yellow peppers; and the hot fruit gratin, with its tangy citrus, sweet caramelized dates, and gratinéed crème anglaise. For this reason I once chose the menu for some food photographs. The meal looked truly elegant, served on one hundred-year-old Italian porcelain dishes. We set the table with silver and crystal on a lace tablecloth, poured the deep red Bandol wine into cut-glass carafes, and filled vases with extravagant red roses.

After this heartwarming, decidedly Italian dinner, one of my guests wrote in my Supper Club guest book that it had been "a fitting meal for a cold and rainy winter night." In February that's about the only kind of night we get, but who cares when the table looks beautiful and the food tastes so good.

RAVIOLI AND BROCCOLI SALAD

Salade de Raviolis et de Brocolis

FOR THE SALAD

¾ ounce (20 g) small dried mushrooms, such as mousserons, chanterelles, or shiitakes

1 pound (500 g) broccoli florets

1 tablespoon unsalted butter or olive oil

1 clove garlic, minced or put through a press

1 teaspoon soy sauce

1 tablespoon vegetable or olive oil

Salt

¾ pound (340 g) small ravioli or tortellini with cheese or cheese-and-herb filling (available in most pasta shops)

3 to 4 scallions, sliced very thin

1 tablespoon chopped fresh chives (optional)

2 tablespoons chopped fresh basil or parsley

2 to 3 tablespoons freshly grated Parmesan cheese

This was initially inspired by a Craig Claiborne recipe, which a friend clipped from the *New York Times.* I added small dried mushrooms called *mousserons,* which could be replaced by dried shiitake mushrooms. It's not too difficult to find cheese-filled ravioli or tortellini, with all the pasta shops now springing up around the country. I use ravioli with a delicious basil-cheese filling, which I found in a pasta shop I discovered one day on the rue Monge, near Place Maubert in the 5th arrondissement. Ravioli has less dough than tortellini, and because it's lighter, I think it works better here.

MAKING THE SALAD: Place the dried mushrooms in a bowl and pour on boiling water to cover. Let them sit while you prepare the remaining ingredients, about 20 to 30 minutes.

If the broccoli florets are very large, break or cut them into smaller pieces. Steam 5 minutes, or until crisp-tender, and refresh under cold water. Set aside.

Drain the mushrooms, saving the soaking liquid, and rinse them thoroughly. Strain the soaking liquid through a coffee filter or a sieve lined with a double thickness of paper towels, and set aside (you will add it to the pasta water). Squeeze the mushrooms dry and remove their woody stems. Heat the butter or oil in a skillet and add the garlic and mushrooms. Sauté for about 5 minutes and add the soy sauce. Remove from the heat.

Fill a large pot with fresh water and the soaking liquid from the mushrooms. Bring to a rolling boil, add a generous amount of salt, a spoonful of oil (any kind), and the ravioli or tortellini. Cook al dente, which should take from 3 to 5 minutes for fresh pasta and up to 10 minutes for dried. Drain and rinse with cold water. Shake out the excess water and transfer to a salad bowl. Add the other salad ingredients and gently toss together.

MAKING THE DRESSING: Mix together the vinegar, mustard, garlic, tarragon, and salt and pepper, and whisk in the oil.

Just before serving, toss the salad with the dressing. Garnish each serving with a few sprigs of watercress and some radish roses.

TO PREPARE AHEAD OF TIME: All the components for the salad can be prepared several hours in advance. Hold in covered containers in the refrigerator. If you are holding the dish in the refrigerator, toss the cooked ravioli with a couple of tablespoons of olive oil so they don't stick together, and cover.

SERVES 6 TO 8

FOR THE DRESSING
1/4 cup (60 ml) good-quality red wine vinegar or balsamic vinegar
1 teaspoon Dijon mustard
1 clove garlic, minced or put through a press
1/4 teaspoon dried tarragon
Salt and freshly ground pepper to taste
3/4 cup (180 ml) good-quality olive oil

FOR GARNISH
Watercress and radishes

DEEP-DISH EGGPLANT TORTE
Torte aux Aubergines

This rich, double-crusted torte has very good staying power, which was confirmed when I made it to be photographed. Food photography takes hours, and the torte continued to look beautiful throughout the day. We ate it for dinner that night; the following night we ate the back-up one, which was even better, although the crust had begun to get a little soggy. The torte also freezes well. It is very hearty and makes a warming, filling winter meal.

The one drawback to this dish is that it is time consuming, so you shouldn't plan to make it for dinner after work. The first time I tried it I was cooking for three hours. You can, however, make some of the components, like the crust and the tomato sauce, in advance. This is what I did for Supper Club,

FOR THE CRUST

2 cups (225 g) whole-wheat
   pastry flour plus 1 cup
   (115 g) unbleached white
   flour, or use 3 cups (340 g)
   whole-wheat pastry flour in
   all
1/2 teaspoon salt
1 1/2 sticks (6 ounces, 170 g)
   butter
1 large egg yolk
4 to 6 tablespoons ice-cold
   water, as necessary

FOR THE TOMATO SAUCE

1 tablespoon olive oil
1 onion, finely chopped
4 to 5 cloves garlic, minced or
   put through a press
3 pounds (1 1/2 kg) fresh
   tomatoes peeled, seeded, and
   chopped, or three 28-ounce
   (780 g) cans drained,
   seeded, and chopped
1/4 cup (60 ml) tomato paste
Salt and freshly ground
   pepper to taste
1/4 teaspoon mild-flavored
   honey or sugar
1/4 teaspoon dried thyme
1 teaspoon dried oregano
1 tablespoon chopped fresh
   basil or 1 teaspoon dried
Pinch of ground cinnamon
Tiny pinch of cayenne
   (optional), for a piquant
   sauce

SUPPER CLUB
CHEZ MARTHA ROSE

and the assembly went fairly quickly. You can assemble the torte hours before you bake it, and you can keep it in the refrigerator or freezer until you put it into the oven.

The dried mushrooms here are optional. They add a very distinctive flavor that surprises the palate, but the torte is still marvelous without them.

MAKING THE PIE DOUGH: Mix together the flours and salt, then cut in the butter. When the mixture has the consistency of coarse cornmeal, add the egg yolk, then the water by tablespoons. Gather into a ball, wrap tightly in plastic, and refrigerate for 2 hours or overnight.

PREPARING THE EGGPLANT: Slice the eggplant, salt the slices, and place in a colander or on an oven rack over the sink. Set a board on top of the slices and a pot of water or something else that heavy on the board, and let sit for 1 hour while you prepare the sauce and dried mushrooms, if using.

PREPARING THE SAUCE: Heat the olive oil in a large, heavy-bottomed Dutch oven and sauté the onion with half the garlic until the onion begins to turn golden. Add the tomatoes, tomato paste, remaining garlic, salt (3/4 to 1 teaspoon or more, to taste), and honey or sugar, and bring to a simmer. Simmer, covered, for 1 hour. Remove the lid, taste, and add more salt and garlic if you wish, then add the herbs. Continue to cook, uncovered, stirring occasionally, for another 30 minutes or so, until the sauce is no longer watery. Add the cinnamon and the optional cayenne and remove from the heat.

PREPARING THE OPTIONAL DRIED MUSHROOMS: Place the dried mushrooms in a bowl and pour on boiling water to cover. Let them sit 20 to 30 minutes. Drain and rinse thoroughly, then squeeze dry and chop. Heat the 2 teaspoons of butter in a small skillet and add the cèpes and the garlic. Saute for about 3 minutes and season with a little soy sauce. Remove from the heat and stir into the tomato sauce.

COOKING THE EGGPLANT: Preheat the oven to 450° F (230° C, gas mark 8). Rinse the eggplant slices and pat dry with a towel (this is definitely the most tedious part of the operation). Place the slices on oiled baking sheets and brush the top sides with a little olive oil. Bake 8 to 10 minutes, until cooked through and fragrant. Be careful not to burn them. Remove from the oven and turn down the oven to 375° F (190° C, gas mark 5).

ROLLING OUT THE CRUST AND ASSEMBLING THE TORTE: Roll out two-thirds of the piecrust (easiest between pieces of wax paper) and line the bottom and sides of a very well buttered 10- to 12-inch (25 to 30 cm) springform pan or cake pan. (See general directions for whole-wheat crusts, page 39). Beat one of the eggs, brush the crust, and prebake for 7 minutes in the heated oven (retain the remaining beaten egg for the top crust). Remove from the heat.

Layer one-third of the eggplant slices over the crust, slightly overlapping. Top this with a layer of one-third of the mozzarella, then a layer of one-third of the tomato sauce, then one-third each of the breadcrumbs and Parmesan. Repeat the layers two more times, ending with the sauce, breadcrumbs, and Parmesan. Beat the remaining 3 eggs in another bowl and pour over the top of the torte (the beaten eggs will sink into the torte as it bakes and hold everything together).

Roll out the remaining dough and place it over the top of the torte. Fold over the edge and shape an attractive lip by gently pinching all the way around the rim of the pan.

Brush the top crust with the remaining beaten egg you used for the bottom crust, and bake 1 hour, until golden brown. Let sit 15 to 20 minutes before cutting into wedges to serve.

TO PREPARE AHEAD OF TIME: The dough for the crust can be mixed up several days in advance and refrigerated or frozen. The tomato sauce will hold for 2 days in the refrigerator in a covered bowl. All of the ingredients can be prepared up

FOR THE EGGPLANT

4 medium-size eggplants, sliced ¼ inch thick
Salt
Olive oil as necessary

FOR THE MUSHROOMS (OPTIONAL)

½ to ¾ ounce (15 to 20 g) dried cèpes or other dried mushrooms
2 teaspoons butter
1 clove garlic, minced or put through a press
Soy sauce to taste

FOR ASSEMBLING THE TORTE

4 eggs
6 ounces (170 g) skim-milk or fresh mozzarella, sliced thin
2 ounces (55 g) whole-wheat breadcrumbs (½ cup)
6 ounces (170 g) Parmesan cheese, freshly grated (1½ cups)

to a day in advance. The entire torte can be assembled up to a day in advance and held in the refrigerator or freezer. Transfer directly to the preheated oven and bake 1 hour, 20 minutes, or until the crust is golden brown.

SERVES 8 GENEROUSLY

SAUTÉED RED AND YELLOW PEPPERS
Poivrons Rouges et Jaunes Poêlés

2 tablespoons olive oil

2 large sweet yellow peppers, cut in half, seeds removed, then cut in thin lengthwise strips

2 large sweet red peppers, cut in half, seeds removed, then cut in thin lengthwise strips

1 to 2 cloves garlic, to taste, minced or put through a press

1/4 teaspoon fresh thyme leaves (optional)

Salt and freshly ground pepper to taste

These make a gorgeous, light side dish. They go especially well with my richer entrees, like the Deep-Dish Eggplant Torte in this menu or Green Lasagne with Spinach Filling (page 105), but they would go equally well with lighter fish dishes.

Heat the oil in a large skillet or wok and add the peppers and the garlic. Sauté over medium-high heat until crisp-tender, 10 to 15 minutes. Add the thyme and salt and pepper to taste and serve as a side dish.

SERVES 4 TO 6

CITRUS AND DATE GRATIN
Gratin de Fruits d'Hiver

This is one of the most amazing desserts I've ever made. The dates add the crowning touch. When you bake the gratin they caramelize, and the combination of flavors is heavenly. A beautiful hot dessert for a winter feast.

Squeeze the juice from one orange and one grapefruit, strain and set the juice aside.

Remove the peel and zest from the remaining oranges and grapefruit and cut the fruit into quarters or eighths. Distribute, along with the dates, among 4 to 6 small gratin dishes, or toss together and place in a 1- or 2-quart (1 or 2 L) gratin dish.

Heat the juice to the boiling point in a small saucepan. Meanwhile, beat together the egg yolks and honey until thick and lemon colored. Slowly pour in the hot juice, beating. Return the mixture to the saucepan and place over medium heat. Heat through, stirring constantly with a wooden spoon, until the custard thickens and coats the spoon like thick cream. In the beginning it will be foamy on the top, so it will be hard to see it thickening. To be safe, keep removing it from the heat once wisps of steam begin to appear, spooning a little out and checking. When thick, remove from the heat and stir in the rum, vanilla, and cinnamon. Set the crème fraîche aside, covered.

Preheat the broiler 15 minutes before you wish to serve. Beat the crème fraîche in a bowl and beat in the crème anglaise. Spoon over the fruit and place under the broiler for 3 to 6 minutes, until the sauce begins to brown. Remove from the heat and serve.

TO PREPARE AHEAD OF TIME: The crème anglaise will hold

5 oranges
2 grapefruit
12 dates, as fresh as you can get them, pitted and quartered
5 large egg yolks
6 tablespoons mild-flavored honey
2 tablespoons rum
1 tablespoon vanilla
1 teaspoon ground cinnamon
½ cup (120 ml) crème fraîche

for several hours or overnight in the refrigerator. Allow it to cool and cover tightly. The fruit can be prepared several hours before assembling and refrigerated.

SERVES 4 TO 6

March

Beaujolais Nouveau, Gamay Primeur

CURLY ENDIVE SALAD WITH BAKED GOAT CHEESE
Salade de Frisée au Chèvre Rôti

SOURDOUGH COUNTRY BREAD (PAGE 18)
Pain de Campagne

PROVENÇAL-STYLE FISH SOUP
"Chowder" à la Provençale

TEXAS CORNBREAD (PAGE 35)
Pain de Mais à l'Américaine

PEAR CRISP WITH GINGER CRÈME ANGLAISE
Délice de Poires avec Crème Anglaise au Gingembre

Bandol Rosé Domaine Tempier, 1984
JON WINROTH'S WINE SUGGESTIONS: BOURGUEIL OR CHINON ROSÉ

I have served this meal at every season of the year, in France, San Francisco, Texas, and New York, and it's always a hit. You can make the soup anywhere you can find fresh fish, and vary the other ingredients according to season and availability of produce. Any firm white-fleshed fish will do; in France, at one time or another, I've used cod, sea bass, monkfish, ling cod, gurnard, turbot, conger eel, and redfish. In the States I've used Pacific red snapper, redfish, and cod. In France I garnish the soup with mussels, whereas in the States I usually opt for clams. As for the vegetables, in fall and winter I use pumpkin, a lovely idea I got from a Portuguese recipe, whereas in spring and summer I add zucchini and sweet corn.

This menu is a perfect example of how I like to marry French and American gastronomy in a meal. The salad is clearly a traditional French dish, and it's an excellent entree for the fish soup. The soup is called a "chowder" because I begin with the idea of a Manhattan-style chowder, with lots of tomatoes and potatoes; but the flavors are distinctly Provençal, with all the garlic, the hint of cayenne, the saffron, and the *soupçon* of orange peel. So in the end the soup is more reminiscent of bouillabaisse than of clam chowder. But then I serve it with Texas cornbread, which brings us back to the U.S.A., and cornbread couldn't be a better accompaniment for this heartwarming dish. It always elicits a lot of table conversation. The French are enchanted with any bread that is *comme gâteau,* like cake; and the Americans, ecstatic to be eating their beloved cornbread instead of baguettes, have questions and comments, like "How did you get it to be so light? It's not like my mother's, but then, my mother uses a lot of chicken grease in hers," or "Why isn't it a brighter color yellow?" (answer: because of the whole-wheat flour).

The warm pear crisp with its sweet, nutty topping and ginger-flavored crème anglaise is especially popular with Americans and the British, Irish, and Scots, who love "crumbles." I have also served apple pie for dessert with this soup, and other kinds of cobblers or crisps, depending on the season and what's available.

A southern French wine, either a rosé or a red, goes well with this meal. But so does a light red or rosé from the Loire. I particularly like the wines from Domaine Tempier in Bandol, and usually serve their rosé. At this particular dinner I served Domaine Tempier for a special reason: Laurence Peyraud, whose family makes the wine, was one of the guests.

One of the great advantages of this meal is that so much of it can be done in advance. The salad greens can be washed and dried as far ahead as the day before, the remaining vegetables and vinaigrette prepared hours in advance. The goat cheese is marinated for a day, so everything for the salad is ready to be put together just before you serve it. The breads will hold for a day or two if tightly wrapped, and the crème anglaise can be made a day in advance. You can do everything for the soup, right up to the addition of the fish and saffron, several hours before serving time. The vegetables take only about 15 minutes to cook, and the fish cooks so quickly that you can add it between courses. The mussel or clam garnish can be steamed hours before in the white wine. The pear crisp shouldn't sit too long, as the topping might get soggy, but it will hold for several hours, and can be reheated.

CURLY ENDIVE SALAD WITH BAKED GOAT CHEESE
Salade de Frisée au Chèvre Rôti

I always eat this salad as my main course when I go to my local bistro, Le Bistro Henri, on the rue Princesse. Mine is a little different from Henri's because I don't use as much chèvre; I don't want my guests to be too full for the next course. And I make sure to use the least salty goat cheese on the market. The ones to avoid are Bûcheron and the aged, harder goat cheeses. Generally the soft, moist, fresh ones are less salty. I use St. Christophe when I can find it. In the States, try local fresh goat cheeses if you are lucky enough to find them. If you can't find curly endive or watercress, use other lettuces; that shouldn't stop you from making this marvelous dish. And if you're eating the salad as a main course, you could increase the cheese.

Marinate the rounds of goat cheese in the ⅓ cup (90 ml) olive oil for a day, along with the sprigs of thyme and the rosemary. Turn from time to time.

Make the vinaigrette. Mix together the vinegar, lemon juice, mustard, garlic, and tarragon. Whisk in the oils and add salt and freshly ground pepper to taste.

Shortly before serving, preheat the oven to 425° F (220° C, gas mark 7). Place the garlic croutons on a baking sheet and top with the marinated cheese. Sprinkle with thyme. Bake 6 minutes, until the cheese is bubbling. Meanwhile toss the lettuces, chervil, and optional red pepper and mushrooms together with the dressing and distribute among 6 salad plates.

Top the salads with the croutons and hot cheese, garnish with radishes, and serve.

FOR THE SALAD

Twelve ½-inch (1.5 cm) thick rounds of fresh goat cheese, such as St. Christophe or Ste. Maure

⅓ cup (90 ml) fruity olive oil

4 sprigs fresh thyme

¼ teaspoon chopped fresh rosemary (optional)

12 Garlic Croutons (page 46), preferably made with sourdough bread

½ teaspoon fresh or dried thyme

½ large or 1 smaller curly endive, leaves separated and thoroughly washed and dried

2 generous handfuls watercress, stems trimmed

12 to 15 sprigs fresh chervil, if available

1 sweet red pepper, seeded and sliced thin (optional)

¼ pound (115 g) mushrooms, cleaned and sliced thin (optional)

FOR THE DRESSING

2 to 3 tablespoons red wine vinegar, to taste

1 tablespoon fresh lemon juice

1 teaspoon Dijon mustard

1 small clove garlic, minced or put through a press (optional)

1 teaspoon chopped fresh tarragon or ¼ teaspoon dried

7 tablespoons olive oil (use the cheese marinade and add to make up 7 tablespoons)

2 tablespoons walnut oil

Salt and freshly ground pepper to taste

FOR GARNISH

12 radish roses or tiny radishes

TO PREPARE AHEAD OF TIME: The croutons can be toasted a day in advance. Store in a sealed plastic container. The lettuces can be washed and thoroughly dried up to a day in advance. Wrap in towels, then seal in plastic bags. You can prepare the remaining vegetables and hold them for several hours in the refrigerator. The cheese is marinated for a day (you can do this the night before), and the dressing will hold for several hours.

SERVES 6

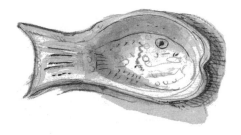

PROVENÇAL-STYLE FISH SOUP
"Chowder" à la Provençale

This is an intensely satisfying soup. Even though I call it a "chowder," it has a decidedly Mediterranean flavor, with all the garlic, the saffron, and the special perfume of the orange peel, which is added close to the end of the cooking.

You can prepare this soup, up to the addition of the saffron, orange peel and fish, well in advance of serving it. This makes it a great dish for a dinner party, as the fumet and the tomato sauce with the vegetables are easy and straightforward. The orange peel and saffron can be added before you sit down to the first course, and the fish can be added between courses. The chowder, with cornbread or crusty *pain de campagne,* is a meal I never tire of and have served time and again at my Supper Club, to the delight of my guests.

MAKING THE FUMET: Combine the fish trimmings, quartered onion, carrot, celery, leek, garlic, parsley, bay leaf, thyme, water, and salt in a large soup pot or saucepan and bring to a simmer over medium heat. Skim off all the foam that rises (the foam is bitter). Continue to skim until no foam remains, then cover, reduce the heat, and simmer 15 minutes. Add the wine and simmer another 15 minutes, covered. Remove from the heat and strain at once through a fine sieve or a strainer lined with cheesecloth. Don't cook any longer than this or the fumet will be bitter.

MAKING THE TOMATO STEW: Heat the olive oil in a large, heavy-bottomed soup pot or flameproof casserole and sauté the onion with the garlic until the onion is tender. Add the tomatoes, tomato paste, dried basil (if using), and thyme and simmer 15 minutes. Add the fumet, bay leaf, and salt to taste. Bring to a simmer and cook, uncovered, for 30 minutes. Add

FOR THE FUMET
1 pound (500 g) fish trimmings (heads and bones), rinsed
1 onion, quartered
1 carrot, sliced
1 stalk celery, sliced
1 leek, white part only, cleaned and sliced
2 cloves garlic, peeled
2 sprigs fresh parsley
1 bay leaf
1 sprig fresh thyme
1 quart (1 L) water
Salt to taste
1 cup (225 ml) dry white wine

FOR THE TOMATO STEW
1 to 2 tablespoons olive oil, as necessary
1 large onion, chopped
4 cloves garlic (or more, to taste), minced or put through a press
Two 28-ounce (760 g) cans tomatoes, with their juice, seeded and chopped
2 tablespoons tomato paste
1 tablespoon minced fresh basil or ½ to 1 teaspoon dried
½ to 1 teaspoon dried thyme

1 bay leaf
Salt to taste
¾ pound (340 g) new
   potatoes, diced
1 pound (500 g) pumpkin,
   peeled, seeded, and diced, or
   zucchini, sliced
Fresh corn kernels from 2 to 3
   ears, if in season (optional)
Pinch or two of cayenne, or
   ¼ teaspoon crushed red
   pepper
Freshly ground pepper to taste
2 wide strips orange peel,
   without pith
Generous pinch of saffron
Additional water if necessary
2 to 2½ (1 to 1.25 kg)
   pounds fish fillets or steaks,
   such as cod, striped bass,
   monkfish, tilefish, snapper,
   redfish, bream, turbot, or
   conger, cut in 2-inch cubes
   (you can use a combination
   of several kinds)

FOR GARNISH

½ pound (250 g) mussels or
   clams (enough for 4 per
   bowl)
1 cup (225 ml) dry white
   wine
½ cup (120 ml) water
3 tablespoons chopped fresh
   parsley
Lemon wedges

the potatoes, cover, and simmer 10 to 15 minutes (you cover the soup now because you want to cook the vegetables without letting any more of the liquid evaporate), or until the potatoes are cooked through but still have some texture. Add the pumpkin or zucchini, the optional corn and fresh basil (if using), cover, and simmer another 15 minutes, or until the pumpkin is tender. Add cayenne and pepper and adjust seasonings, adding salt, garlic, or more herbs if you wish. At this point you may remove the soup from the heat and let it sit until shortly before serving, when you will bring it back to a simmer and cook the fish.

PREPARING THE MUSSELS OR CLAMS: While the stew is simmering, clean the mussels or clams well, in several rinses of cold water (see instructions for cleaning mussels, page 204). Bring the wine and water to boil in a large lidded pot and add the mussels or clams. Steam 5 minutes, or until the shells open up, shaking the pan once to distribute evenly. Remove from the heat, drain, and set aside. Discard any that have not opened.

FINISHING THE SOUP: Fifteen to 20 minutes before you wish to serve, bring the soup to a simmer and add the orange peel and saffron. Adjust seasonings and add water if the broth seems too thick, or if there's not enough of it to cover the seafood. If you add water, make sure to adjust the seasonings again. Add the fish, cover, and simmer 10 minutes, until the flesh is opaque and falls apart. Serve at once, garnishing each bowl with mussels or clams, chopped fresh parsley, and a lemon wedge.

TO PREPARE AHEAD OF TIME: The fumet, the tomato sauce base, and the finished soup, up to the addition of the saffron, orange peel, and fish, will all hold for several hours. The tomato sauce could even be made the day before and held, covered, in the refrigerator.

SERVES 4 TO 6

PEAR CRISP WITH GINGER CRÈME ANGLAISE

Délice de Poires avec Crème Anglaise au Gingembre

Everybody loves a crisp or a crumble. This is such an American idea, but the crème anglaise, with its hint of ginger, and the pear eau de vie or liqueur give it a special exotic twist. This is one of those scrumptious desserts that I find myself eating for breakfast (if any remains) the next day, and picking at until there's none left. I love the rich nutty flavor of the pecan topping.

MAKING THE FRUIT MIXTURE, PREPARING THE TOPPING: Preheat the oven to 375° F (190° C, gas mark 5). Butter a 2-quart (2 L) baking dish.

Place the currants in a bowl and toss with 2 tablespoons of the eau de vie de poire or pear liqueur. Let them sit while you prepare the pears and other ingredients.

Place the pecans in a dry skillet and toast over a medium flame just until they begin to brown and smell toasty, stirring constantly. Remove from the heat.

Mix together the oats, flour, raw brown sugar, nutmeg, and salt. Cut in the butter and work to a crumbly consistency. Stir in the pecans and lemon zest (this can all be done in a food processor).

Toss together the pears, 2 tablespoons of the lemon juice, the currants and honey. Dissolve the cornstarch in the remaining 1 tablespoon each lemon juice and eau de vie de poire or pear liqueur and toss with the pears. Turn into the buttered baking dish. Sprinkle the topping over in an even layer.

BAKING THE CRISP: Bake in the preheated oven for 35 to 45 minutes, until crisp and beginning to brown on the top. To finish browning the top, run the crisp under the broiler, watch-

FOR THE CRISP
1/4 cup (45 g) currants

3 tablespoons eau de vie de poire or pear liqueur

1/2 cup (55 g) chopped pecans

1/2 cup (55 g) rolled oats

1/2 cup (55 g) whole-wheat pastry flour

1/4 cup (30 g) raw brown sugar

1/4 teaspoon freshly grated nutmeg

1/4 teaspoon salt

3 ounces (85 g) cold unsalted butter

2 teaspoons grated lemon zest

2 1/2 pounds (1.2 kg) Bosc or Comice pears, peeled, cored, and sliced

3 tablespoons fresh lemon juice

1 tablespoon mild-flavored honey

1 tablespoon cornstarch

FOR THE CRÈME ANGLAISE

4 large egg yolks
⅓ cup (90 ml) mild-flavored honey
1 ¼ cups (285 ml) milk
½ to ¾ teaspoon ground ginger, to taste
½ teaspoon vanilla

ing closely, for 2 to 3 minutes. Serve warm, with the ginger crème anglaise.

MAKING THE CRÈME ANGLAISE: Beat the egg yolks until lemon colored and add the honey. Beat until thick. Meanwhile, heat the milk in a heavy-bottomed saucepan to the simmering point. Being careful that the milk is not boiling, beat it into the egg-honey mixture. Return this mixture to the saucepan and heat over a medium-low flame, stirring constantly with a wooden spoon. Do not allow the mixture to boil. The crème anglaise is ready when it reaches the consistency of thick cream and coats both sides of your spoon evenly. Remove from the heat and strain into a bowl. Whisk in the ginger and vanilla.

TO PREPARE AHEAD OF TIME: The ginger crème anglaise can be made a day in advance. Cool, cover, and refrigerate. Serve it cold or warm with the crisp. Do not bake the crisp too far ahead of time so the topping remains crunchy. You can warm this in a low oven before serving.

SERVES 6

April

❧

SALUT PRINTEMPS

Sauvignon Touraine

GREEN BEANS VINAIGRETTE
Haricots Verts en Vinaigrette

SOURDOUGH COUNTRY BREAD (PAGE 5)
Pain de Campagne

CANNELLONI WITH CHARD, HERB, AND RICOTTA FILLING
Cannellonis Printanières

PAN-FRIED MUSHROOMS
Champignons Poêlés

STRAWBERRIES AND ORANGES WITH COINTREAU
Salade d'Oranges et de Fraises au Cointreau

CRISP ALMOND COOKIES (PAGE 89)
My Biscotti di Prato

Coteaux de Tricastin 1983, Paul Truffaut
JON WINROTH'S WINE SUGGESTIONS: CÔLES DU RHÔNE, GIGONDAS

April in Paris ain't what it's cracked up to be. It's a frustrating month: the weather is almost always cold and damp. You have a few warmish days of "false spring," enough to allow the trees to bud and to give you hope that the winter will end. But usually it gets cool and nasty again and remains that way until mid-May.

So I tried to evoke the spring with this menu, beginning with a chilled, pale dry Sauvignon Blanc served as an aperitif. The green bean salad is the color of new leaves. The light, beautiful cannelloni *printanières,* pale green with specks of parsley in the pasta, are filled with Swiss chard, an abundance of fresh parsley, and a mixture of ricotta, goat cheese, and Parmesan, with more emphasis on the vegetables and herbs than the cheese. The mushrooms served on the side have a meaty, savory quality that complements the soft cannelloni. And who can resist the first strawberries of the year? They look irresistible alongside the oranges and make a fine finale with the *biscotti,* after the cannelloni.

GREEN BEANS VINAIGRETTE
Haricots Verts en Vinaigrette

FOR THE BEANS

2 ounces (55 g) slivered almonds (optional)

1 ½ pounds (750 g) tender green beans, trimmed and cut in half if very long

2 tablespoons chopped fresh parsley

FOR THE VINAIGRETTE

5 tablespoons good-quality red wine vinegar

2 teaspoons Dijon mustard

1 small clove garlic, minced or put through a press

Salt and freshly ground pepper to taste

¼ teaspoon tarragon

¾ cup (180 ml) olive oil, or use half olive oil, half safflower oil

FOR GARNISH

Fresh tomatoes, in season, cut in wedges

One of my favorite bistros in Paris is a little place on the rue Princesse called Le Bistro Henri. It's a peppy neighborhood bistro with a black and white tile floor and French doors that look out onto the narrow little street. Henri cooks everything to order on a two-burner stovetop behind a little counter. There isn't even a sign on the door; you just have to know about the place. Henri has a prix-fixe menu with several choices of entrees and main dishes, all simple meat dishes. I always order the same things, both from the hors d'oeuvres. I start with his *salade de haricots verts* and continue with a green salad topped with a generous portion of baked goat cheese on toasted Poilane bread (see my version on page 18). Henri serves his famous scalloped potatoes, *gratin dauphinois,* a rich, buttery mixture of sliced potatoes and crème fraîche, baked until crisp on top, along with all orders, and all of this makes a great and filling dinner. I always drink the bistro's good Beaujolais or Bourgueil with this meal.

I think I appreciate Henri the most for his healthy green bean salad. Henri has never overcooked a bean. His vinaigrette is sharp and mustardy. Sometimes I add toasted almonds to my green bean salad, and I hope it's as good as his.

MAKING THE SALAD: If you're using the almonds, roast them in a dry skillet over medium-high heat, stirring constantly, until they begin to smell toasty. Remove from the heat and transfer to a bowl.

Bring a large pot of water to a rolling boil. Add a generous amount of salt and the beans. As soon as the water comes back to the boil, count to 20, taste one bean, and if it tastes cooked but is still crunchy, drain at once and rinse with cold water. If you want the beans a little better done, cook another half minute to a minute and drain. Set aside.

MAKING THE VINAIGRETTE: Mix together the ingredients for the dressing. Taste and add more vinegar or mustard, if you desire. Just before serving, toss with the beans, parsley, and optional almonds. Garnish the salad, or each serving, with fresh tomato wedges.

TO PREPARE AHEAD OF TIME: You can trim and blanch the beans a day ahead of time and hold them in a plastic bag in the refrigerator. The toasted almonds will hold for several days in a tightly covered jar. The dressing can be made several hours in advance and held in or out of the refrigerator.

Variation: Green Bean Vinaigrette with Beet Garnish

This is the version I served at my April Supper Club. I didn't want to repeat the tomatoes that were in the cannelloni sauce, or the almonds in the *biscotti,* so I omitted the almonds and substituted steamed beets for tomatoes. Use 2 to 3 medium beets for this recipe; steam until tender and slice in very thin rounds. Toss with a few tablespoons of the vinaigrette. Surround the beans with the sliced beets. The contrast of colors is beautiful.

SERVES 4 TO 6

CANNELLONI WITH CHARD, HERB, AND RICOTTA FILLING
Cannellonis Printanières

FOR THE PASTA

Whole-Wheat Pasta, Spinach Pasta, or Herb Pasta made with parsley (pages 36-39)
1 tablespoon salt
1 teaspoon vegetable or olive oil

FOR THE FILLING

1 pound Swiss chard leaves (3 pounds chard, with stalks)
1 cup (30 g) finely chopped fresh Italian flat-leafed parsley
1/2 cup (15 g) finely chopped fresh basil, if available (use 1 1/2 cups parsley in all if basil isn't available)
1 pound (500 g) fresh ricotta
1/2 pound (250 g) fresh goat cheese, not too salty (such as St. Christophe, Ste. Maure, or a fresh local variety, if available)
2 1/2 ounces (70 g) Parmesan cheese, freshly grated (2/3 cup)

These demand a lot of time, and I suggest you make them with a friend. I remember vividly the first time I made the cannelloni for Supper Club. Siena Herrera, my assistant at the time, a beautiful, golden-haired, precise French woman of Cuban origin who was studying to be a fashion designer, rolled and cut neat squares, all the same size (mine are never that even). I cooked the squares, and a woman who was renting a room in my apartment for a few weeks (an editor from New York named Martha Levin, who didn't mind being conscripted into my kitchen on a Wednesday night) filled them with the chard, cheese, and herb mixture I'd put together that afternoon. We worked late into the night, held the cannelloni in a covered dish in the refrigerator, and I finished them with the sauce just before baking and serving. Upon tasting this dish the following evening, my assistants agreed that the labor of love had been worthwhile.

The cannelloni are light and springlike, alive with the taste of fresh herbs and chard. They can be made with parsley, spinach, or whole-wheat pasta. I think the green-speckled parsley cannelloni are the prettiest.

ORDER OF STEPS: There are a number of choices here, as literally all of the components can be made a day ahead of time (or even 2 days, for the tomato sauce). The order listed below works well if you are assembling the pasta a day ahead of time. If you are making a large quantity of the cannelloni and need to stack them, do so between sheets of aluminum foil, lightly oiled with olive oil, and heat the sauce separately on the stove. Sauce the cannelloni when you serve them. You must have the filling ready before you roll out and cook the pasta, since you must fill the pasta as soon as it is cooked. The entire dish is then baked in the oven.

MIXING UP THE PASTA DOUGH: Mix up the pasta dough of your choice, according to the directions on pages 36-39. Knead and allow it to rest 30 minutes while you make the filling.

MAKING THE FILLING: Wash the chard, separate the leaves from the stalks, weigh out 1 pound (500 g), and place in a large, dry skillet. Cook over high heat in the liquid left on the leaves after washing, just until it wilts. Remove from the pan, rinse with cold water, and squeeze very dry in a towel. Chop fine, either by hand or in a food processor, and blend together with the remaining filling ingredients, either in a food processor or mixer or in a large bowl, stirring well with a wooden spoon.

ROLLING, CUTTING, COOKING, AND FILLING THE PASTA: Roll the pasta out into long, wide sheets. Cut these into squares about 4 ½ by 5 ½ inches (12 × 15 cm). Allow them to dry for about 20 minutes on towels.

Bring a large pot of water to a rolling boil and add a tablespoon of salt and a teaspoon of oil. Have a bowlful of cold water next to the pot. Drop the pasta squares into the boiling water, a few at a time, and cook for about 1 minute, or until they float up to the surface of the boiling water. Remove from the pot with a slotted spoon and place in the cold water to stop the cooking, then drain on a towel. Continue until you have cooked all the squares.

Oil a large (3 quarts, 3 L) baking dish. Place 2 heaping tablespoons of filling along the longer edge of each sheet and roll it up. Place the cannelloni side by side in the baking dish, seam side up. (You may need two baking dishes.)

MAKING THE TOMATO SAUCE: Heat 1 tablespoon of the olive oil in a heavy-bottomed Dutch oven or saucepan and

½ teaspoon dried thyme
½ to 1 teaspoon minced fresh rosemary, or ¼ to ½ teaspoon dried, to taste
2 cloves garlic, minced or put through a press
⅛ teaspoon freshly grated nutmeg
2 large eggs, beaten

FOR THE TOMATO SAUCE
1 to 2 tablespoons olive oil, as necessary
1 small or medium onion, minced
3 large cloves garlic, minced or put through a press
3 pounds (1.5 kg) fresh tomatoes, peeled, seeded and chopped, or three 28-ounce (780 g) cans
¼ teaspoon honey or sugar
Salt to taste
1 to 2 tablespoons chopped fresh basil, if available, or ½ to 1 teaspoon dried, to taste
Pinch of ground cinnamon
Freshly ground pepper to taste

FOR THE TOPPING
2 to 4 ounces (55 to 115 g) Parmesan cheese, freshly grated (½ to 1 cup)
2 to 3 tablespoons chopped fresh parsley

sauté the onion and 1 clove of the garlic until the onion is golden and translucent. Add the tomatoes, sugar, salt to taste, and the remaining garlic, and bring to a simmer. Simmer over medium heat, stirring occasionally, for 30 minutes. Add the basil and cinnamon and simmer another 20 minutes. Correct the salt and add freshly ground pepper to taste. For the best texture, puree through the medium blade of a food mill. Taste and adjust seasonings.

FINAL ASSEMBLING AND BAKING: Preheat the oven to 375° F (190° C, gas mark 5). Top the cannelloni with a layer of tomato sauce, then a sprinkling of grated Parmesan. Bake for 20 to 30 minutes in the preheated oven, until the cheese is melted and the sauce is bubbling. Sprinkle with parsley and serve.

TO PREPARE AHEAD OF TIME: The tomato sauce can be made up to a day ahead of time, but is best made the day you are serving.

The chard filling can be made a day ahead of time and held in a covered bowl in the refrigerator.

The cannelloni can be made and filled a day ahead of time and held in the refrigerator. Oil the baking dish or dishes well and cover tightly with lightly oiled foil.

SERVES 6 (18 CANNELLONI)

PAN-FRIED MUSHROOMS
Champignons Poêlés

This is a convenient side dish and is especially good with hefty main dishes. Regular or fresh wild mushrooms are both suitable.

Heat the butter and oil in a large, heavy-bottomed skillet and add the mushrooms and shallots. Sauté over medium heat until the mushrooms begin to release their liquid, about 5 minutes. Add the garlic and sauté about 2 minutes, then add the wine and the soy sauce. Raise the heat and cook, stirring, until most of the liquid has evaporated, about 5 to 10 minutes. Lower the heat a little and add the herbs and salt and freshly ground pepper to taste. Cook, stirring, for another few minutes. Taste and adjust seasonings, adding more garlic, soy sauce, or herbs, if you wish. Remove from the heat, stir in the parsley, and serve, or cool and heat through again just before serving. Stir in the parsley just before serving.

TO PREPARE AHEAD OF TIME: All the ingredients can be prepared and held in covered containers in the refrigerator for several hours. The entire dish will hold for several hours on top of the stove. In this case, don't add the parsley until you reheat the mushrooms.

SERVES 4 TO 6

1 tablespoon unsalted butter

1 tablespoon olive oil

1 1/2 pounds (750 g) regular or wild mushrooms (such as cèpes, chanterelles or pleurottes), or a combination, cleaned, trimmed, and thickly sliced or quartered

2 shallots, minced

3 cloves garlic, minced or put through a press

1/4 cup (60 ml) dry white wine

2 to 3 teaspoons soy sauce

1 teaspoon fresh or 1/2 teaspoon dried thyme

1 teaspoon fresh or 1/2 teaspoon dried rosemary

Salt and freshly ground pepper to taste

2 tablespoons chopped fresh parsley (optional)

STRAWBERRIES AND ORANGES WITH COINTREAU
Salade d'Oranges et de Fraises au Cointreau

1 ½ pounds (150 g) ripe
  strawberries (2 pints),
  trimmed and quartered or
  cut in half
1 tablespoon mild-flavored
  honey
Juice of 2 oranges
4 navel oranges, or 2 blood
  oranges and 3 navels,
  peeled, white pith removed,
  and cut in wedges
¼ cup (60 ml) Cointreau
3 tablespoons chopped fresh
  mint

This is a salad for early spring, when the strawberries are coming in and the oranges are going out. The colors are gorgeous, like the red and orange tulips that also appear at this time. I like to use the blood oranges we get here, which come from North Africa and Israel, as well as navel oranges. The blood oranges are tart and dark red, the navels sweet and bright orange.

Prepare the strawberries and toss with the honey and orange juice. Cover and refrigerate for at least 1 hour.

Toss together the strawberries, oranges, Cointreau, and mint. Refrigerate until ready to serve.

TO PREPARE AHEAD OF TIME: This can be prepared several hours before serving. Cover and chill.

SERVES 6

May

VIVA MEXICO ENCORE ENCORE

MARGARITAS (PAGE 51)

CEVICHE

CUMIN AND CORNMEAL BREAD (PAGE 28)
Pain au Cumin

CHALUPAS EXTRAORDINAIRES

PAN-FRIED ZUCCHINI WITH PARSLEY BUTTER
Courgettes Poêlées

STRAWBERRY SHERBET
Sorbet aux Fraises

TEXAS TEA CAKES (PAGE 122)
Galiettes Texanes

Domaine du Pavillon, Maurice Lutz viticulteur
JON WINROTH'S WINE SUGGESTIONS: BEAUJOLAIS, GAMAY TOURAINE

This is my standard Tex-Mex buffet, and it never gets old. I have made this meal for six people, for my regular twenty-five Supper Club guests, for parties of fifty and a hundred fifty. The larger buffets include more dishes (see recipes on pages 111–123), but everything centers around the black bean Chalupas Extraordinaires.

I've made this menu so many times that I can practically do it with my eyes closed. For that reason I often choose it when I know I'm going to be distracted by deadlines or out-of-town visitors. In May 1986, my close friends Marianne Schmink and Chuck Wood were in town. They had been charter members of the original Austin Supper Club; Marianne, in fact, had been my roommate, and used to set the tables every Thursday. It was exciting to show them the Paris version, and to demonstrate that during my years in Paris I hadn't forgotten how to cook Mexican food.

Chalupas Extraordinaires show up at least once a year at Supper Club, and they are my standard fare for catered events, whether large or small. They are convenient in that everything except the guacamole can be prepared hours in advance. I usually soak the beans two days before the dinner and cook and refry them the day before. They reheat easily in a moderate oven, and their flavor improves overnight.

At Supper Club my assistants and I make up the chalupas at the buffet and run them to the tables. But at larger events the chalupa buffet is part of the party. My assistants and I stand behind long tables, making up the chalupas as guests move through the line.

I'll never forget the first time we catered a big *International Herald Tribune* staff party for a hundred fifty people. The party was on a large barge that left from Boulogne-Billan-court, just outside of Paris, and moved up the Seine, around the Île-St.-Louis and back, a four-hour ride. It was a very hot summer night in July of 1983, and everybody was up for a party. The guests stood around drinking margaritas and eating crudités while we passed *moules à la mexicaine* (see page 195 for the recipe) for about an hour, until everybody was there. Then there was a great moment when the boat began to move, the Tex-Mex band I'd hired (called the Transcontinental Cow-boys) began to play, and we started serving chalupas. People moved through the line, then came back for seconds, and my crew and I didn't look up for a couple of hours.

When things slowed down a little I went up on the top deck, just as the boat was passing under the ornate Pont Alex-andre, Paris's most beautiful bridge. It leads over to the Grand Palais, with its *belle époque* glass roof, another one of Paris's breathtaking monuments. Everything was perfect at that mo-ment—the air was soft and warm, the city was lit up, the chalupas were a hit, and I was doing a big catering job on a boat on the Seine in Paris.

CEVICHE

This is one of the purest, heal-thiest ways I can think of to serve fish. Ceviches are made with various kinds of seafood; the traditional Mexican ceviche, ac-cording to Diana Kennedy, calls for mackerel or sierra; other recipes call for bay scallops. But I prefer a lighter, less oily fish, like cod or whiting. Both of these fish have a mild, subtle flavor, and they are inexpensive.

Ceviche is always popular at my Supper Club. It isn't too *picante,* as it often is in Mexico and Texas—I have to keep the conservative French palate in mind. I also don't want to interfere too much with all the other flavors in the dish. What distinguishes my ceviche from many others is the quantity of vegetables—the avocados, tomatoes, onions—which give it a variety of textures and fresh flavors.

Cut the fish fillets into ½-inch (1.5 cm) cubes and place in a bowl. Pour on the lime juice and toss together well. Marinate the fish in the lime juice, making sure it is completely submerged, for 7 hours, covered, in the refrigerator. The fish should be opaque.

Add the onion, garlic, chilis, chopped tomatoes, salt and pepper, diced avocado, and olive oil and refrigerate another hour or more. Just before serving, toss with the chopped coriander and adjust seasonings.

Line individual salad plates with leaves of spinach or lettuce. Top with the ceviche. Garnish with slices of avocado, lime and tomato, the optional radish roses, and the optional corn on the cob. Sprinkle with additional sprigs of coriander and serve.

TO PREPARE AHEAD OF TIME: This *must* be made 8 hours before serving.

SERVES 6

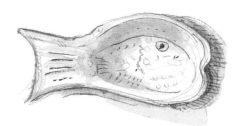

FOR THE CEVICHE

1 ½ pounds (750 g) very fresh fish fillets, such as cod, red snapper, whiting, redfish, mackerel, or sierra

Juice of 7 large limes—1 ½ to 2 cups

1 small onion, sliced

1 clove garlic, minced or put through a press

1 to 2 fresh or canned jalapeño or serrano peppers, to taste, seeded and chopped

2 medium tomatoes, chopped

Salt and freshly ground pepper to taste

1 large or 2 small ripe avocados, peeled, seeded and diced

¼ cup (60 ml) olive oil

4 tablespoons chopped fresh coriander

FOR THE PLATE

Either 6 ounces (170 g) large spinach leaves, washed and stemmed, or 1 head Boston or leaf lettuce

1 small avocado, peeled, seeded, and sliced

Thin slices of lime

2 tomatoes, sliced

2 ears corn, cooked and broken into 3-inch pieces (optional)

Radish roses (optional)

Fresh coriander sprigs

CHALUPAS EXTRAORDINAIRES

This recipe hasn't changed too much since I first published it in *The Vegetarian Feast.* The chalupas are still extraordinary; maybe even better than the original. In France I substitute *fromage blanc,* a kind of whipped cottage cheese, for the yogurt/ricotta mixture I used in my American version, and I use shredded lettuce instead of sprouts. Instead of Cheddar cheese I use Cantal, and I use chopped toasted almonds instead of sunflower seeds.

Black Bean Frijoles (page 54)
½ cup (115 g) ricotta or cottage cheese
½ cup (120 ml) plain low-fat yogurt
½ pound (250 g) white Cheddar cheese
1 recipe Salsa Fresca (page 53) (or more, to taste)
½ cup (55 g) almonds
1 small head leaf lettuce or romaine
Guacamole (page 55)
12 Chalupa chips (for homemade, see page 44)

Soak the beans overnight, then cook and refry according to the recipe.

Whip the ricotta or cottage cheese in a food processor or mixer and stir in the yogurt (don't blend them together or the mixture will be too runny). Grate the cheese. Hold in separate bowls, covered, in the refrigerator.

After making the salsa, cover and refrigerate until ready to serve.

Roast the almonds in a dry skillet over medium heat, or in the oven, just until they begin to brown and smell toasty. Remove from the heat and chop, not too coarse but not too fine (you need them for texture and a nutty taste). Set aside.

Wash the lettuce, dry it, and cut in chiffonade. Refrigerate in a plastic bag.

Make the guacamole, as close to serving time as possible, and refrigerate, covered, until ready to serve.

Forty minutes before serving time, preheat the oven to 350° F (180° C, gas mark 4). Douse the refried beans with a little liquid you've saved from the cooking, and cover with foil. Reheat for 30 minutes in the oven.

ASSEMBLING THE CHALUPAS: A chalupa buffet is a lovely sight. Have the beans in an attractive baking dish and all the other ingredients in pretty bowls. Spread a generous spoonful of the frijoles on each chalupa crisp. Top with a sprinkling of the grated cheese, then a spoonful of guacamole. Top the guacamole with a spoonful of the yogurt-ricotta mixture, then shredded lettuce, then a generous spoonful of salsa, and finally a light sprinkling of chopped almonds. Serve two to a plate, and pass extra salsa on the side.

TO PREPARE AHEAD OF TIME: The beans will hold for up to three days, covered, in the refrigerator. They also freeze well. Place a layer of plastic or wax paper between the beans and the foil so the beans won't react with the aluminum, but remember to remove the plastic before you reheat the beans.

The ingredients for the salsa can be prepared a day in advance and held in covered containers in the refrigerator. The salsa can be assembled and held in the refrigerator for several hours. The cheese can be grated and the ricotta and yogurt mixed up a day ahead of time. These can be refrigerated, covered, in the bowls you will be serving from. The chalupa crisps can be fried and the lettuce cut in chiffonade several hours in advance.

SERVES 6

PAN-FRIED ZUCCHINI WITH PARSLEY BUTTER
Courgettes Poêlées

Steam the zucchini until crisp-tender, about 5 minutes. It should just be starting to become translucent. Refresh under cold water. This can be done in advance and the zucchini held in a bowl.

Heat the butter in a wide skillet and add the zucchini. Sauté, stirring with a wooden spoon, until the squash is heated through. Add salt and freshly ground pepper to taste, stir in the parsley, and serve.

SERVES 4 TO 6

1 to 1½ pounds (500 to 750 g) zucchini, sliced thin
1 tablespoon unsalted butter
Salt and freshly ground pepper to taste
2 tablespoons minced fresh parsley

STRAWBERRY SHERBET
Sorbet aux Fraises

Here's another one of my easy sherbet recipes. This is a dish for spring and summer, when strawberries are at their best. It's tangy and perfect after a rich or spicy meal (or any meal, for that matter).

½ cup (120 ml) mild-flavored honey

1⅔ cups (375 ml) water

2¼ pounds (1 kg, or 3 pints) strawberries, washed, stems removed

½ cup (120 ml) fresh orange juice, strained

3 tablespoons fresh lemon juice, strained

2 tablespoons crème de cassis liqueur

Fresh mint for garnish

Combine the honey and water in a large saucepan (the honey boils up drastically) and bring to a simmer. Simmer 10 minutes and allow to cool.

Puree the strawberries in a food processor or blender until smooth. Add the orange juice, lemon juice, crème de cassis, and two-thirds of the honey syrup. Taste and add the rest of the syrup if the mixture isn't sweet enough. Freeze in an ice cream maker or a sorbetière, or still-freeze according to the instructions in the note on page 59.

Transfer to individual serving dishes, a mold, or an attractive bowl, cover each serving dish, or the bowl, with plastic, then foil, and freeze. Work quickly so the mixture doesn't melt. Allow to soften in the refrigerator for 20 minutes before serving. Garnish each serving with fresh mint leaves.

TO PREPARE AHEAD OF TIME: The sherbet should be made at least a day in advance and will last for weeks in the freezer.

SERVES 6 TO 8

June

CHAMPAGNE AND GRAPEFRUIT JUICE PUNCH
Punch au Champagne, Pamplemousse, et Cassis

ORIENTAL SALAD WITH HOMEMADE BUCKWHEAT PASTA (PAGE 25)
Salade Orientale aux Pâtes Maison

COUNTRY BREAD WITH OLIVES (PAGE 32)
Pain aux Olives

POACHED FILLETS OF SOLE WITH PUREED TOMATO SAUCE
Filets de Sole Pochés à la Sauce Vierge

STEAMED ZUCCHINI
Courgettes à la Vapeur

STRAWBERRY "SOUP"
Soupe aux Fraises

HONEY-LEMON REFRIGERATOR COOKIES (PAGE 60)
Galettes au Miel et au Citron

Pinot Chardonnay, Haut-Poitou
JON WINROTH'S WINE SUGGESTIONS: SAUVIGNON TOURAINE, ENTRE-DEUX
MERS, GRAVES BLANC

This is a late spring or early summer dinner; you can't do it before sweet, red, ripe tomatoes and strawberries are available. I remember walking around Paris on a rare and welcome warm June day in 1985, during one of those springtimes that was more like winter, envisaging what the plates would look like for each course: pasta salad with a rainbow of green and red vegetables, served on a bed of lettuce; delicate fish fillets in a satiny tomato sauce, garnished with a steamed vegetable; something fruity and unexpected for dessert. Chilled white wine, yellow and white daisies on the table, colorful Italian pottery instead of my usual white porcelain. I sat in the sun at a sidewalk café on the Boulevard Port-Royale, drank *citron pressé* (fresh lemonade), and wrote shopping lists.

The cold poached fish with *sauce vierge,* an uncooked puree of tomato sauce, is my version of a recipe I had come across years ago in Roy Andries de Groot's *Revolutionizing French Cooking.* The original recipe is by Michel Guérard. My *sauce vierge* has additional herbs, a touch of balsamic vinegar, and a julienne of orange zest, the finishing touch added at the end. It is a lively, easy dish. A simple steamed vegetable, zucchini in this case—but green beans, fresh peas, or snow peas would also be nice—is all you need to accompany the fish.

The salad is sublime, with delicate homemade noodles, pungent sauce, fresh coriander and crisp, bright snow peas, shiny red peppers and a shrimp garnish. The delicious Strawberry "Soup," served with honey-lemon cookies, makes a perfect finale to this meal.

CHAMPAGNE AND GRAPEFRUIT JUICE PUNCH
Punch au Champagne, Pamplemousse, et Cassis

1 quart canned or bottled grapefruit juice
1 bottle dry Champagne
3 tablespoons crème de cassis liqueur
Ice cubes
Sliced citrus and strawberries for garnish

This is the punch I always served in Austin, Texas, for my big parties. It's great because it seems you can drink a fair amount without becoming too inebriated, probably because of the large proportion of citrus juice.

Mix together the grapefruit juice, Champagne, and liqueur in a punch bowl. Chill with ice cubes, garnish with the fruit, and serve.

SERVES 6

ORIENTAL SALAD WITH HOMEMADE BUCKWHEAT PASTA
Salade Orientale aux Pâtes Maison

FOR THE SALAD
Buckwheat Pasta (page 37) or ½ pound (250 g) buckwheat noodles (soba; can be found in Japanese markets and natural foods stores)
2 tablespoons Chinese sesame oil

This is a convenient salad for a dinner party because all the components can be prepared in advance. Just before serving, toss it with the dressing. It is as beautiful as it is delicious, and could be eaten as a simple meal as well as a starter. You can, of course, buy the noodles, but I have given you my recipe on page 36, in case you want to make them yourself.

Make the pasta and cook until al dente, just firm to the bite, and toss with the 2 tablespoons sesame oil. Set aside.

Steam the snow peas until crisp-tender and refresh under cold water (or you can blanch them; see page 81). Toss with the noodles and all the remaining salad ingredients. Chill until ready to serve, or serve at room temperature.

Mix together all the ingredients for the dressing in a blender until smooth. Adjust seasonings. Shortly before serving, toss with the noodles. Taste and adjust seasonings, adding more salt, pepper, soy sauce, or cayenne if you wish.

Line plates or a platter with the lettuce leaves. Top with the salad, and place 4 to 6 shrimp on the top of each serving. Sprinkle with additional coriander and serve.

TO PREPARE AHEAD OF TIME: The noodles can be made a day or two in advance and dried. They can be cooked several hours ahead of time, tossed with the sesame oil in a bowl, and refrigerated. The dressing can be made a day in advance; refrigerate in a covered jar. The vegetables can be prepared several hours in advance and refrigerated in plastic bags or covered containers.

SERVES 4 TO 6

½ pound (250 g) snow peas, trimmed
1 sweet red pepper, seeded and cut in thin strips
2 tablespoons minced chives
3 tablespoons minced fresh coriander

FOR THE DRESSING
2 tablespoons lemon juice
2 tablespoons cider vinegar (or more, to taste)
2 tablespoons water
1 tablespoon tamari or Kikkoman soy sauce
1 teaspoon dry sherry
1 teaspoon mild-flavored honey (optional)
1 teaspoon minced or grated fresh ginger
1 clove garlic, minced or put through a press
1 teaspoon sesame tahini
3 tablespoons safflower oil
3 tablespoons Chinese sesame oil
Salt and freshly ground pepper to taste
Pinch of cayenne

FOR THE PLATES
24 to 30 small shrimp, cooked and peeled, for garnish (optional)
Leaf lettuce
Additional chopped coriander

POACHED FILLETS OF SOLE WITH PUREED TOMATO SAUCE

Fillets de Sole Pochés à la Sauce Vierge

Here is another perfect do-ahead dish for a dinner party. Every portion of it can be prepared (must be prepared) well in advance, unless you are serving the fish hot. Even then, it's just a question of 5 to 10 minutes' work. Since you are relying on ripe, fresh tomatoes, this is a spring or summer dish, and for this reason I like to serve the fish at room temperature. I poach them in the morning, chill them, and an hour or so before serving, remove them from the refrigerator.

Everybody loves the flavor of the basil and the hint of orange in this elegant dish.

FOR THE FISH

Vinegar Court Bouillon (page 170)

1 to 1½ pounds (500 to 750 g) sole fillets (allow 4 ounces, 115 g, per person)

2 to 3 teaspoons olive oil, for the serving dish

Salt and freshly ground pepper to taste

Juice of ½ lemon

Thin strips of zest from ½ orange

First make the vinegar court bouillon and allow it to cool. If you are serving the fish cold, it doesn't matter whether you poach the fish or make the sauce first. If you are serving the fish hot, make the sauce first.

PREPARING THE FISH: Rinse the fillets and pat them dry. Place them on a cutting board and slap with the flat side of a large knife. This breaks down the muscle fibers so they won't curl when you poach them. Make a few diagonal slashes, about ⅛ inch (.25 cm) deep, across each one.

Spread 2 to 3 teaspoons olive oil over the bottom of an attractive flat or oval serving dish or casserole.

Butter a deep, flat frying pan or flameproof gratin and add the court bouillon, which should be at room temperature or warm, but not too hot. Add the fish fillets in an even layer. Bring to a simmer over low heat. Never let the court bouillon actually boil; it should be just trembling. When it reaches this point, count 5 minutes for each ½ inch (1.5 cm) of thickness in the layer of fish (fillets are usually ½ inch—1.5 cm—thick). After 5 minutes the fish should be opaque and should break apart easily with a fork. Carefully remove the fillets from the poaching liquid with a slotted spatula and place in the oiled casserole. Lightly salt and pepper, then sprinkle with the lemon juice and orange zest.

PREPARING THE SAUCE: Blend the tomatoes, garlic, chervil, parsley, half the basil, and the vinegar together in a food processor or blender until smooth. Add salt and freshly ground pepper to taste. If you wish, add a bit more balsamic vinegar.

Transfer the mixture to an electric mixer or a large bowl, and using a wire whisk to incorporate air and lighten the sauce as you slowly drizzle in the olive oil. This step gives the sauce a silky texture. Taste and correct seasonings. Set aside in the refrigerator in a covered bowl if serving the next day, or at room temperature if serving in a few hours.

Shortly before serving, stir in the remaining basil and the orange zest. Correct seasonings.

IF SERVING COLD: Cover the fish with plastic or foil and refrigerate. An hour or two before serving, remove from the refrigerator. Pour on half the sauce and let sit at room temperature until ready to serve. At serving time, place the fillets and some of the sauce on each plate, and top with more sauce.

IF SERVING HOT: After poaching and sprinkling the fish with the lemon juice, orange zest, salt and pepper, garnish with about a third of the sauce. Bring to the table and serve, topping each serving with another spoonful of sauce.

NOTE: You could also cool the fish in its poaching liquid. In this case, poach for only 3 to 4 minutes and remove the casserole from the heat. The fish will have a slightly more vinegary taste.

TO PREPARE AHEAD OF TIME: The sauce will hold for a day in the refrigerator; the flavors actually ripen overnight, al-

FOR THE SAUCE

1 ½ pounds (750 g) tomatoes, peeled and seeded

2 large cloves garlic, peeled

1 tablespoon fresh chervil leaves

1 tablespoon chopped fresh parsley

2 tablespoons chopped fresh basil leaves

1 tablespoon balsamic vinegar (or more, to taste)

Salt and freshly ground pepper to taste

3 tablespoons fruity olive oil (optional)

Thin strips of zest from ½ orange

though the last of the basil and orange zest should be added close to the time of serving. The fish can be poached in the morning for an evening meal. If the fish is to be served cold, it must be poached several hours before serving and stored in the refrigerator. The court bouillon can be made a day or two in advance and refrigerated in a covered bowl or jar.

SERVES 4 TO 6

VINEGAR COURT BOUILLON

1 quart (1 L) water
1/2 cup (120 ml) good-quality
 red wine vinegar
1 onion, sliced
2 leeks, cleaned and sliced
1 carrot, sliced
1 stalk celery, sliced
2 whole cloves garlic, peeled
1 sprig fresh parsley
1 sprig fresh thyme
1 bay leaf
1 teaspoon salt (or more or
 less, to taste)
6 peppercorns

This is a good poaching medium for fish if you are going to serve the fish cold, especially with an acidy sauce like the *sauce vierge*.

Combine all the ingredients except the peppercorns in a large saucepan or soup pot. Bring to a boil, reduce the heat, cover, and simmer 30 minutes. Add the peppercorns and simmer another 15 to 30 minutes. Strain and retain the broth. Use for poaching fish.

This will keep for a day or two in the refrigerator and can be frozen.

MAKES ABOUT 1 QUART

STRAWBERRY SOUP
Soupe aux Fraises

This is a simple *concassée* of strawberries: the berries are crushed in a mixer (not pureed) and mixed with orange juice, honey, and a good eau de vie. Into this go whole or halved strawberries that have been marinating in lemon juice and honey to bring out their sweetness and flavor. It's essential to find sweet, red-ripe strawberries.

Divide the berries in half, including all crushed less-than-perfect berries in one of the halves; you will use this one for the *concassée*.

Cut the large berries from the "good-looking" half in halves or quarters and toss them with the lemon juice and 1 to 2 tablespoons honey, to taste. Cover and refrigerate.

Place the remaining strawberries in the bowl of your mixer or in a large bowl. Using the mixing beater, a fork, or a pestle, crush the berries to a coarse puree. Beat in the orange juice, eau de vie, and 1 to 2 tablespoons honey, to taste. Set aside until ready to serve. This can be done hours in advance and stored in the refrigerator.

Just before serving, stir the chopped mint into the *concassée*. To serve, ladle a generous portion of the *concassée* into each bowl. Give the whole strawberries a toss and add them to each serving. Garnish with fresh mint leaves and serve.

TO PREPARE AHEAD OF TIME: The soup can be made hours in advance, up to the addition of the mint, and stored in the refrigerator in a covered bowl. You can, however, chop the fresh mint and refrigerate it, wrapped in plastic, for several hours. I have even served the soup the next day, but the strawberries don't look as good.

SERVES 4 TO 6

2¼ pounds (1 kg, or 3 pints) strawberries, hulled
Juice of 1 lemon
2 to 4 tablespoons mild-flavored honey in all, to taste
Juice of 1 orange
1 tablespoon good-quality kirsch or eau de vie d'abricot (apricot eau de vie)
2 tablespoons chopped fresh mint
Fresh mint leaves for garnish

Two July Menus

❧

FOR A HOT EVENING

CRAZY SALAD WITH TUNA TARTARE
Salade Folle

SOURDOUGH COUNTRY BREAD (PAGE 5)
Pain de Campagne

COLD STEAMED FISH FILLETS WITH TOMATO-CAPER SAUCE
Filets de Poisson à la Marseillaise

NEW POTATOES EN PAPILLOTE
Pommes de Terres Nouvelles en Papillote

PEACH TART
Tarte aux Pêches

FOR A COOLER SUMMER EVENING

VEGETABLES À LA GRECQUE
Légumes à la Grecque

COUNTRY BREAD WITH OLIVES (PAGE 32)
Pain de Campagne aux Olives

BAKED WHITING WITH TOMATO-CAPER SAUCE
Merlans à la Marseillaise

PASTA WITH SWEET PEAS AND HERB BUTTER

PEACH TART
Tarte aux Pêches

Côteaux de Tricastin 1983, Paul Truffaut
JON WINROTH'S WINE SUGGESTION: CHÂTEANEUF-DU-PAPE BLANC

July in Paris can be crazy; it can start out cold and wet, then become very hot and humid. The first menu here is a meal for a hot night, and when I served this in 1986 hot weather was upon us. A few years before, for a July Supper Club, it had been cold for so long I felt like trying to force the summer with vegetables. That year I served hot baked whitings with the same *sauce marseillaise,* and several vegetable dishes. I'm including both menus in this chapter.

The salad for the hot-weather meal was inspired by a salad Laurie and I had made for dinner the weekend before my Supper Club. I'd been working with tuna, and had made *lardons de thon* (small crisp-fried pieces of tuna), *tartare de thon* (marinated raw tuna), and broiled fresh tuna, all of which I'd thrown into a wild salad containing all sorts of leftovers and beautiful lettuces we'd gotten at various markets. It was so good I decided that would be the first course the following Thursday, using only the raw tuna and adding as many colorful vegetables as possible.

The weekend I worked with the tuna I had discovered a marvelous fish market on the rue du Bac, the best I've found in the neighborhood. The freshness of their fish is undisputable, and their choice is even better than the Poissonerie du Dôme, which I'd considered the best in my neighborhood. They have rockfish for bouillabaisse, squid and cuttlefish, and all kinds of shellfish. I asked their advice for a fish to serve cold, one that would hold and be solid enough to support a spicy sauce like the marseillaise. They suggested the same two fish I had tested almost a year before to go with *salsa fresca,* rascasse (like redfish or snapper) and lingue (ling cod). I tested them both again, and preferred the rascasse. It works especially well, with lots of gelatin and body.

People are very laid back at summer Supper Clubs, especially if the weather is good. Life in Paris is relaxed during July and August, with so many people out of town. My soirees often continue late into the night; it's still light when we sit down to dinner, and if it's balmy guests linger on the balcony after the meal.

CRAZY SALAD WITH TUNA TARTARE
Salade Folle

FOR THE TUNA TARTARE

¾ *pound (340 g) fresh tuna, skin and bones removed*

3 cloves garlic, peeled

¼ *cup (60 ml) fresh lemon juice*

6 tablespoons olive oil

Salt and freshly ground pepper to taste

Leaves from 3 sprigs fresh parsley, chopped

2 teaspoons chopped chives

1 avocado

FOR THE SALAD

1 large head or the equivalent of a combination of lettuces, such as red tip, romaine, Boston, oak leaf

1 cucumber, peeled and thinly sliced

SUPPER CLUB
CHEZ MARTHA ROSE

This is a "crazy salad" because of all the different colors and ingredients—lettuce, sweet baby peas, brilliant red peppers, and ripe tomatoes. I make it in early summer when there is a great variety of produce in the markets. You don't have to be limited to the ingredients here. It could be a "clean out the refrigerator" salad. What makes it truly special, though, is the raw tuna, which is marinated for several hours in lemon juice, crushed garlic, and olive oil, then tossed with diced avocado just before serving. You must use the freshest possible tuna for this.

MAKING THE TUNA TARTARE: At least 3 hours before you wish to serve, cut the tuna into ½ inch (1.5 cm) dice. Crush the garlic with the flat side of a knife and combine in a bowl with the lemon juice, olive oil, and salt and pepper to taste. Add the tuna, parsley, and chives and toss thoroughly. Cover and refrigerate for 3 hours. Stir from time to time; taste and adjust seasonings.

PREPARING THE SALAD INGREDIENTS AND THE DRESS-ING: Wash and dry the lettuces. Tear in large pieces and wrap in a towel, then in a plastic bag, and refrigerate until ready to use.

Prepare the remaining vegetables, herbs, and the croutons and toss together in a large bowl.

Make the salad dressing. Combine the lemon juice and vinegar, the garlic, mustard, and salt and pepper, and mix together. Whisk in the oil or oils and combine well.

Just before serving, dice the avocado and stir into the tuna. Toss with 2 tablespoons of the salad dressing.

If serving on individual plates, toss the lettuces in one bowl with half the dressing, and the other ingredients in a separate bowl with the other half. Line salad plates with the lettuce and top with the vegetable mixture. Top this with the tuna and avocado, and serve. If you are serving the salad from a big bowl, toss together the lettuce and vegetable mixture, top with the tuna and avocado, and serve.

TO PREPARE AHEAD OF TIME: The tuna must be prepared several hours in advance. The peas can be shelled and the croutons made a day in advance. Hold the peas in a plastic bag or container in the refrigerator, and the croutons in a well-sealed container. The vegetables and salad dressing can be prepared several hours in advance. Refrigerate the vegetables in plastic bags or covered containers, and the dressing in a jar or bowl.

SERVES 6

1 to 2 sweet red peppers, seeded and thinly sliced

1/2 pound (250 g) fresh peas (unshelled weight), shelled

1/2 pound (250 g) carrots, peeled and grated

1 bunch radishes, cut in half lengthwise and thickly sliced

1/4 pound (115 g) mushrooms, cleaned, trimmed, and sliced

3 to 4 tomatoes, cut in wedges

4 to 6 tablespoons, to taste, one or more chopped fresh herbs such as tarragon, basil, chives, parsley, dill

1 cup (115 g) diced garlic croutons (see page 46)

FOR THE DRESSING

Juice of 1 medium or large lemon

1/4 cup (60 ml) red wine vinegar

1 to 2 cloves of the crushed garlic from the tuna tartare, to taste, minced or put through a press

1 heaping teaspoon Dijon mustard

Salt and freshly ground pepper to taste

3/4 to 1 cup (180 to 225 ml) olive oil, to taste; or use half olive oil, half safflower or vegetable oil

COLD STEAMED FISH FILLETS WITH TOMATO-CAPER SAUCE

Filets de Poisson à la Marseillaise

I've served the sauce that goes with this fish with tuna, with baked whitefish, and here, chilled, with cold steamed rascasse fillets, which could be replaced by redfish, red snapper, or cod. It's a zesty Mediterranean tomato sauce, pungent with garlic and capers.

FOR THE TOMATO-CAPER SAUCE

1 tablespoon olive oil

1 small or ½ medium onion, finely chopped

½ cup (150 g) capers, rinsed and chopped in a food processor or mashed in a mortar and pestle

4 to 6 cloves garlic, chopped (can be chopped or mashed along with the capers)

2½ pounds (1.25 kg) tomatoes, seeded and chopped

Pinch of sugar

Salt and freshly ground pepper to taste

2 to 3 teaspoons chopped fresh basil

¼ to ½ teaspoon fresh thyme leaves or ¼ tsp dried

MAKING THE SAUCE: Heat the olive oil in a large, heavy-bottomed skillet and add the onion. Sauté for a few minutes and add the garlic and capers. Sauté, stirring, for 5 minutes, then add the tomatoes and a pinch of sugar. Cook over moderate heat, stirring occasionally, for 20 to 30 minutes. Season to taste with salt and freshly ground pepper, and stir in the basil and thyme. Allow to cool, then cover and chill.

STEAMING THE FISH: First prepare the fillets by slapping them with the flat side of a knife, to break down the muscle fibers so they don't curl when they are exposed to the heat. Score each fillet on the diagonal, three or four times, about ¼ inch (.75 cm) deep. Lightly salt and pepper and place on an oiled steaming rack. Bring a small amount of water, to which you have added a few leaves of fresh basil, to a boil in your steaming pot. Place the steaming rack over the boiling water, cover, and steam 5 minutes per ½-inch (1.5 cm) thickness (the fillets I get in Paris take about 7 minutes). The fish should be opaque and flake easily with a fork. Immediately transfer the fillets to an oiled platter or casserole and allow them to cool. Cover and refrigerate until 30 minutes before serving time.

Thirty minutes before serving, remove the fish and the sauce from the refrigerator. The fish should be cold, but not so cold that you can't taste it. Serve each fillet partially covered with the sauce, with more sauce on the plate. This is excellent with potatoes or fresh pasta on the side.

TO PREPARE AHEAD OF TIME: The sauce can be made a day ahead. Cool, then transfer to a bowl or serving dish, cover, and refrigerate. The fish can be steamed several hours in advance, but should be bought the day you are serving it. Once steamed, cover and refrigerate.

SERVES 6

FOR THE FISH

6 redfish or red snapper fillets, about 6 ounces (170 g) each

Salt and freshly ground pepper to taste

1 large sprig fresh basil for the steaming water

NEW POTATOES EN PAPILLOTE
Pommes de Terres Nouvelles en Papillote

If you are increasing this recipe by a substantial amount, make several papillotes. If you crowd the potatoes they take longer to bake. I learned this the hard way at Supper Club, when my assistant followed my directions and removed the potatoes from the foil after 25 minutes, and served them rock hard. I died a hundred deaths.

Preheat the oven to 425° F (220° C, gas mark 7).
Scrub the potatoes, dry, and cut in 1-inch (2.5 cm) pieces.
Cut a double-thick square of aluminum foil large enough to form a loose pouch for the potatoes. Butter or oil the foil generously and place the potatoes on top. Salt and pepper, add the thyme and remaining butter, and fold the foil over the potatoes. Crimp the edges of the foil together tightly. Bake in the oven 25 to 30 minutes. Remove from the oven and open the foil. Check to see that the potatoes are tender. If they are not, close up and bake another 5 to 10 minutes. Remove from the foil, toss with the parsley in a serving dish, and serve hot.

SERVES 6

1 1/2 pounds (750 g) new potatoes, the smaller the better

2 tablespoons unsalted butter or olive oil

Salt and freshly ground pepper to taste

2 sprigs fresh thyme

2 tablespoons chopped fresh parsley

PEACH TART
Tarte aux Pêches

The taste of this juicy peach tart, with its crunchy, almondy crust, is sublime. There is, however, a problem that I can't seem to get around with my fruit tarts: the crust underneath the fruit will get soggy very quickly. It's because whole-wheat pastries are more penetrable than those made with white flour. Yet the taste is so good. It helps considerably to brush the crust generously with beaten egg before you prebake it. But I recommend that you make this as close to serving time as possible.

Sweet Almond Piecrust (page 41)
1 large egg, beaten
Juice of 1 lemon
2 tablespoons mild-flavored honey
2½ pounds (1.2 kilos) peaches (or a mixture of peaches and apricots), peeled, pitted and thinly sliced
2 tablespoons apricot preserves (optional)

Make the piecrust. Refrigerate until ready to prebake.

Preheat the oven to 375° F (190° C, gas mark 5). Brush the crust generously with the beaten egg and prick with a fork in several places. Prebake 20 minutes, until the bottom is cooked through and the edges are beginning to brown. Remove from the oven.

Mix together the lemon juice and honey in a large bowl. Toss the sliced peaches, or combination of peaches and apricots, with the lemon-honey mixture. Arrange the fruit on the prebaked crust. Retain any liquid remaining in the bowl. Return the tart to the oven and bake another 10 to 15 minutes, or until the crust is brown and the fruit is heated through.

Transfer the liquid from the fruit to a saucepan and reduce over medium-high heat until you have a thick syrup. Add the optional apricot preserves and melt together with the syrup.

Remove the tart from the oven and brush the fruit gently with the syrup. Serve warm or cooled.

SERVES 8

VEGETABLES À LA GRECQUE
Légumes à la Grecque

This recipe was inspired by a dish I ate at the Paris restaurant l'Ambroisie my first year here. Theirs is called *étuvée de légumes au coriandre,* a fancy name for a dish that was a brilliant version of the traditional vegetables à la Grecque. The vegetables are stewed in a heady bouillon, with lots of crushed coriander seeds, then marinated in the same broth. The broth is later reduced and poured over the vegetables, and the dish is quite stunning and fragrant with the intensified flavors in the bouillon.

Combine all the ingredients for the bouillon in a large flameproof casserole or stockpot and bring to a simmer. Simmer, covered, while you prepare the vegetables.

Cut off the stems of the artichokes, pull off all the tough outer leaves around the bottoms, and slice off the tops where the artichokes begin to curve inward. Rub continuously with lemon juice to prevent discoloration. Trim the bottoms of the artichokes by rotating them against the sharp blade of a knife, so that all the tough green skin is cut away and the white fleshy part underneath the leaves is exposed. Rub these cut surfaces with lemon juice and drop the artichokes into a bowl of water acidulated with the juice of 1 lemon.

Drop the artichokes, fennel, onions, and garlic cloves into the simmering bouillon. After 15 minutes add the cauliflower and carrots. Add the zucchini spears after another 10 minutes, and simmer everything together for another 10 minutes.

Remove the vegetables from the bouillon and place in a bowl. Take out the artichoke bottoms, allow them to cool, and cut in half. Using a small spoon, gently scoop out the chokes. Put the artichokes back in the bowl with the other vegetables,

FOR THE BOUILLON/MARINADE

2 1/2 cups (600 ml) water
1 1/2 cups (350 ml) dry white wine
Juice of 2 large lemons
2 tablespoons vinegar
1/2 cup (120 ml) olive oil
3 cloves garlic
1 dozen peppercorns
1 tablespoon coriander seeds
1 bay leaf
4 sprigs fresh parsley
1/2 teaspoon fennel seeds
1/2 teaspoon salt
1 large shallot, chopped
4 ounces (115 g) raisins

FOR THE VEGETABLES

2 to 3 large globe artichokes
Juice of about 2 lemons
One 1-pound (500 g) fennel bulb, cut lengthwise into eighths
20 small boiling onions, peeled
8 whole cloves garlic, peeled
1 small cauliflower, broken into florets
1/2 pound (250 g) carrots, peeled and cut in 3-inch (8-cm) spears

½ *pound (250 g) zucchini,*
cut in 3-inch (8-cm) spears

FOR THE PLATES
Lettuce leaves (optional)
Sprigs of fresh chervil or
chopped fresh parsley
Radish roses
Thin slices of lemon

pour on the bouillon, cover, and refrigerate for 2 hours, or overnight.

Drain the vegetables and strain the marinade. Place the marinade in a saucepan and bring to a boil over high heat. Reduce by two-thirds. If you wish, line individual plates with lettuce leaves. Distribute the vegetables in equal portions over the plates. Pour on the reduced marinade and garnish with sprigs of chervil or chopped fresh parsley, radish roses, and thin slices of lemon. Serve.

TO PREPARE AHEAD OF TIME: Obviously this has to be done a few hours in advance, and will hold for a day or two in the refrigerator.

SERVES 6 TO 8 GENEROUSLY

BAKED WHITING WITH TOMATO-CAPER SAUCE
Merlans à la Marseillaise

In cooler weather I serve the Tomato-Caper sauce and fish hot. Whole small whiting baked in a little white wine have a subtle taste and go nicely with the lusty sauce.

The tomato-caper sauce from
the recipe on page 178
6 small whiting, cleaned,
heads removed
Salt and freshly ground
pepper to taste
½ *cup (120 ml) dry white*
wine

First make the sauce according to the directions in the recipe and set it aside.

Preheat the oven to 425° F (220° C, gas mark 7). Butter a rectangular or oval baking dish large enough for all the fish to fit in a single layer. Wipe the fish and pat them dry with a dishtowel. Lay them side by side, alternating head end to tail end, in the buttered baking dish. Salt and pepper lightly. Place the wine in a saucepan, bring to a simmer, and pour over the fish. Cover with buttered parchment paper or foil and bake 10 to 15 minutes in the preheated oven, until the flesh is opaque and flakes easily with a fork. While the fish is baking, reheat the sauce. Serve the fish with some of the sauce on top and more on the side.

TO PREPARE AHEAD OF TIME: Just as for the cold fish fillets with tomato-caper sauce, the sauce will hold for a day in the refrigerator. The fish can be prepared in their baking dish hours in advance, covered, and refrigerated. Remove from the refrigerator 30 minutes before baking.

SERVES 6

PASTA WITH SWEET PEAS AND HERB BUTTER

This simple, fragrant pasta is lovely as a side dish with fish, but could also be served as a first course.

Make an herb butter by combining the butter, parsley, basil, chives, and garlic. Add a little salt, to taste.

Steam the peas until tender, 5 to 10 minutes. Refresh under cold water and set aside.

Bring a large pot of water to a rolling boil. Add a teaspoon of salt, a tablespoon of oil, and the pasta. Cook al dente, just until firm to the bite. This will take 3 to 5 minutes, depending on the width, or seconds if it is fresh pasta. Drain and toss in a warm serving dish with the herb butter and peas. Serve at once.

TO PREPARE AHEAD OF TIME: The herb butter can be made several hours before serving time and held in the refrigerator. The noodles are cooked and tossed with the herb butter just before serving.

SERVES 4 TO 6

5 tablespoons softened unsalted butter
1/4 cup (10 g) chopped fresh parsley
1/4 cup (10 g) chopped fresh basil
2 tablespoons minced chives
1 small clove garlic, pureed or put through a press
Salt to taste
1 pound (500 g) fresh peas (unshelled weight)
1 tablespoon olive or vegetable oil
3/4 pound (240 g) spaghettini

August

Crémant de Bourgogne

PASTA PRIMAVERA WITH ROASTED RED PEPPERS AND GOAT CHEESE
Pâtés Printanières aux Poivrons Rotis et au Chèvre

COUNTRY BREAD WITH OLIVES (PAGE 32)
Pain de Campagne aux Olives

WHOLE-WHEAT HERB BREAD (PAGE 30)
Pain aux Herbes

COLD POACHED FILLETS OF FISH WITH EGG-LEMON SAUCE
Turbot ou Barbue Froid à la Sauce Avgolimone

BAKED TOMATOES
Tomates au Four

STEAMED ZUCCHINI
Courgettes à la Vapeur

MIXED PLUM AND APRICOT TART
Tarte aux Quetsches, Reines-Claudes, et Abricots

Sancerre
JON WINROTH'S WINE SUGGESTIONS: ANY OTHER SAUVIGNON WINE, SUCH AS
ENTRE-DEUX-MERS, QUINCY

Here's another cold summer meal with a pasta salad and fish. This pasta, however, with its Mediterranean flavors—sweet basil, roasted red peppers, and goat cheese—is very different from the Oriental pasta salad I served in June. So is the fish, and really, in an unair-conditioned apartment in the city, there is no better choice for an August menu. Each course is as exquisite to look at as it is tasty. The fragrant pasta salad sparkles with bright peas, asparagus, and roasted peppers. The colors in the main dish are pale and summery: lemon yellow–sauced fish fillets topped with dark green sprigs of tarragon; roasted tomatoes and barely steamed zucchini decorating the plate like a fan. The flavors of the savory olive and herb breads make a nice contrast to the delicately seasoned fish. And the tart is like a pinwheel of multicolored fruit.

I came upon the fish dish in Elizabeth David's *Summer Meals.* She uses sole and calls the dish *sole à la juive.* I like the dish with sole, but prefer a slightly more substantial flatfish, like turbot or brill. The first time I served it at Supper Club I tested the recipe with brill and liked it, so I ordered the brill and xeroxed all my menus with "Barbue à la Sauce Avgolimone." Early Thursday morning when I got to the Poissonerie du Dôme, behind the Boulevard Montparnasse, they told me they hadn't been able to get the brill but were preparing turbot (and were giving me the same price—a deal). I was upset, but what could I do? I went and drank a coffee at Le Select while they filleted the fish. When I got home and cooked the fillets I discovered that I liked turbot even better than brill, and changed all the menus.

August is the time in France for irresistible plums—*reines claudes*, which are small, marvelously sweet and juicy green-gages; deep-purple prunes; and the sweet-tart, reddish purple *quetsches*. Apricots are still sweet and abundant, and they look beautiful interspersed with the plums.

PASTA PRIMAVERA WITH ROASTED RED PEPPERS AND GOAT CHEESE
Pâtés Printanières aux Poivrons Rotis et au Chèvre

The pasta you use for this can be fresh or dried, and you can choose any shape you fancy. I've made the salad with fettuccine, thinner tagliarini, spiral pasta, and spaghetti.

FOR THE VEGETABLES AND HERBS

3 sweet red peppers
1 pound (500 g) fresh peas (unshelled weight)
1 pound (500 g) fresh asparagus
2 tablespoons olive oil
1 clove garlic, minced or put through a press
Coarse salt
1 bunch fresh basil
1/2 cup (15 g) chopped fresh parsley, preferably flat-leaf

PREPARING THE VEGETABLES: First roast two of the red peppers. Either roast them under a broiler or above a burner flame, turning until charred on all sides. Remove from the heat and place in a paper bag or damp towel. Allow to cool.

Meanwhile shell the peas and cut the tips of the asparagus off, about 2 inches (5 cm) down from the top. Trim off the tough base of the asparagus and cut the remaining stalks into pieces about 1/2 inch (1.5 cm) long. Keep the tops separate from the stalks. Seed the remaining red pepper and cut into thin lengthwise strips, then cut these strips in half or into thirds.

When the roasted peppers are cool enough to handle, remove the skins, rinse under cold water, and pat dry. Remove the stems, seeds, and membranes, and cut into thin strips. Place in a bowl and toss with 2 tablespoons of olive oil, a minced or pressed clove of garlic, about 1/4 teaspoon coarse salt, and 8 large leaves of the basil, cut in slivers. Toss together, cover, and refrigerate for at least 1 hour.

Mince the remaining basil and the parsley and set aside. Steam the peas, asparagus tips, and asparagus stalks separately, just until crisp-tender, about 5 minutes for the asparagus, 5 to 10 minutes for the peas. Refresh under cold water and set aside.

COOKING THE PASTA: Bring a large pot of water to a boil and cook the pasta al dente. Drain and toss with the remaining 5 tablespoons olive oil, which you have mixed with 1 clove garlic, minced or put through a press. Refrigerate until shortly before ready to serve, or leave at room temperature if serving soon.

ASSEMBLING AND SERVING THE DISH: Shortly before serving, toss the pasta with the steamed peas and asparagus stalks, the sliced raw pepper, the minced basil, parsley, Parmesan, and goat cheese. Taste and adjust salt and pepper.

Serve on individual plates and top each portion with a spoonful of roasted red peppers. Arrange asparagus tops and a few radishes on the side, and serve.

TO PREPARE AHEAD OF TIME: You can roast the red peppers and marinate them a day in advance. Refrigerate in a covered bowl. You can also prepare all of the vegetables a day in advance. Store them in plastic bags or covered containers in the refrigerator. The pasta can be cooked several hours in advance; toss with the olive oil and garlic, cover and refrigerate until ready to toss with the remaining ingredients. The salad will hold, all assembled, for an hour or two.

SERVES 6

FOR THE PASTA AND THE REST OF THE DISH

½ pound (250 g) spinach pasta, herb pasta, or whole-wheat pasta

5 tablespoons olive oil

1 clove garlic, minced or put through a press

4 ounces (115 g) goat cheese, diced or crumbled

4 ounces (115 g) Parmesan cheese, freshly grated (1 cup)

Salt and freshly ground pepper to taste

Radish roses for garnish

COLD POACHED FILLETS OF FISH WITH EGG-LEMON SAUCE

Turbot ou Barbue Froid à la Sauce Avgolimone

I prefer this dish cold, but you can also serve it hot. It can be made well in advance, and it's easy. The sweet/pungent tarragon sets off the tangy egg-lemon sauce in a lovely way. If fresh tarragon is difficult to find, substitute chopped fresh chervil, basil, or parsley.

My favorite fish for this is turbot, but any white-fleshed flatfish will work. Brill and sole are quite good. Accompany the fish with a baked tomato and a fan of steamed zucchini slices.

The leftovers, if you have any, have an added feature. The fumet will gelatinize overnight in the refrigerator, and the gelatin has a marvelous flavor. If you place your leftovers in a tureen and pour the leftover sauce over them, then refrigerate overnight, you'll have a lovely terrine for lunch the next day.

MAKING THE FUMET: Combine 1 pound (500 g) of the fish bones and heads in a large soup pot with the water, onion, carrot, celery, garlic, leek, peppercorns, and bouquet garni. Bring to a boil. Skim off all the foam that rises, and when there is no longer any foam, cover and simmer over low heat for 15 minutes. Add the white wine and salt to taste, cover, and simmer another 15 minutes. Drain and strain the stock through a dish towel or a double layer of cheesecloth. Set aside and cool to lukewarm or colder.

PREPARING AND COOKING THE FISH: Rinse the fish fillets and pat them dry with paper towels. Using the flat side of a large knife, slap the fillets to break down the muscle fibers so they won't curl when you poach them. Now make two or three diagonal slashes, about ⅛ inch (.5 cm) deep, across the fillets on the skin side.

Butter a large, flat flameproof casserole large enough to accommodate the fish fillets in one layer. Lay the fish fillets in the casserole and add 3 cups (340 g) of the fumet, or enough to cover the fish. Cover with a piece of buttered parchment and bring to a bare simmer over medium heat. Reduce the heat and poach the fish for 8 to 10 minutes, or 5 minutes for each ½ inch (1.5 cm) of thickness, until the fillets are opaque and flake easily. Remove the fish from the liquid with a slotted spatula and place on an attractive serving dish. Keep warm in a very low oven if serving hot.

MAKING THE SAUCE: Strain the poaching liquid into a saucepan. Turn up the heat and reduce to about 1 cup (225 ml). Remove from the heat and cool a moment.

Beat together the egg yolks and lemon juice (use the juice of 1 lemon at first, then add more if you want a more lemony sauce); add a ladleful or so of the hot stock to this, stir together well and return the mixture to the remaining stock. Stir over low heat until the mixture reaches a creamy consistency, being careful not to bring to a simmer or the eggs will scramble. Remove from the heat and adjust the lemon juice, salt and pepper. Pour over the fish fillets, cover, and refrigerate until 15 to 30 minutes before you wish to serve, depending on how cold you want the fish to be.

TO SERVE: Just before serving, sprinkle the tarragon over the fish. Serve two fillets per person, first spooning a little extra sauce over the plate underneath the fillet, and garnishing with a sprig of tarragon or parsley and a lemon slice.

If you wish to serve the dish hot, once the sauce is ready, pour it over the fish, sprinkle with the tarragon, and serve, garnishing as above.

Chill any leftovers in a tureen.

TO PREPARE AHEAD OF TIME: The fumet will hold for several hours. Strain it and hold in a covered pot. The entire dish should be made several hours in advance when you are serving it cold. Cover with plastic wrap and refrigerate.

SERVES 4

2 large flat white fish, such as turbot, sole, brill, or flounder, filleted, skins removed, heads and bones reserved (you should have 1 pound (500 g) of fillets in all)
1 quart (1 L) water
1 onion, quartered
1 carrot, coarsely sliced
1 stalk celery, coarsely sliced
2 cloves garlic, peeled
1 leek, white part only, cleaned and sliced
4 black peppercorns
Bouquet garni made with 1 bay leaf, a couple of sprigs of fresh parsley, and a sprig of fresh thyme
1 cup (225 ml) dry white wine
Salt to taste
4 large egg yolks
Juice of 1 to 2 large lemons, to taste
2 tablespoons chopped fresh tarragon

FOR GARNISH
Thin slices of lemon
Sprigs of fresh parsley or tarragon

BAKED TOMATOES
Tomates au Four

6 medium or large firm, ripe
  tomatoes
Salt and freshly ground
  pepper to taste
Olive oil
2 shallots, minced
2 tablespoons pesto (page 293)
  or chopped fresh herbs such
  as basil, thyme, parsley,
  rosemary, oregano

Preheat the oven to 375° F (190° C, gas mark 5). Oil a baking dish.

Cut the stems out of the tomatoes. Salt and pepper lightly and drizzle on a little olive oil. Sprinkle with the chopped shallots, and place a spoonful of pesto or chopped herbs in the cone-shaped cavity where you cut out the stem.

Bake 20 to 30 minutes in the preheated oven, until the tomatoes are bubbling and the skin is beginning to shrivel. Spoon any of the juices accumulated in the pan over the tomatoes, and serve.

SERVES 6

MIXED PLUM AND APRICOT TART
Tarte aux Quetsches, Reines-Claudes et Abricots

There are two techniques for this exquisite tart: in the first the fruit is briefly baked on the prebaked pastry, and in the second the assembled tart is run under the broiler, just until the tips of the fruit begin to carmelize. In either version the fruit should not cook very long, or the plums will lose their lively colors.

Mix the pastry dough, wrap it in plastic, and refrigerate for several hours or overnight.

Cut the fruit in half or in wedges and discard the pits. Combine the plum brandy, honey, and vanilla in a large bowl and toss the fruit in this mixture. Marinate for an hour or more.

FOR METHOD 1, IN WHICH THE FRUIT IS BAKED: Preheat the oven to 375° F (190° C, gas mark 5). Roll out the piecrust and line a buttered 12- to 14-inch (30 to 35 cm) tart pan. Beat the egg and brush the surface of the pastry generously. Prick in several places with a fork, and bake 20 minutes in the preheated oven, until the surface and edges are brown. Remove from the oven. Raise the oven heat to 400° F (200° C, gas mark 6).

Drain the fruit in a colander over a bowl. Place the liquid in a saucepan—at least twice the volume of the liquid to avoid its boiling over—and bring it to a boil. Reduce this by half, and stir in the apricot jam.

Arrange the drained fruit in the prebaked piecrust, alternating colors and overlapping the fruit if necessary. Gently brush with the reduced marinade–apricot jam mixture.

Sweet Almond Piecrust (page 41)

¾ pound (340 g) greengage plums

¾ pound (340 g) fresh prunes or purple plums (use 1½ pounds—750 g—prunes or purple plums if you can't find greengages)

¼ cup (60 ml) plum brandy

2 tablespoons mild-flavored honey

½ teaspoon vanilla

1 pound (500 g) fresh apricots

1 large egg

1 tablespoon apricot jam

Bake the tart for 10 to 12 minutes, until the crust is a rich brown color. Remove from the heat and brush the fruit gently again with the marinade. Serve cool or warm.

FOR METHOD 2, USING THE BROILER: Proceed as above, but blind-bake the pastry shell for 30 minutes. After you arrange the drained fruit in the baked pastry shell, brush with the glaze and run the tart under the broiler for 4 to 5 minutes, just until the tips of the fruit are beginning to brown. Remove from the heat, gently brush again, and allow to cool or serve warm.

SERVES 8

Part II:
Special Events

TEX-MEX IN PARIS

I was known in Paris for my Tex-Mex meals long before I began my Supper Club. I have forced my friend Serge Orenbush to lug a *comal* (a Mexican griddle), a tortilla press, and kilos of black beans up a mountain in the French Alps so I could make enchiladas during a week-long ski trip in Avoriaz; and I've dragged the same equipment and ingredients to Saint Moritz so that I could make Mexican food for Niki de Saint-Phalle and her friends when I was working for her. I knew there would be a need for all those Mexican cooking supplies when I packed them into my car in Austin. I've never come back from the States without at least ten pounds of black beans in my suitcase.

My reputation for Tex-Mex food in Paris began our first October here with a Migathon. "Migathon" is a term coined by Maggie Megaw and Steve Monas; it was what they called the Mexican brunches they were in the habit of throwing in Austin, Texas, before they moved to New York (where they continued the tradition). The main dish was always *migas,* Mexican-style eggs scrambled with onions, tomatoes, chili peppers, and crisp strips of fried corn tortilla.

When we all came over to Paris in the fall of 1981, we hadn't been here for more than a month when we decided it was high time we gave a party. Why not introduce the Migathon to Paris? Each of us invited the few people we knew. I had come over with most of the ingredients we needed, and Fauchon supplied the rest. The food was a big hit; nobody can dispute the genius of Steve's *migas.*

Two days after our brunch I got a phone call from the wife of Lee Huebner, the publisher of the *International Herald Tribune.* My friend and colleague, Patricia Wells, had been at the brunch, and had told her about our great Mexican food. Mrs. Huebner wanted to know if we would cater a birthday party for her husband that Friday. How could we resist? Yellow Rose Catering was born.

I've catered a number of Tex-Mex events since that first small dinner party. The most challenging have been the two *International Herald Tribune* staff parties held on a barge in July of 1983 and 1984. These are terrific parties, although transporting food for a hundred fifty people in my Volkswagen is hell. The people who run the boat aren't too happy about letting caterers other than their own use the kitchen, so they limit our refrigerator and work space and don't even let us use their sponges or brooms. But we manage.

I always do my chalupa buffets for large groups, with crudités and my goat cheese dip, and Mussels à la Mexicaine as hors d'oeuvres. In addition to the chalupas I often serve a Mexican rice salad and green pepper "boats" filled with sautéed zucchini and diced red pepper. Dessert is usually a big watermelon fruit basket, or fruit marinated in sweet white wine. One of my roommates, Ronnie Kaufman, was trying to get a chocolate-chip cookie business off the ground during the period of the *Herald Tribune* parties, and we always passed chocolate-chip cookies and brownies in big baskets after the buffet. Hers are the best around, but she won't divulge the recipe.

Below are the Migathon and one of the *Herald Tribune* party menus. The Migathon menu rarely changes, as I found out to my delight when Maggie and Steve gave a Migathon in New York for Christine Picasso, when she visited for the first time in 1986.

THE MIGATHON

MARGARITAS (PAGE 51)

TORTILLA CHIPS

STUFFED JALAPEÑOS
Piments Farcis

GUACAMOLE NACHOS (PAGE 115)

BLACK BEAN NACHOS
Nachos aux Haricots Noirs

STEVE'S MIGAS

HOMEMADE TORTILLAS (PAGE 43)
Tortilllas Maison

MEXICAN RICE (PAGE 57)
Riz à la Mexicaine

BLACK BEAN FRIJOLES (PAGE 54)
Frijoles aux Haricots Noirs

FRUIT SALAD
Salade aux Fruits

TEXAS TEA CAKES (PAGE 122)
Galettes Texanes

TEX-MEX BUFFET FOR AN INTERNATIONAL HERALD TRIBUNE STAFF PARTY

MARGARITAS (PAGE 51)

CRUDITÉS WITH GOAT CHEESE AND HERB DIP
Crudités aux Chèvre

MEXICAN-STYLE MUSSELS ON THE HALF SHELL
Moules à la Mexicaine

CHALUPAS EXTRAORDINAIRES (PAGE 160)

MEXICAN RICE SALAD
Salade de Riz à la Mexicaine

SAUTÉED ZUCCHINI AND RED PEPPERS IN BELL PEPPER BOATS
Courgettes et Poivrons Rouges Poélés dans ses Barquettes de Poivrons

WATERMELON FRUIT BASKET
Panier de Pasteques aux Fruits

MANGOS, PEACHES, AND BERRIES IN SWEET WHITE WINE
Mangues, Pèches, et Fruits Rouges au Vin Doux

CHOCOLATE CHIP COOKIES, BROWNIES, AND TEXAS TEA CAKES
Les Cookies, Brownies, et Galettes Texanes

Wine suggestions are the same as for the May Supper Club menu (page 155). Jon Winroth also suggests Gewürtztraminer.

STUFFED JALAPEÑOS
Piments Farcis

Eating these is a challenge for those sensitive to heat, but it's a dream for people like my friends Sam Okoshken, a Paris lawyer, and Patricia Wells; for them, the hotter the better.

Wearing rubber gloves so the peppers don't irritate your hands, cut the jalapeños in half and discard the seeds.

Mash the two cheeses together in a bowl. Put the mixture into a pastry bag and pipe it into the jalapeño shells (or fill them with a spoon). Arrange on a plate and garnish with the coriander.

SERVES 4 TO 6

6 canned pickled jalapeño peppers
¼ pound (100 g) ricotta cheese
¼ pound (100 g) goat cheese
Chopped fresh coriander for garnish

STEVE'S MIGAS

We usually made two batches of *migas,* one hot and one mild, as tolerance for *picante* varies from palate to palate. Some cooks add cheese to their *migas,* but Steve insists it makes them "too busy."

12 large eggs
Salt and freshly ground
    pepper to taste
1/2 cup (120 ml) safflower or
    vegetable oil
6 corn tortillas (for
    homemade, see recipe page
    31; may be stale), cut into
    strips
1 small onion, minced
2 to 4 fresh or canned
    jalapeño or serrano peppers,
    to taste, seeded and chopped
4 medium-size tomatoes (1
    pound—500 g) seeded and
    chopped
3 tablespoons unsalted butter
1 tablespoon chopped fresh
    coriander

Beat the eggs lightly in a large bowl. Do not overbeat; you want both white and yellow in the resulting dish. Add salt and freshly ground pepper and set aside.

Heat the oil in a large, wide frying pan over high heat to 360° F (190° C). Add the tortilla strips and fry until they are crisp and golden brown. This should only take a few seconds. Drain on paper towels.

Discard all but 2 tablespoons of the oil and allow it to cool for a few minutes. Reduce heat to low. Add the onion and peppers and sauté until the onion is soft but not brown. Add the tomatoes and cook very briefly, about 1 minute. Season with a little salt, and transfer to a bowl.

Melt the butter in the frying pan over low heat and add the eggs. Cook slowly over low heat, stirring. When the eggs are somewhat set, stir in the vegetables. Just before the eggs are set, stir in the fried tortilla strips. Stir in the chopped fresh coriander and serve at once.

SERVES 6

CRUDITÉS WITH GOAT CHEESE AND HERB DIP
Crudités aux Chèvre

Prepare the vegetables. Cut the zucchini in spears or rounds and break the broccoli and cauliflower into florets. Steam until bright green or blanch the broccoli, green beans, and zucchini; peel and cut the carrots in rounds or sticks, cut the peppers into strips, the cucumbers into rounds or sticks.

Beat the cottage cheese and goat cheese together in a food processor or a mixer and stir in the yogurt. Don't use the food processor to stir in the yogurt or the mixture will be too runny. Combine well and stir in the optional garlic, herbs, and freshly ground pepper. Transfer to a bowl, cover, and refrigerate until ready to use.

Arrange the vegetables attractively on a decorative platter. Place the dip in a bowl in the middle.

SERVES 12

3 to 4 pounds (1.5 to 2 kg) assorted vegetables in season, such as zucchini, broccoli, cauliflower, green beans, carrots, red and green peppers, cucumbers

1/2 pound (250 g) cottage cheese

1/4 pound (115 g) goat cheese

1 cup (225 ml) plain low-fat yogurt

1 to 2 cloves garlic, minced or put through a press (optional)

1/4 to 1/2 cup (10 to 15 g), or more, to taste, chopped fresh herbs, such as tarragon, basil, parsley, dill, chives

Freshly ground pepper to taste

MEXICAN-STYLE MUSSELS ON THE HALF SHELL
Moules à la Mexicaine

This is one of the tastiest mussel dishes I've ever had. It was served at the opening night party at Café Pacifico, but unfortunately the restaurant didn't put the item on their menu. Perhaps it's too labor intensive a dish; you do have to clean and cook all the mussels, then remove them from their shells. (There's no way getting around it: cleaning mussels is tedious. But cleaning them carefully is essential for two important reasons. First of all, by handling the mussels individually you will detect any with broken or open shells; these are no longer alive and must be discarded. Second, there is nothing worse than gritty mussels —except gritty lettuce.) I have assistants to help me when I make it for my Tex-Mex catering jobs. Even so, when I'm cooking for a large crowd, like the *Herald Tribune* staff, it can be a nightmare. I serve it anyway, because it's so good, making just enough so everybody can eat two or three while they're waiting for the chalupas.

1 quart (1 L) mussels
1 cup (225 ml) dry white
  wine
1 cup (225 ml) water
2 shallots or 1 onion, chopped
2 cloves garlic, crushed
A few sprigs parsley
Fresh coriander for garnish
Double recipe of Salsa Fresca
  (page 53)

CLEANING THE MUSSELS: Place the mussels in a large bowl of cold water. Brush them with a wire brush and pull out their "beards." Drain the water and fill the bowl again, adding 2 tablespoons salt or vinegar. Let the mussels sit in the water for 15 minutes. The mussels will spit out much of their sand because they don't like the salt or vinegar. Drain, rinse in fresh water, brush the mussels once more, and discard any that have broken shells or are opened. Soak one more time for 15 minutes in vinegar or salt water, drain, and rinse thoroughly.

COOKING THE MUSSELS: Combine the wine, water, onion or shallots, garlic, and parsley in a large pot and bring to a boil. Add the mussels, cover tightly, and steam 5 minutes, shaking the pan halfway through to redistribute the mussels. The mussels should be open after 5 minutes. Drain the mussels, straining the cooking liquid into a bowl, and discard any mussels that haven't opened. Set the strained liquid aside.

ASSEMBLING THE DISH: Combine all the ingredients for the salsa and adjust seasonings. Remove the mussels from their shells, but retain the shells. Add the mussels to the salsa, along with ½ cup (120 ml) of their cooking liquid. Stir together, cover, and chill for an hour or more. Rinse the shells.

To serve, place a mussel on a half shell and spoon on some of the salsa. Garnish with fresh coriander. Place on a platter and serve as finger food.

SERVES 6 AS AN HORS D'OEUVRE

MEXICAN RICE SALAD
Salade de Riz à la Mexicaine

This is a great buffet salad for a few reasons beyond its wonderful taste and variety of textures. First of all, it's so colorful, with the saffron-tinted rice and all of the vegetables. Also, it has good staying power. It will hold for several hours in the refrigerator, but toss the green vegetables with the rice and cumin-flavored vinaigrette just before serving; otherwise they will lose their bright color.

To make the salad, bring the water to a boil and add the rice, saffron, and salt. Cover and reduce the heat until cooked al dente, 20 to 25 minutes for white rice, 35 to 40 minutes for brown rice. Remove from the heat, drain off the excess water, and cool.

Toss the rice with the vegetables.

Mix together the vinegar, lemon juice, garlic, mustard and cumin for the dressing. Whisk in the oils and season to taste with salt and pepper. Taste and adjust seasonings.

Toss the rice, vegetables, and coriander with the dressing. Refrigerate for an hour or so. If you are holding the salad for several hours, keep the green beans separate and toss with the salad shortly before serving.

Arrange leaf lettuce on plates, then spoon the salad over the lettuce. Garnish with tomato wedges and radish roses.

TO PREPARE AHEAD OF TIME: The vegetables, rice and dressing can all be prepared a day in advance and refrigerated in separate plastic bags or containers. The salad, without the green vegetables, will hold for several hours, and with the green vegetables for an hour.

SERVES 6 TO 8

FOR THE SALAD

3 cups (750 ml) water
1 1/2 cups (340 g) long-grain white rice or brown rice
1/2 teaspoon saffron threads
1/4 teaspoon salt
1/2 pound (250 g) green beans, trimmed and blanched
1 sweet red pepper, seeded and cut in thin strips
4 scallions, thinly sliced
5 tablespoons pine nuts or chopped almonds
1 small cucumber, peeled, seeded, and chopped
5 radishes, thinly sliced
4 to 5 tablespoons chopped fresh coriander

FOR THE DRESSING

3 tablespoons wine or cider vinegar
Juice of 1 large lemon
1 clove garlic, minced or put through a press
1 teaspoon Dijon mustard
1 teaspoon ground cumin
3/4 cup (180 ml) safflower oil
1/4 cup (60 ml) olive oil
Salt and freshly ground pepper to taste

FOR THE PLATES

Leaf lettuce
3 to 4 tomatoes, cut in wedges
Radish roses

SAUTÉED ZUCCHINI AND RED PEPPERS IN BELL PEPPER BOATS

Courgettes et Poivrons Rouges Poélés dans ses Barquettes de Poivrons

These are a treat for the eye as well as the palate. The little specks of red pepper set off the glistening zucchini, and are beautifully presented in the little half-pepper "boats."

2 tablespoons olive or safflower oil

1 medium onion, minced

1 to 2 cloves garlic, minced or put through a press

1½ pounds (750 g) zucchini, diced small

1 large sweet red pepper, seeded and diced small

Salt and freshly ground pepper to taste

3 small sweet green or red peppers, cut in half lengthwise, seeds and membranes removed

Heat the oil and sauté the onion with 1 clove of the garlic until the onion is beginning to brown. Add the zucchini, chopped red pepper, and the remaining garlic and sauté over moderate heat, stirring, for about 15 minutes, until the zucchini is bright green and tender. Season to taste with salt and freshly ground pepper and remove from the heat.

Spoon into the pepper shells and serve, or hold in a covered dish and heat through in a 325°F (170°C, mark 3) oven for 20 minutes before serving.

TO PREPARE AHEAD OF TIME: The pepper boats can be assembled hours in advance and held in a covered dish. Reheat in the oven as directed above shortly before serving.

SERVES 4 TO 6

WATERMELON FRUIT BASKET
Panier de Pasteques aux Fruits

Feel free to use whatever fruits are ripe and available. In the States I always add Thompson grapes, which add color as well as their sweet, juicy taste. In spring, cherries would be welcome. Sometimes I use peaches, but they tend to discolor and fall apart a bit. Kiwi makes a nice addition, again adding color and taste.

MAKING THE WATERMELON BASKET: Set the watermelon on a table to figure out what side it sits on most steadily. If the melon seems unstable, you can cut a very fine sliver out of the bottom to assure that it won't roll.

Draw a "handle" across the top of the watermelon. Cut down the sides of the handle, then cut the melon crosswise in half, stopping at the handle. Lift off the melon on either side of the handle, and cut away the flesh underneath; save the flesh. Remove the watermelon from the bowl of the "basket" with a melon baller. Place in a bowl. With a small, sharp knife, scallop the edges of the basket, but not the handle. Refrigerate until shortly before serving.

PREPARING THE FRUIT: Seed the reserved watermelon flesh and make balls, using a melon baller; place the balls in a large bowl. Make melon balls of the cantaloupe and honeydew. Toss with the watermelon balls, apricots, and strawberries. Quarter the pineapple, remove the core and skin and cut in 1-inch (2.5-cm) pieces. Toss with the other fruit. Retain a tablespoon of whole mint leaves and chop the remaining leaves. Toss the chopped mint with the fruit. Refrigerate the fruit separately from the watermelon basket.

1 small watermelon

½ cantaloupe, halved and seeded

½ honeydew melon, halved and seeded

½ pound (250 g) fresh apricots, halved and pitted

¾ pound (350 g—1 pint) strawberries, hulled and cut in half

½ small ripe pineapple

2 tablespoons fresh mint leaves

ASSEMBLING THE DESSERT: Shortly before serving, give the fruit a toss and fill the watermelon basket. Place it on a large platter and surround with the fruit that wouldn't fit into the basket. Garnish with the whole mint leaves.

TO PREPARE AHEAD OF TIME: The fruit will hold for several hours in the refrigerator.

SERVES 12

MANGOS, PEACHES, AND BERRIES IN SWEET WHITE WINE

Mangues, Pèches, et Fruits Rouges au Vin Doux

4 ripe peaches, pitted and sliced

2 mangos, peeled and diced or sliced

3/4 pound (340 g) strawberries (1 pint), hulled and cut in half, or other berries of your choice (blueberries, blackberries, raspberries, or try red currants if you can find them)

1 full wineglass sweet white wine

You can use other fruits in season for this dish, such as melon and nectarines. The mango is especially nice. As for the choice of wine, it should be sweet like a Sauternes, but it doesn't have to *be* a Sauternes. I've used other white Bordeaux, and particularly liked a wine that Jon Winroth gave me, a "Moelleux" from Gaillac, in southwestern France, made by Robert Plageoles.

Prepare the fruit and toss together. Pour on the wine, toss, and chill. Remove from the refrigerator about 15 minutes before serving so the fruit won't be too cold.

TO PREPARE AHEAD OF TIME: This will hold for a couple of hours in the refrigerator.

SERVES 6

NEW YEAR'S EVE CHEZ MARTHA
Le Reveillon chez Martha

CHAMPAGNE

BLACK-EYED PEA SALAD À LA MEXICAINE

OR

ENDIVE, APPLE, AND WALNUT SALAD
Salade d'Endives et Pommes aux Noix

MEXICAN BEAN SALAD
Salade de Haricots à la Mexicaine

FENNEL, LEMON, AND MUSHROOM SALAD
Salade de Fenouil, Citron, et Champignons

BLINI WITH SALMON AND FROMAGE BLANC, EGG, AND CAVIAR FILLING
Blini au Saumon, Fromage Blanc, Oeufs et Caviar

HUMMUS

ASSORTED HOMEMADE BREADS
Pains Assortis

ASSORTED FRESH VEGETABLES

ASSORTED CHEESES—*Fromages Assortis*

ASSORTED DESSERTS (BROUGHT BY FRIENDS)
Tangerines—Clémentines
Désserts Assortis

I love to celebrate and dance on New Year's Eve, but I hate to go out into the jammed Paris streets. My way of getting around that is to throw an annual New Year's Eve party. I provide the dance floor, guests bring Champagne and something to eat. But I always prepare a spread as well, so the buffet is lavish.

I give this New Year's Eve party with a couple of friends, who invite their friends (who invite *their* friends) and help with the organization and some of the preparation. The number of people at the party grows every year: the last count was about a hundred fifty. That estimate was based on the number of empty Champagne bottles left after everybody had gone home. My sister Melody lined them up in my long hallway between the entrance hall and the kitchen; seventy-five bottles made two long rows and a great Polaroid picture.

People begin arriving after ten; by midnight the party is peaking. But waves of arrivals continue through the night. Mine is just one in a long list of parties for the people who arrive after twelve. Parisians usually go out *en groupe* on New Year's Eve, with old friends, often the old *bande* from college or even high school days. So if I invite one friend, and she brings her boyfriend, they usually come with the rest of the group they've been out with all night. The party goes on until the following morning: the last to leave wait for the first metros to begin running. It was at seven A.M., January 1, 1986, after everybody had left, that my sister took the picture of all the empty Champagne bottles. We stayed up until about eight-thirty picking up confetti and streamers (never again will I allow *that*) so that Laurie could teach a dance class the next day, then slept until three-thirty and got up to go to another party.

Both of my two long tables in the big dining room serve as buffets at these events. One is for desserts; people bring beautiful cakes and tarts from Paris bakeries, and Peters Day, an American illustrator who did the drawings for this book, makes his unparalleled *tarte tatins* in big copper pans. The other table is packed with colorful salads, cheeses, my breads and blini, crudités, dips, pâtés, etc. In the middle of the room are two immense plastic tubs, which I bought when I catered the *Herald Tribune* parties. A friend named Rob Anderson, who is a graphic designer here, is "the iceman" every year. He picks up a twenty-kilo sack of ice at Paris's one ice depot, and the ice and Champagne go into the tubs. Since everybody has been instructed to bring Champagne, and I have a substantial stash of my own, there is no danger of running out. There are always guests who take it upon themselves to be barmen for a while, and they don't stop popping corks.

Once I start dancing I don't stop, so I choose foods that are both festive and don't need tending, like the blini. The most important of the dishes I prepare are those containing black-eyed peas. In Texas it is a tradition to eat black-eyed peas on New Year's Day for good luck (as people don't begin to arrive until after ten, most of the eating goes on after midnight), and being a superstitious woman, I stick to it. Americans familiar with the custom, and that means all Southern and black Americans, are always thrilled to see the peas. But I don't prepare them in the traditional way, with ham hocks and greens. I make a salad with a cumin vinaigrette, sort of *à la mexicaine,* with lots of fresh coriander and crunchy green peppers. Sometimes I combine the black-eyed peas with other kinds of beans, other years I use them exclusively. Both salads are scrumptious. As one black American dancer from South Chicago commented last year, "Except for my mother's, these are the best black-eyed peas I've ever tasted."

ENDIVE, APPLE, AND WALNUT SALAD
Salade d'Endives et de Pommes aux Noix

I eat this salad all through the winter. Endive is a convenient lettuce to have on hand, because it lasts longer in the refrigerator than other lettuces. I love the textures and sweet and nutty combination of flavors in this salad.

Wash the endives and pat them dry. Either cut them in thick slices or separate the leaves. If the leaves are still wet, dry them in a salad spinner. Toss with the other salad ingredients.

Mix together the vinegar, lemon juice, mustard, salt and pepper, and tarragon. Whisk in the oils and combine thoroughly. Toss with the salad just before serving.

TO PREPARE AHEAD OF TIME: All the ingredients except the apples can be prepared several hours in advance (the apples should be cut at the last minute or they will turn brown). Wrap the endives in paper towels and seal in plastic bags. Place the other ingredients in a tightly covered container. The dressing will hold for several hours.

SERVES 4

FOR THE SALAD

1 pound (500 g) Belgian endives

2 tart apples, cored and sliced

5 to 6 medium or large mushrooms, cleaned and sliced

6 tablespoons broken walnut pieces

2 ounces (55 g) Gruyère cheese, cut in thin slivers, or blue cheese, crumbled

2 tablespoons chopped fresh parsley

FOR THE DRESSING

2 tablespoons red wine vinegar

3 tablespoons fresh lemon juice

1 teaspoon Dijon mustard

Salt and freshly ground pepper to taste

1/4 teaspoon dried tarragon

5 tablespoons walnut oil

6 to 8 tablespoons olive or safflower oil, to taste

MEXICAN BEAN SALAD
Salade de Haricots à la Mexicaine

This is a more colorful version of the black-eyed pea salad on page 215. The different-colored beans contrast beautifully, and the cumin vinaigrette and fresh coriander give the dish a decidedly Mexican flavor. The fresh green and red peppers add crunchy texture. The first time I served this to the French they were very impressed, because they don't work very much with dried beans. "You really must know what you're doing," said one tactless friend. "You could have produced something really dull."

FOR THE BEANS

½ cup (115 g) black-eyed peas, washed and picked over

½ cup (115 g) red or kidney beans, washed and picked over

½ cup (115 g) black beans, washed and picked over

½ cup (115 g) chick-peas (garbanzos), washed and picked over

1 tablespoon safflower oil

1 large onion, chopped

4 cloves garlic, minced or put through a press

2 quarts (2 L) water

2 bay leaves

Salt to taste

PREPARING AND COOKING THE BEANS: Because black-eyed peas cook much faster than the other beans, they will be cooked separately. They require no soaking.

Soak the other beans, in four times their volume of water, overnight or for at least 6 hours. Drain.

Heat 1 tablespoon safflower oil over medium heat in a large, heavy-bottomed saucepan or Dutch oven and sauté the onion with 3 cloves of garlic until the onion is tender. Add the soaked, drained beans and 2 quarts (2 L) water, raise the heat, and bring to a boil. Reduce the heat, add 1 bay leaf, cover, and cook 1 to 1½ hours, until the beans are tender but not mushy. Add salt to taste.

Meanwhile, in a separate pot combine the black-eyed peas, 2 cups (450 ml) of water, the remaining garlic and bay leaf, and bring to a boil. Reduce the heat, cover, and cook 45 minutes, or until tender. Add salt to taste.

Drain all the beans over a bowl and retain their cooking liquid.

MAKING THE DRESSING: Mix together the lemon juice, vinegar, garlic, mustard, cumin, salt and pepper. Whisk in the safflower oil and ¼ cup (60 ml) liquid from the beans.

ASSEMBLING THE SALAD: Place the beans in a bowl and toss with the dressing. Add the chives and fresh coriander and refrigerate for an hour or two, unless you are serving the salad warm. Shortly before serving, toss with the chopped green and red pepper (the vinegar will dull the bright green of the pepper if they are in contact for too long). Taste and adjust seasonings, adding liquid from the beans, vinegar, or salt and pepper, if desired.

Line a bowl or plates with the lettuce leaves and top with the beans. Garnish with strips of red pepper and serve.

TO PREPARE AHEAD OF TIME: See Black-Eyed Pea Salad à la Mexicaine (page 215).

SERVES 4 TO 6

FOR THE VINAIGRETTE

Juice of 1 large lemon
6 tablespoons red wine vinegar
1 clove garlic, minced or put through a press
1 heaping teaspoon Dijon mustard
1 teaspoon ground cumin
Salt and freshly ground pepper to taste
¾ cup (180 ml) safflower oil
¼ cup (60 ml) liquid from the beans

FOR THE SALAD

2 to 3 tablespoons chopped chives
4 tablespoons chopped fresh coriander
1 sweet green pepper, seeded and chopped
1 small sweet red pepper, seeded and half chopped, half cut in thin strips for garnish
Boston or leaf lettuce

BLACK-EYED PEA SALAD À LA MEXICAINE

COOKING THE PEAS: Heat 1 tablespoon safflower oil in a large, heavy-bottomed saucepan or Dutch oven and sauté the onion with 3 cloves of garlic until the onion is tender. Add the black-eyed peas and the water and bring to a boil. Reduce the

FOR THE BEANS

1 tablespoon safflower oil

1 large onion, chopped

*3 to 4 cloves garlic, to taste,
  minced or put through a
  press*

*1 pound (500 g) black-eyed
  peas, washed and picked*

2 quarts (2 L) water

1 bay leaf

Salt to taste

FOR THE VINAIGRETTE

Juice of 1 large lemon

*1/4 cup (60 ml) red wine
  vinegar*

*1 clove garlic, minced or put
  through a press*

*1 heaping teaspoon Dijon
  mustard*

1 teaspoon ground cumin

*Salt and freshly ground
  pepper to taste*

3/4 cup (180 ml) safflower oil

FOR THE SALAD

*2 to 3 tablespoons chopped
  fresh chives*

*1/4 cup (10 g) chopped fresh
  coriander*

*1 sweet green pepper, seeded
  and chopped*

*1 small sweet red pepper,
  seeded and half chopped,
  half cut in thin strips for
  garnish*

Boston or leaf lettuce

heat, add the bay leaf, cover, and cook 45 minutes, or until the beans are tender but not mushy. Add salt and more garlic to taste. Drain the beans over a bowl and retain the cooking liquid.

MAKING THE VINAIGRETTE: Mix together the lemon juice, vinegar, garlic, mustard, cumin, salt and pepper for the dressing. Whisk in the safflower oil and 1/4 cup (60 ml) liquid from the beans.

ASSEMBLING THE SALAD: Place the beans in a bowl and toss with the dressing. Add the chives and fresh coriander and refrigerate for an hour or two, unless you are serving the salad warm. Shortly before serving, toss with the chopped green and red peppers (the vinegar will dull the bright green of the pepper if they are in contact for too long). Taste and adjust seasonings, adding liquid from the beans, lemon juice or vinegar, and salt and pepper, if desired.

Line a bowl or plates with the lettuce leaves and top with the beans. Garnish with strips of red pepper and serve.

TO PREPARE AHEAD OF TIME: The vinegar acts as a kind of preservative, so the beans can be cooked up to 3 days in advance and marinated in the dressing. Refrigerate in a covered bowl. The completed salad will hold for an hour or two in the refrigerator.

SERVES 6

FENNEL, LEMON, AND MUSHROOM SALAD
Salade de Fenouil, Citron, et Champignons

Fennel is such a refreshing vegetable. This salad is great for a buffet because it doesn't wilt.

Mix together the fennel, mushrooms, lemon, red pepper, and parsley.

Whisk together the lemon juice, vinegar, mustard, optional garlic, salt and freshly ground pepper. Whisk in the oils. Toss with the salad and serve.

TO PREPARE AHEAD OF TIME: This salad will hold for several hours in the refrigerator.

SERVES 6 TO 8

FOR THE SALAD

2 pounds (1 g) fennel bulbs, quartered and sliced thin

1/2 pound (250 g) mushrooms, cleaned and sliced thin

1 lemon, peel and white pith removed, sliced very thin

2 sweet red peppers, seeded and sliced

1/4 cup (10 g) chopped fresh parsley

FOR THE DRESSING

1/4 cup (60 ml) fresh lemon juice

2 tablespoons red wine vinegar

1 to 2 teaspoons Dijon mustard, to taste

1 small clove garlic, minced or put through a press (optional)

Salt and freshly ground pepper to taste

1/2 cup (120 ml) safflower or sunflower seed oil

3 tablespoons olive oil

BLINI WITH SALMON AND FROMAGE BLANC, EGG, AND CAVIAR FILLING

Blini au Saumon, Fromage Blanc, Oeufs, et Caviar

Blini (page 45)
*¾ pound (340 g) low-fat
    cottage cheese*
*⅔ cup (140 ml) plain
    low-fat yogurt*
3 hard-boiled eggs, chopped
1 small onion, finely minced
*1 small jar black lumpfish
    caviar*
*Salt and freshly ground
    pepper to taste*
*½ pound (250 g) smoked
    salmon, thinly sliced*

FOR GARNISH
Lemons, cut in wedges
Chopped chives
Fresh lemon juice to taste

I love making blini for parties because they hold very nicely, so I can make them well in advance. I freeze the leftovers and always have the makings for an impromptu cocktail party on hand. The egg, caviar, and fromage blanc filling couldn't be easier. When I serve blini as part of a buffet, as I do for New Year's Eve, I make small ones for finger food. The blini are on one platter, the egg and caviar filling on another, and smoked salmon on another.

Make the blini and set aside.

Beat the cottage cheese in a food processor or electric mixer until smooth, and blend in the yogurt. Stir in the chopped hard-boiled egg, onion, and the caviar. Add salt and freshly ground pepper to taste.

To serve, top each blini with smoked salmon and the cheese, egg, and caviar filling. Garnish with lemon wedges and chives and squeeze on lemon juice to taste. (Salmon and crème fraîche with lemon is good, too.)

SERVES 6 TO 8

HUMMUS

I've made hummus so many times I can practically do it with my eyes closed. Yet I never tire of it. I always make sure I'm a little hungry when I make it, because I can't resist tasting. Time and again it gets raves from guests. This version is much less oily than traditional hummus. I thin it with low-fat yogurt instead of olive oil. The secret ingredient here is the ground cumin. The hummus can be served on bread or piped onto rounds of cucumber and strips of sweet red and green pepper. I usually do both: I make platters of the cucumber and peppers, with the decorative hummus topping, and place the remainder in a bowl, decorated with olives, chopped parsley, and cherry tomatoes or radishes. Next to the bowl are baskets with assorted breads.

SOAKING AND COOKING THE CHICK-PEAS: Soak the chick-peas overnight in about 4 cups (1 L) of water.

In the morning, drain the beans and combine in a large pot with another 4 cups (1 L) water. Bring to a boil, reduce the heat, cover, and simmer 2 hours, until the beans are tender. Add 1 teaspoon of the salt at the end of the cooking time.

MAKING THE HUMMUS: Drain the beans and puree them in a food processor or blender, or through a food mill, along with the garlic. Add the lemon juice, olive oil, sesame tahini, cumin, salt, and yogurt, and blend until thoroughly smooth. Taste and adjust seasonings, adding more salt, garlic, or lemon juice, if you wish. Transfer to a serving bowl and cover. Refrigerate until ready to serve.

TO PREPARE AHEAD OF TIME: Hummus will hold for 3 to 4 days in the refrigerator but is best the day after you make it. It can also be frozen.

SERVES 12

½ pound (250 g) dried chick-peas (garbanzos), washed and picked over
8 cups (2 L) water
Salt to taste
2 large cloves garlic
4 to 6 tablespoons fresh lemon juice, to taste
¼ cup (60 ml) olive oil
4 to 6 tablespoons sesame tahini, to taste
½ teaspoon ground cumin
¼ to ½ cup (60 to 120 ml) plain low-fat yogurt, depending on how stiff you want your hummus (stiffer it's easier to pipe, less stiff it's more refined)

A PICNIC ON THE SEINE

TOMATOES WITH PESTO
Tomates au Pistou

NIÇOISE SALAD HERO SANDWICHES
Pain Bagnat

VEGETABLES AND EGGS WITH OLIVE PASTE (PAGE 68)
Tapenade en Barquettes

RATATOUILLE

PROVENÇAL ONION PIZZA
Pissaladière

ASSORTED CHEESES

SOURDOUGH COUNTRY BREAD (PAGE 18)
Pain de Campagne

ASSORTED FRUITS

JON WINROTH'S WINE SUGGESTION: BANDOL OR ANY OTHER ROSÉ FROM THE
SOUTH OF FRANCE

On a warm summer night I like to picnic on the Seine, either on the cobbled banks underneath the Quai d'Orleans on the Île-St.-Louis, or across the river on the banks below the Quai de la Tournelle. This is where Paris looks most like illuminated pages in a beautifully illustrated fairy tale. I love to look at the back of Nôtre Dame, with its flying buttresses, and watch the Bateaux Mouches, the tour boats, go by. The light in Paris is at its best in the late evening, as the sun sets behind the cathedral. When the weather is good the sky becomes pink and orange, sometimes streaked with gold. The buildings glow; it's magic. In the summer the sun sets late—between nine-thirty and eleven, depending on the month, and then you get twilight, followed by the Paris city lights and the moon. Nôtre Dame is a spectacle, highlighted regularly by ultra-bright pink-yellow lights from the Bateaux Mouches. Somehow I'm not rattled by these lights or by the sound of the guides, who, heavily miked, point out all the monuments in good French and bad other languages as they go by. I've taken many a Bateau Mouche myself, and love to think of how many have made their tour, hour after hour, year after year, and how many people have looked at Paris from the middle of the river.

My picnic on the Seine is a real treat for summer visitors, and I like to take them on one soon after their arrival. If they are too jet-lagged the first night, I plan it, weather permitting, for their second. There will be much eating in restaurants later, and this is such a dreamy way to see the city. I pack up baskets with Provençal tablecloths, silverware, plates, wine, water, and plastic cups, and food that's easy to carry and eat —*pain bagnat* (the Niçoise salad sandwich), ratatouille, *tape-*

nade en barquettes, tomatoes with pesto, *pissaladière,* fruit, cheese, bread. The dishes are almost all Provençal in spirit, probably because my earliest picnics in France were in Provence. Everyone takes a basket, and we either walk or take the number 87 or 63 bus up the Boulevard St.-Germain to rue Cardinal Lemoine, then it's a short walk to the river.

Sometimes, of course, my picnics are spontaneous. Then my menu is a little different: bread, cheese, tomatoes, crudités, and fruit. Maybe I'll stop at a charcuterie and get *carottes rapées* (grated carrot salad) and cooked artichokes. If I have an hour, I'll throw together a *salade niçoise,* or even make *tapenade.* How can anything taste bad when you're in Paris, eating on the banks of the Seine in the soft summer evening light?

Packing a Picnic Basket

I've always wanted one of those elegant wicker picnic baskets with silver servers and china plates, but I still don't have one. I use my market baskets and L. L. Bean canvas shoulder bags for my Paris outings, and they serve me well.

Use one bag for plates, tablecloths, silverware, wine, etc. Pack up salads in plastic containers, jars, or bowls with tight-fitting lids. Set them in bags or baskets, and lay *pain bagnat,* cheeses, fruits, bread—the crushable items—on top. Carry attractive platters and bowls separately and transfer food to them once you've arrived at your picnic spot. For stuffed vegetables like the *tapenade en barquettes* (Vegetables and Eggs with Olive Paste, page 68), it may be neater to carry the filling separately and stuff the vegetables and eggs at the picnic.

PICNIC CHECKLIST

Plates
Forks, knives, bread knife,
*   serving spoons*
Napkins
Cups
Wine
Water
Corkscrew, bottle opener
Cutting board
Dishtowels
Trash bags
Serving bowls
Light platters
Candles
Flashlight
Salt and pepper
Mustard

TOMATOES WITH PESTO
Tomates au Pistou

These are like the *tapenade en barquettes* on page 68, but filled with pesto instead.

Cut the tops of the tomatoes off, about ½ inch (1.5 cm) down. Gently squeeze out the seeds. Spread with a generous helping of pesto.

6 medium or 12 small tomatoes
½ recipe Pesto (page 293)

TO PACK FOR A PICNIC: Place the tomatoes side by side in a shallow plastic container with a tight-fitting lid. Or don't fill the tomatoes until you reach your destination. Keep the hollowed-out tomatoes in one container and the pesto in another.

SERVES 6

FOR THE SANDWICH

3 baguettes or 6 roll-size pain
    de campagnes
1 clove garlic, cut in half
Olive oil
Red wine vinegar
1 small head Boston lettuce,
    leaves separated and
    washed, then broken into
    small pieces
½ pound (250 g) carrots,
    peeled and grated
1 pound (500 g) tomatoes,
    sliced
½ pound (250 g) tender
    green beans, trimmed and
    blanched
1 small cucumber, peeled,
    seeded, and thinly sliced
6 hard-boiled eggs, sliced
24 imported black olives,
    halved and pitted
1 7½-ounce can tuna packed
    in water, drained
12 anchovy fillets (optional)

FOR THE VINAIGRETTE

¼ cup (60 ml) red wine
    vinegar
1 clove garlic, minced or put
    through a press
1 teaspoon Dijon mustard
2 tablespoons chopped fresh
    herbs
Salt and freshly ground
    pepper to taste
⅔ cup (140 ml) olive oil

NIÇOISE SALAD HERO SANDWICHES
Pain Bagnat

A *pain bagnat* is like a Niçoise salad on a hero. The quality of the bread will determine how good your *pain bagnat* is. If made on a banal, cottony baguette, the salad part might be great, but as a sandwich it will be nothing to write home about. But a crusty sourdough baguette or *pain de campagne,* infused with vinaigrette, will result in something truly mouthwatering.

Cut the rolls or baguettes in half and scoop out some of the bread. Rub the inside of the bread halves with a cut clove of garlic and drizzle on a small amount of olive oil and vinegar. Toss the crumbs from the inside of the bread together with the vegetables, olives, tuna, and anchovies.

For the dressing, combine the vinegar, garlic, mustard, herbs, and salt and pepper. Whisk in the olive oil. Toss with the salad. Mound the salad in one half of the bread, lay egg slices over the salad, and top with the other half. Cut each sandwich into three equal pieces. Squeeze together well and wrap tightly in plastic or foil. Refrigerate for an hour before eating.

TO PREPARE AHEAD OF TIME: These will hold for several hours in the refrigerator. Wrap them tightly as directed above.

SERVES 6

RATATOUILLE

My stepmother used to make ratatouille for us when I was a teenager, and when I began cooking at the age of seventeen, it was one of the first dishes I asked her to teach me. I already had a penchant for Mediterranean flavors. I've changed my recipe again and again. The most memorable ratatouille I've ever eaten was in a restaurant in Cassis called Chez Gilbert. All the vegetables in Gilbert's ratatouille are coarsely chopped and glazed with their reduced cooking juices. The chef won't divulge his recipe, but in researching this dish I found that food writer Richard Olney's version seems to come pretty close, and mine is based on his. My friend Lulu Peyraud, at the Bandol winery Domaine Tempier, makes another great ratatouille; she insists it's because she cooks it in an earthenware pot.

Ratatouille should be made the day before you wish to serve it. It is good hot or cold, and is perfect for picnics or the first course of a summer meal.

Place the cubed eggplant in a colander and sprinkle with salt. Let sit 30 minutes while you prepare the other vegetables, then rinse and pat dry with paper towels.

Heat half the oil in a very large, heavy-bottomed flameproof casserole or Dutch oven and sauté the onion with half the garlic over medium-low heat until the onion is softened and translucent. Add the remaining oil, the peppers, and eggplant and continue to cook over medium-low heat for about 10 minutes, stirring with a wooden spoon. Add the tomato wedges, the remaining garlic, salt to taste, the dried herbs, and bay leaf. Continue to cook over low heat, stirring the vegetables gently until they are almost submerged in their own liquid. Raise the heat and bring these juices to a boil, stirring, then immediately lower the heat, cover partially, and simmer 1 hour, stirring occasionally. Add the zucchini, chopped

1 pound (500 g) eggplant, cubed

Salt

6 tablespoons olive oil

1 pound (500 g) medium-size onions, sliced

6 cloves garlic, minced or put through a press

½ pound (250 g) sweet red peppers, seeded and cut in half crosswise, then in wide strips

½ pound (250 g) sweet green peppers, seeded and cut in half crosswise, then in wide strips

6 ripe tomatoes (about 1 ½ pounds, 750 g) peeled and seeded, 4 tomatoes cut in wedges and the remainder chopped

Freshly ground pepper to taste

1 teaspoon dried oregano, or a mixture of dried or fresh thyme and dried oregano

1 bay leaf

1 pound (500 g) zucchini, thickly sliced

3 tablespoons chopped fresh basil, in season

Pinch of cayenne (optional)

FOR GARNISH

Chopped fresh parsley

Vinaigrette or olive oil (for cold ratatouille)

Chopped fresh basil or parsley (for cold ratatouille)

Lettuce leaves (for cold ratatouille)

Ripe tomatoes, cut in quarters (for cold ratatouille)

tomatoes, and basil, and continue to simmer another 20 to 30 minutes, or until the zucchini is tender but still bright green.

Place a colander over a bowl and drain the ratatouille. Allow it to drain 10 minutes, then return the vegetables to the casserole. Place the liquid in a saucepan and reduce it over high heat, stirring often, until syrupy. Pour the liquid back over the vegetables, stir, and simmer together for a few minutes. Taste and adjust salt, pepper, and garlic. If you wish, add a small pinch of cayenne. Transfer to a bowl and cool. Cover and refrigerate overnight.

If you are serving the ratatouille hot, bring it back to a simmer over low heat. Serve, topping each helping with chopped fresh parsley. If you are serving it cold, douse it if you wish with a mild vinaigrette or simply with olive oil and chopped fresh basil or parsley. Serve over lettuce leaves, garnished with tomato wedges.

SERVES 6

PROVENÇAL ONION PIZZA
Pissaladière

There are many versions of this recipe. Some people make theirs in a pastry crust, while others use a pizza crust, which I prefer. Sometimes it is thick with onions, other times the layer is thin. The important thing is to cook the onions until they become sweet and slightly caramelized.

BEGINNING THE CRUST: Dissolve the yeast in the lukewarm water. Let it sit 10 minutes, or until the mixture begins to bubble. Stir in the salt and oil. Add the flour, a cup at a time, and mix thoroughly, first with a whisk, and then, when it becomes too thick for a whisk, with a large wooden spoon.

Turn the dough out onto a lightly floured board and knead for 10 minutes, adding only enough flour to keep it from sticking. If you work briskly and use a pastry scraper to manipulate the dough, it won't stick too much. Shape it into a ball, then place in a lightly oiled bowl, rounded side down first, then rounded side up. Cover with a damp towel or plastic wrap and set in a warm place to rise until doubled in bulk, 1 to 1 1/2 hours.

PREPARING THE ONIONS: While the dough rises, heat the olive oil and butter in a large frying pan over low heat. Add the onions and cook over low heat, stirring from time to time, until they are translucent. Add the honey, wine, and thyme and cook gently, stirring occasionally, for 1 to 1 1/2 hours, until the onions are golden brown and beginning to caramelize. Add salt and freshly ground pepper to taste. The onions should not brown or stick to the pan. Add oil or butter as needed.

When the dough has doubled in size, punch it down and let it rise another 40 minutes (the onions will still be cooking).

BAKING THE PISSALADIÈRE: Preheat the oven to 450° F (220° C, gas mark 8). Turn the dough out onto a lightly floured work surface. Roll out to about 1/4 inch (.75 cm) thick, or a little thinner. Oil a 12- to 14-inch (30 to 35 cm) pizza pan or tart pan and line it with the pizza dough. Pinch a lip around the edge.

Prebake the crust for 7 to 10 minutes, until the surface is crisp and the edges are beginning to brown. Spread with the onions, then top with anchovies and olives and bake for 15 minutes, or until the crust is browned and crisp. Remove from the oven and serve hot, or cool and serve at room temperature.

TO TRANSPORT FOR A PICNIC: Keep it in the pizza pan, but cut into pieces. Cover tightly with foil.

SERVES 8

FOR THE CRUST

2 teaspoons active dry yeast

3/4 cup (180 ml) lukewarm water

3/4 teaspoon salt

2 tablespoons olive oil

2 cups (225 g) whole-wheat flour or whole-wheat pastry flour, or use half whole-wheat, half unbleached white

Unbleached white flour, as necessary for kneading

FOR THE FILLING

2 tablespoons olive oil (or more, as necessary)

1 tablespoon unsalted butter

4 pounds (2 kg) onions, sliced very thin

2 teaspoons mild-flavored honey

1/4 cup (60 ml) dry red wine

1/4 teaspoon dried thyme (or more, to taste)

Salt and freshly ground pepper to taste

1 small can anchovy fillets

1/3 to 1/2 cup (about 50 g) black Niçoise olives

Part III:
Special People

Chez Christine

SWEET AND SOUR RED PEPPERS
Poivrons Aigres-Doux

SALAD OF SWEET AND SOUR PEPPERS AND AVOCADO

CHRISTINE'S CREAMY CUCUMBER SALAD
Crème de Concombres

ARTICHOKES WITH TOMATOES, GARLIC, AND PROVENÇAL HERBS
Artichaut à la Barigoule

IRANIAN RICE WITH MONKFISH RAGOUT
Riz à l'Iranienne au Ragoût de Lotte

IRANIAN OMELET WITH PARSLEY AND MINT
Coucou à l'Iranienne

SALMON TROUT EN PAPILLOTE
Truite Saumonée en Papillote

CHERRY CLAFOUTI
Clafouti aux Cerises

ALSATIAN APPLE CAKE
Gâteau Alsacien aux Pommes

PEACHES IN RED WINE WITH HONEY AND CINNAMON
Pêches au Vin Rouge

PEACH AND APRICOT SALAD WITH CURRANTS
Salade de Pêches et Abricots aux Raisins de Corinthe

CHRISTINE'S WINE CHOICES: BANDOL ROSÉ, CÔTES DU VENTOUX ROSÉ OR RED, CÔTES DU LUBERON ROSÉ OR RED

JON WINROTH'S WINE SUGGESTIONS: SYLVANER OR PINOT BLANC (KLEVNER)

The recipes in this chapter are dishes I have learned from my landlady and very dear friend, Christine. Christine Ruiz Picasso is the widow of Paulo Picasso, Pablo Picasso's first son. She is an extraordinary woman who knows much about life, and it is my great fortune to know her.

When you first meet Christine you are immediately struck by her beauty: her wide-set, soft blue eyes, ever so slightly Oriental; her high, Slavic cheekbones; her clear, shining complexion, dark eyebrows and silver-gray hair; her wide, sensuous mouth, from which issues a voice that has the melodic timbre of a bell and a vocabulary and turn of phrase so rich you hang on every word. If I speak French with any precision at all, it comes from being around Christine. Even people who don't speak the language are impressed by the clarity of her speech, and get a sense of what she's talking about. She is so direct and so much fun that anyone with half a sense of humor can communicate with her. And God knows she's been put to the test, for I am forever bringing non-French-speaking friends with me on my visits.

So many attributes come together in Christine's marvelous personality. She is hilariously funny and even bawdy, and at the same time she is a woman of great refinement and sensitivity. She is tender, motherly, and loving; honorable, sentimental, and wise; both spiritual and down-to-earth. Nature and humanity are equally fascinating to her; nothing goes unnoticed.

I met Christine in July of 1980, when I was renting La Sara, the farmhouse near Bonnieux, in the Luberon. The Luberon is a chain of low mountains that runs through the north-

ern Provençal department of the Vaucluse, east of Avignon and about forty kilometers north of Aix-en-Provence. This is one of the most beautiful areas in France. Bonnieux is on the northern slope of the Luberon and looks out over a wide valley and smaller mountain chain, called the Petit Luberon. The country here is dotted with vineyards and lavender fields, and the earth has a red-ocher hue. The perfection in the landscape, the rich colors—greens, reds, and purples—and the amazing Provençal light, always stop me in my tracks. As you move further east, beyond a town called Apt and north into the hills, the land becomes more rugged: the lavender fields continue, but vineyards give way to pastures and grain crops. Most of the towns in the Vaucluse are Roman and medieval hill towns, and they look almost like carved outcroppings of the mountain rock.

By the end of the seventies, Christine had had enough of Paris. Her husband had died in 1975, and she was ready to begin a new life, alone and in the country. It was in this part of France that she had decided to make her home, and she was in the process of buying a farm when we met her. She had a friend named Nina Engels, who was our neighbor, and who had found her the farm. Christine was staying with Nina while the former tenants moved out and the house was being readied for her, and we would occasionally all have drinks or dinner together.

The day after Christine moved into her extraordinary stone house, she invited us all for lunch. She didn't have any real furnishings yet, so we brought a picnic. Nina led us there —a good thing, as we would never have found the place on our own. When we finally arrived, after twisting and turning up an unpaved road for what seemed like quite a long time, we found ourselves in "God's country." The house itself, a three-hundred-year-old, three-story, rectangular *mas*—the term used in this area for the stone and stucco farmhouses you see everywhere—is quite grand, but it's the vast countryside that takes your breath away. To the south are the mountains of the Luberon; closer, to the southwest, are hills and dales displaying a patchwork of fields, yellow with hay, purple with lavender, and many shades of green. The little town of Saint-Michel-l'Observatoire sits on one of these hills, just close enough to reassure you that you aren't completely cut off from humanity. East of the house, the land slopes upward to a small plateau, and then abruptly up to a high ridge and another plateau. To the north, the Petit Luberon with its patchwork fields slopes more gently upward, but directly behind the house there is a dramatic canyon and divide, which Christine fondly refers to as her own Texas.

Christine is building a second house just below the eastern plateau, smaller and even more extraordinary than the *mas.* When it is finished she'll move into it, leaving the larger house for guests.

Little did I know, on that hot July afternoon as we sat around eating Cavaillon melons and Nina's onion tarts and famous chocolate cake, then climbed and walked along the ridge, that a year later I would be moving into Christine's Paris apartment. And that this was the beginning of a long and special friendship and a deep love that would be nurtured by my frequent, unforgettable visits to her Provencal home.

Christine has come into her own since moving to the Vaucluse. The land around her house is now a working farm. Her caretakers, Bernard and Brigitte LeBecq, are specialists in natural medicine and organic farming, and over the years Bernard has been revitalizing the earth, denatured after years of neglect, and planting grain crops and vegetable gardens. A couple of years after Christine moved in, she and Bernard planted three hundred fifty truffle oaks on the middle plateau east of the house. These are small scrub oaks whose roots have been injected with microorganisms that will eventually spawn truffles. If all goes well, in five years the oaks will bear, providing Christine with not only an enviable larder, but also a handsome source of revenue. Christine likes the image of herself as truffle cultivator: "I've been a lot of things in my life; first I was a ceramicist, then in Paris I had a hotel on the rue de Rennes, and after that I had a fancy button and accessories store on the rue du Dragon. I will go out a *trufficultrice.*"

CHRISTINE THE HOSTESS

Every summer, and at various times during the year, Christine has a house full of guests. She is the kind of hostess who will hardly let you lift a finger. Each day, while you are waking up or swimming in the pool, sunbathing or hiking, reading or touring the region, she produces three fabulous meals. Yet her efforts are invisible; it is as if there were two of her, one laughing by the pool with you or watering the garden, and one in the kitchen. If the weather is fine you eat outside, at lunchtime under a big white parasol. Christine hammers the stand into the ground and opens the parasol over one of her two stone tables, made from the large, flat yellow-white stones *(lauze)* of the region. At dinner she sets candles in large blown-glass lanterns and serves dinner under the stars. If it's too windy, chilly, or hot (as it can be on summer afternoons), you eat in her friendly dining room in front of the stucco hearth. Christine is a fabulous cook, and the meals are long and leisurely; great food, great conversation—even when half the people don't speak French!—and always, much laughter.

Breakfast consists of tea or coffee, fresh-squeezed juice, and toasted whole-wheat bread with the inimitable lavender honey from the region and Christine's marvelous homemade preserves—cherry, apricot, strawberry, plum, peach, marmalade.

Christine has a way with vegetables, and each year she grows more in her garden. At lunch we eat salads of home-grown lettuces tossed with herbs and baby onions, one or two vegetable dishes (usually Provençal or Mediterranean in character), freshly picked tomatoes, cold meats, or one of the fragrant Iranian dishes she has learned from her architect, Nasarine. Summer lunches usually begin with sweet, juicy melons from Cavaillon, and end with a fresh fruit salad or tart.

We drink chilled white or rosé wine from the cooperative at Apt, light and refreshing Côtes du Lubéron or Côtes du Ventoux. Afterwards we sleep.

At around eight or eight-thirty, the "pink time" in the Vaucluse sky, we find ourselves at the table again, eating little olives from the region, watching the sunset, and drinking aperitifs—pastis, Martini Bianco, or chilled rosé wine. Christine then performs her magic act again, and we set the table for dinner.

If we've eaten a big lunch, dinner is light—a green salad with roasted goat cheese, maybe a fruit tart or *clafouti.* Usually, though, it's substantial: meat or fish (either poached in a court bouillon or cooked *en papillote*), potatoes from the garden, or pasta tossed with whatever herbs and vegetables are on hand, salad, fruit or dessert. If we're having fish we'll drink rosé from the region, otherwise we'll drink the fruity, light red.

Like so many French women I've met, once Christine makes a dish the recipe is imprinted in her memory. How many times have I remarked at table, "This is great! How do you make it?" to have her recite the exact recipe. Sometimes I get back to Paris and call her on the phone to find out about something she served when I was there, and it's as if she were reading from a cookbook. She is so precise with her language that hearing her explain a recipe in that bell-like voice always gives me great pleasure.

I've visited Christine's paradise at every season of the year. Summer is the most fun because of the sun, the pool in its exquisite setting, the purple lavender fields, and the fact that you can eat outside morning, noon, and night. But each season has its special charm. I was there after a heavy blizzard in February, and was enchanted by the silence, the birds, and the dazzling snow. Springtime explodes with wildflowers— fields of red poppies and broom—and bright yellow sunshine. In autumn the light is the purest; it's as if the land and air had been swept clean after the hot August haze. The minute I arrive I feel tranquil and expansive; but that's because of Christine just as much as the place.

SWEET AND SOUR RED PEPPERS

Poivrons Aigres-Doux

Christine serves these beguiling red peppers on their own, and they are marvelous with no further embellishment. I have served them alone and as a salad, over lettuce, garnished with avocado, radishes, and herbs (see recipe following). Every time I have red peppers left over from a dinner or catering job, this is how I preserve them. They will hold for weeks in the refrigerator.

Combine the water, vinegar, honey, onions, garlic, bay leaves and peppercorns in a large pot and bring to a boil. Add the cut peppers and thyme and cook over a fairly high flame for 15 minutes. Remove from the heat, cool, cover, and refrigerate.

SERVES 6

3 cups (750 ml) water
1/2 cup (120 ml) good-quality sherry or Champagne vinegar
1/3 cup (80 ml) mild-flavored honey
2 onions, sliced
8 cloves garlic, sliced
2 bay leaves
1/2 teaspoon whole peppercorns
2 pounds (1 kg) sweet red peppers, cut in half, seeded, and cut in very wide strips
4 sprigs fresh thyme

SALAD OF SWEET AND SOUR PEPPERS AND AVOCADO

Make the sweet and sour peppers and chill.

To serve, line salad plates with the lettuce leaves and top with the peppers; discard the garlic cloves. Garnish with radish roses and avocado slices. Strew the chervil over the top. Spoon on some of the liquid remaining from the peppers and serve.

SERVES 6

Sweet and Sour Peppers (recipe above)
1 head red tip or leaf lettuce, leaves separated and washed
1 bunch radishes, made into roses
1 avocado, peeled, pitted, and sliced
18 sprigs fresh chervil

CHRISTINE'S CREAMY CUCUMBER SALAD
Crème de Concombres

1 pound (500 g) creamy cottage cheese (can be low-fat)

2 cups (500 g) yogurt (use a thick yogurt, not a runny one)

4 ounces (115 g) crumbled goat cheese (optional, or more to taste)

1 long English cucumber, peeled and finely minced, or 3 regular cucumbers, peeled, seeded, and finely minced

Salt and lots of freshly ground pepper

Fresh lemon juice (optional)

Chopped fresh mint or tarragon (optional)

I have a vivid mental picture of Christine sitting outside and mincing cucumbers into a bowl of fromage blanc, a kind of creamy cottage cheese. Often we are still talking at the breakfast table when she comes out with her bowl, cucumbers, fromage blanc, and pepper. The salad is a very simple combination, and I look forward to it every time I visit. What makes it special is the quality of the fromage blanc, the tiny cucumber dice, and the abundant freshly ground pepper. Sometimes Christine also adds goat cheese.

In my American version I've substituted cottage cheese and yogurt for the fromage blanc. Since this still isn't as good as the fromage blanc from the *fromagerie* in Apt, I usually add the goat cheese, too.

Using the back of a wooden spoon, mash the cottage cheese in a bowl and mix in the yogurt. Crumble in the goat cheese. Add the cucumbers and lots of freshly ground pepper. Add salt to taste and lemon juice, if desired. You can also stir in chopped fresh mint or tarragon. Chill until ready to serve.

TO PREPARE AHEAD OF TIME: This will hold for 2 or 3 days in the refrigerator in a covered bowl.

SERVES 6 TO 8

ARTICHOKES WITH TOMATOES, GARLIC, AND PROVENÇAL HERBS
Artichauts à la Barigoule

*A*rtichauts à la barigoule is a traditional Provençal dish in which artichokes are simmered slowly in olive oil with tomatoes, onion, garlic, and Provençal herbs, usually thyme, rosemary, and bay leaf. Christine's are the best I've ever tasted. She uses an entire head of garlic, the cloves just peeled and slightly crushed, and adds diced green peppers, which make for a particularly savory dish.

The first time I had this at Christine's, I went home and looked up recipes in eight different French cookbooks, and found eight different versions. In certain cases a glass of white wine is added, some call for mushrooms, others carrots. Each author was quite certain that his or her recipe was the authentic version.

Jacques Médecin, the mayor of Nice, who has written a well-known Niçoise cookbook, writes with great authority that the word *barigoule* derives from the Provençal word *ferigoula,* which means "thyme." Irene Borelli, the author of another Provençal cookbook, says that *barigoule* derives from the Provençal word *berigoulo,* a kind of wild mushroom that was traditionally cooked on a grill; according to her, artichokes were originally cooked in the same fashion. Who's to say what the authentic version is? At any rate, none of these recipes sounded as good as Christine's, so finally I just called her to get her recipe.

8 *small young purple artichokes or 4 globe artichokes*

1 *lemon, cut in half*

3 *tablespoons olive oil*

3 *medium-size white onions, chopped*

1 *small head garlic, cloves separated, crushed slightly, and peeled*

1 *large sweet green pepper or 2 small, seeded and diced*

1 1/2 *pounds (750 g) tomatoes*

1 *tablespoon tomato paste (optional)*

2 *sprigs fresh thyme or 1/4 teaspoon dried*

1 *bay leaf*

Salt and freshly ground pepper to taste

2 *cups (450 ml) simmering water*

Trim the stems off the artichokes, cut off the very tops, trim off the spiny tips of the outer leaves with a scissors, and rub thoroughly with the cut lemon.

Heat the olive oil over medium heat in a large, heavy-bottomed flameproof casserole or Dutch oven and sauté the onion and garlic cloves until the onion begins to turn golden. Add the green pepper and continue to sauté until it softens, about 5 minutes. Add the tomatoes and sauté about 10 minutes, until they have begun to release their juice and cook down. Stir in the tomato paste, then add the artichokes, thyme, bay leaf, salt and pepper, and about ½ cup (60 ml) of simmering water. Cover and simmer 45 minutes to an hour, stirring occasionally and adding water from time to time if the liquid evaporates. When the artichokes are tender, taste and adjust seasonings, and serve. This dish is also good at room temperature or chilled. It will hold for a few days in the refrigerator.

SERVES 4

SALMON TROUT EN PAPILLOTE
Truite Saumonée en Papillote

E very Wednesday Christine goes to a tiny village east of where she lives, just off the N100, to buy fish from a good fishmonger who sells at the weekly market. She usually comes home with several small or one large *truite saumonée,* the pink-fleshed salmon trout. Sometimes she poaches the fish in court bouillon, but more often she bakes it in foil, with her special mixture of Provençal herbs. She insists that the herbs must include cracked fennel, otherwise the dish won't taste as good.

Preheat the oven to 450° F (230° C, gas mark 8).

Cut 4 sheets of heavy-duty aluminum foil, or double sheets of thinner foil, about 12 inches (30 cm) square, and rub the nonshiny side with some of the butter (or use olive oil).

Wipe the trout with paper towels and sprinkle them inside and outside with salt and freshly ground pepper. Place a

4 salmon trout, about ½ pound (250 g) each, cleaned

Salt and freshly ground pepper to taste

2 tablespoons unsalted butter

2 teaspoons herbes de Provence (see note), with cracked fennel

4 sprigs fresh tarragon or rosemary, if available

2 lemons, sliced

SUPPER CLUB
CHEZ MARTHA ROSE

small lump of butter and ½ teaspoon of herbs in each cavity. Add a sprig of tarragon or rosemary.

Lay each trout on a piece of foil and top with a few slices of lemon. Fold the foil up over the trout and crimp the edges together tightly. Place the packets in a baking dish and bake for 10 to 12 minutes, or until the flesh is opaque and flakes easily with a fork (open one packet and test with a fork). Remove from the foil, pour the juices over the fish, and serve.

TO PREPARE AHEAD OF TIME: The papillotes can be assembled several hours ahead of time and held in the refrigerator.

SERVES 4

NOTE: Herbes de Provence is a mixture of thyme, rosemary, and savory, and can also include dried oregano or marjoram, basil, and fennel. Make your own by mixing these herbs in equal proportions. Make sure to include the fennel.

IRANIAN RICE WITH MONKFISH RAGOUT
Riz à l'Iranienne au Ragoût de Lotte

Christine learned this unique, fragrant dish from the Iranian architect who designed the new house she is building on her property. It is one of the most festive dishes she makes, and she makes it almost every time I visit. We always eat too much of it, it's so fascinating and delicious. Served on a big round platter, it looks like a crown of golden rice with a brown, crusty surface. Meat or fish and vegetables are hidden underneath the crust; their juices, which have been drained before adding the rice, are passed on the side, along with yogurt. Each grain of rice is separate, chewy, and tasty, due to a long rinsing process that removes the outer starch. After an initial rinse of 30 minutes, a quick blanch and another rinse, the rice is cooked—actually steamed —in yogurt that has been mixed with powdered saffron. The mixture gives the rice a remarkable color and forms a kind of eggy crust with the rice on the bottom of the pan. Unmolding the rice is tricky, especially when you are using a stainless-steel pan like Christine's; but with patience and a good spatula, you arrive at unmolding the crust in one piece. Enameled cast-iron or nonstick cookware makes this task much easier.

Until a weekend in July of 1986, when I went down to Cavalier to work with Christine on this dish and a few others, Christine had always made the Iranian rice with veal. She'd always said that she thought it would be good with fish, and she was right. We chose monkfish because it's a firm-textured fish that can be cooked for a long time, and made a ragout while the rice was rinsing. Even though there are several steps to this dish, it's really quite simple.

You will need a few pots and pans: a large, wide flame-proof casserole or lidded frying pan for the fish ragout; a large pot for blanching the rice; and a very large, wide, heavy-bottomed casserole or frying pan for the final steaming of the rice and ragout. You will also need a bowl and a colander for rinsing the rice.

This dish is always eaten with a big green salad. Serve a chilled rosé or dry white wine.

PREPARING THE RICE: Place a large pot with the 5 quarts (5 L) water on the stove and heat over a high flame.

Meanwhile, begin rinsing the rice. Place it in a bowl under the faucet and let cold water run over the rice in a slow stream. Rub the rice between your fingers and palms at first, to make sure all the grains are separated. Then just let the water run over the rice for 30 minutes while you prepare and cook the monkfish ragout.

COOKING THE MONKFISH RAGOUT: Heat the butter in a large, wide flameproof casserole or lidded frying pan and add the fish. Salt and pepper generously, brown on all sides, and remove from the pan. Add the onions and garlic, and cook over medium heat for 15 minutes, stirring from time to time. Return the fish to the pan, add the carrots, thyme, bay leaf, bouquet garni, 1/4 teaspoon powdered saffron and the tomatoes, cover, reduce the heat, and simmer 15 minutes. Correct the seasonings. Drain the fish through a large strainer set over a bowl and reserve the liquid. Discard the bay leaf and bouquet garni, and set aside.

BLANCHING, FINAL RINSING, AND STEAMING OF THE RICE: In a bowl, mix together the 1 1/2 cups plain yogurt and the teaspoon of powdered saffron. Make sure the saffron is all dissolved. Set aside.

When the rice has been rinsing for about 30 minutes, place it in a colander and continue to rinse a few more minutes. Pick through the rice and discard any impurities, such as brown hulls and seeds.

When the large pot of water comes to a boil, add 1 tablespoon of salt and the rice. As soon as the water comes

FOR THE RICE

1 1/2 pounds (750 g) Carolina long-grain rice
5 quarts (5 L) water
1 1/2 cups (340 ml) plain yogurt
1 teaspoon powdered saffron
1 tablespoon salt
2 tablespoons unsalted butter, olive, or safflower oil

FOR THE MONKFISH RAGOUT

2 1/2 pounds (1.25 kg) monkfish, cut in 2-inch (5-cm) thick slices
2 tablespoons unsalted butter
3 small or 2 medium onions, chopped
2 large or 4 medium cloves garlic, peeled and left whole
Salt and freshly ground pepper to taste
3 carrots, peeled and sliced
2 sprigs fresh thyme
1 bay leaf
Bouquet garni made with 8 sprigs fresh parsley and 2 sprigs fresh tarragon (if available)
1/4 teaspoon powdered saffron
3 large or 4 medium-size tomatoes, peeled, seeded, and chopped

FOR GARNISH

1 cup (225 ml) plain yogurt
The juices from the fish ragout

back to a boil, drain the rice in a colander and rinse it again under cold water, gently rubbing the rice between your fingers until cooled. Again, pick through for impurities. Shake the rice in the colander to remove excess water.

Heat a large, wide, heavy-bottomed or nonstick casserole over low heat. Add 2 tablespoons butter or olive or safflower oil. Add the yogurt-saffron mixture. Spread it evenly over the bottom of the pan. Now add the rice. Using the back of a large wooden or stainless-steel spoon, make a shallow bowl in the center of the rice. Place the drained contents of the fish ragout —the fish and vegetables—in an even layer, with the fish surrounded by the vegetables in this depression.

Line the underside of the casserole's lid with a large dishtowel, then place the lid, with the towel on the underside and the edges of the towel folded back up over the top, on the casserole. Make sure the heat is very low and let the rice steam for 30 minutes.

UNMOLDING AND SERVING: After 30 minutes, without removing the lid, place the casserole in the sink or in a large bowl with a small amount of cold water. This helps loosen the rice on the bottom.

To serve, remove the lid and gently run a spatula between the sides and bottom of the rice and the edges and bottom of the pan. Invert a large, round platter over the pan, reverse the pan, and unmold the rice. If the crusty layer sticks, don't panic. Just loosen it with a spatula and place it over the rice. It won't look as perfect, but it will taste as good, and anyway, you're going to break up the crust when you serve the dish.

Heat the juices from the fish ragout in a saucepan. Transfer to a bowl and place the plain yogurt for garnish in another bowl. Bring the platter to the table. Serve, including some of the crust, the fish ragout, and more rice with each portion. Pass the yogurt and sauce and spoon them over the rice.

This makes good leftovers, and can be served cold.

SERVES 8 TO 10

IRANIAN OMELET WITH PARSLEY AND MINT

Coucou à l'Iranienne

A *coucou* is the Iranian version of a flat omelet, like a *tortilla española.* This one is filled with a garden of parsley and mint, and contains pine nuts, currants, and a little saffron. I've had them with other herbs, notably chervil, and they are marvelous with fresh walnuts. But Christine's version is the best I've tasted. The eggs are just barely set, and the chopped herbs retain their texture and fragrance. The omelet is even better served cold, a day later—the herbs hold their color and body—so it makes great picnic fare. This version, using eighteen eggs, makes a very large omelet, so you'll have enough to serve it at one meal to six people, and for lunch the next day.

It's important to mix the eggs and filling ingredients an hour or more before you cook the omelet. This gives the herbs time to swell. You also don't want to chop the herbs too fine. "It should be like a vegetable omelet," says Christine.

Like the previous recipe for Iranian rice, this is accompanied by a big green salad.

Wash and dry the herbs. Chop coarsely with a knife, not in a machine. You want them to swell and absorb the egg.

Beat the eggs in a large bowl. Mix in the herbs, pine nuts, and currants, the salt, freshly ground pepper, and saffron, then cover and set aside for 1 to 2 hours in a cool place. If storing in the refrigerator, bring to room temperature before cooking.

To cook, heat a deep, wide frying pan over medium-low heat and add 2 tablespoons olive oil. Stir the egg mixture briskly, and pour it into the pan. Turn the flame to low and cook, lifting the edges and turning the pan until the omelet cooks on the bottom, like a Spanish omelet. Cover the pan, place on a flame tamer or asbestos pad if the flame seems too

2 large bunches parsley, stems removed (about 2 to 3 cups, 60 to 90 g)

1 large bunch mint, stems removed (1 to 1 1/2 cups, 30 to 45 g)

18 large eggs

1/2 cup (50 g) pine nuts

1/3 cup (50 g) dried currants

About 1/2 teaspoon salt, or to taste

Freshly ground pepper to taste

1/4 teaspoon powdered saffron

2 tablespoons olive oil

high (you don't want the bottom of the omelet to stick and burn before it's cooked through), and cook 20 minutes, or until set but still a little runny on the top.

Bring to the table, cut in wedges, and serve, passing salt and a peppermill. Refrigerate whatever is left over for the following day.

SERVES 8 TO 10

CHERRY CLAFOUTI
Clafouti aux Cerises

A *clafouti* is a sort of cross between a flan and a fruit-filled pancake. Christine makes hers in June, when her cherry trees are full of fruit. She makes enormous *clafoutis,* which have good staying power, but with all the guests, they only last a couple of days. I've changed her recipe somewhat, substituting honey for sugar.

Preheat the oven to 350° F (180° C, gas mark 4). Butter a 12-inch (30-cm) tart pan or a 2-quart (2-L) baking dish.

Pit the cherries, if you wish, above a bowl (in France they usually leave the pits, but you might not want to deal with them when you eat the dessert). Place the pitted cherries in a separate bowl, and strain off any juices from the pits.

In a blender or electric mixer, blend together the milk, honey, juice from pitting the cherries, the eggs, vanilla, and salt. Add the flour and continue to blend together for 1 minute, until completely smooth.

Pour into the bowl with the cherries, mix together well, and turn into the buttered baking dish. Bake 45 minutes to an hour, until puffed and browned, and a knife comes out clean when inserted. Remove from the oven and sprinkle the top with the optional sugar. Serve hot or warm, but not cold. The *clafouti* will fall a bit upon cooling.

SERVES 6 TO 8

*1 pound (500 g) dark red or
    black cherries*
1¼ cups (285 ml) milk
*5 tablespoons mild-flavored
    honey*
3 large eggs
1 tablespoon vanilla extract
Pinch of salt
*⅔ cup (160 g) sifted
    unbleached white flour*
*1 tablespoon unsalted butter,
    for the baking dish*
*1 tablespoon brown or white
    sugar (optional)*

ALSATIAN APPLE CAKE
Gâteau Alsacien aux Pommes

Christine made this moist cake during one of my winter visits. I'd been in Monte Carlo at the annual International Television Festival, which always takes place in February. My sixteen-year-old nephew David was living in Tours, and his winter vacation coincided with the end of the festival, so I had him take the train from Tours to Nice, and took him first to visit my winemaker friends in Bandol, and then to Christine's. Christine had been snowed in, and the treacherous road up to her house had just been plowed the day before we arrived. I've never been so terrified in a car, as we slipped and slid up the road. I had no snow tires and the sun was setting fast. Christine's house was a welcome sight. She kept us happy that weekend with her usual delicious meals, served at the dining room table in front of a warm fire, and we ate a great deal of her Alsatian apple cake.

Preheat the oven to 425° F (220° C, gas mark 7). Generously butter a 12-inch (30-cm) cake pan or a 10-inch (25-cm) springform pan.

Peel, core, and cut the apples into eighths. Place in a large bowl.

Mix together the eggs, honey, oil, milk, vanilla, and rum. Mix in the flour, baking powder, baking soda, and salt. Blend well and pour the batter over the apples. Toss everything together and turn into the buttered baking pan.

Bake 30 minutes. Meanwhile, mix together the topping ingredients. After 30 minutes, pour this topping over the cake and spread evenly. Return to the heat and bake another 10 minutes, until caramelized on the top. Cool in the pan on a rack. Serve warm or cool. The cake reheats well.

SERVES 8 GENEROUSLY

FOR THE CAKE

1 tablespoon unsalted butter
4 pounds (2 kg) baking apples or Golden Delicious apples
3 large eggs
1/3 cup (90 ml) mild-flavored honey
1/4 cup (60 ml) safflower or peanut oil
2 tablespoons milk
1 teaspoon vanilla
2 tablespoons rum
1/2 cup plus 2 heaping tablespoons (75 g) sifted unbleached white flour
1 tablespoon baking powder
1 teaspoon baking soda
Pinch of salt

FOR THE TOPPING

1 large egg
2 tablespoons unsalted butter, melted
2 tablespoons brown sugar

PEACHES IN RED WINE WITH HONEY AND CINNAMON
Pêches au Vin Rouge

6 firm, ripe peaches
2 cups (450 ml) full-bodied
   red wine
3 to 4 tablespoons
   mild-flavored honey, to taste
1/2 teaspoon ground cinnamon
   (or more, to taste)
1 teaspoon vanilla
Fresh mint for garnish

Blanch the peaches, run them under cold water, and remove their skins.

Heat the wine to a simmer and remove from the heat. Stir in the honey, cinnamon, and vanilla. Pour into a bowl and slice in the peaches. Refrigerate for several hours.

Serve cold, garnished with fresh mint.

SERVES 6

PEACH AND APRICOT SALAD WITH CURRANTS
Salade de Pêches et Abricots aux Raisins de Corinthe

Juice of 1 lemon
1 tablespoon mild-flavored
   honey or 2 tablespoons
   sugar
4 to 6 firm, ripe peaches,
   sliced
4 to 6 firm, ripe apricots,
   sliced
3 tablespoons dried currants

Mix together the lemon juice and honey or sugar. Toss with the peaches, apricots, and currants. Chill for an hour or more, and serve.

SERVES 4 TO 6

Recipes from Domaine Tempier

SALT COD MOUSSE
Brandade de Morue

SARDINES MARINATED IN VINEGAR
Sardines en Escabeche

TUNA (OR SWORDFISH) WITH TOMATO-CAPER SAUCE
Thon à la Marseillaise

GRILLED SARDINES
Sardines Grillées

LULU'S GRILLED FISH
Poisson Grillé

SQUID RAGOUT
Ragoût de Calmars

LULU'S HUGE VEGETABLE AND FISH PLATTER WITH GARLIC MAYONNAISE
Aïoli Monstre

ORANGE AND OLIVE SALAD WITH CUMIN
Salade D'Oranges et D'Olives au Cumin

LULU'S POTATO GRATIN
Gratin Dauphinois

POTATO GRATIN WITH SORREL
Gratin de Pommes de Terre à l'Oseille

DOMAINE TEMPIER ROSÉS AND RED WINES

These are just some of the recipes I've learned from Lulu Peyraud, the proprietress of the Bandol vineyard Domaine Tempier. Bandol is a seaside town situated about fifty kilometers east of Marseilles, just west of Toulon, in the department of the Var. In this part of France, the Mediterranean coast is lined with small villages, and medieval fortress towns pepper the hills. You can see two of them, Le Castellet and l'Acadière, from Domaine Tempier. The hilly, vineyard-covered countryside is dotted with palm trees, and the sky in this part of France is often a wash of pinks, oranges, purples, blues, greens, and golds. It is all so gorgeous that one wonders why travelers seem to prefer the over-crowded Côte d'Azur to the east.

Domaine Tempier is a country home built in 1835 by Lulu's great-great-grandmother. Lulu and Lucien moved there from Marseilles in 1943, during the war. Times were tough; there was no electricity, no running water. There were three young children to care for (there would be four more) and German soldiers everywhere. Lulu busied herself with her own babies and those of the neighboring farmers. To discourage the German soldiers from setting up camp in her house, she filled it with as many screaming infants as she could find (it worked). Meanwhile, Lucien set to work revitalizing the vineyard. He succeeded in producing a wine worthy of an *appellation,* and today his dry, elegant rosés and fruity, ruby-hued reds are among the most talked about wines in Provence. There are only four *appellations* in Provence, and Bandol is one of them.

Like many winemakers, the Peyrauds are vivacious and passionate. Their eyes twinkle with humor and love. Lulu is a tiny woman with red hair and sparkling blue eyes. Her luncheons are always celebrations, no matter how disparate the group and despite language barriers.

I first went to Domaine Tempier for a festive bouillabaisse luncheon on a sunny July day in 1980, when I was living at La Sara. Nathalie Waag, my landlady, was a great friend of Lulu's, and when she told Lulu about my interest in food, Lulu invited us both to lunch. Nathalie wrote me a note saying "Lulu Peyraud, the best cook I know, would like you to come to lunch next Monday," and gave me directions. I didn't quite know who Lulu Peyraud was, or what Domaine Tempier was; I thought it might be a restaurant. At any rate, early Monday morning I made the beautiful two-hour drive, through the Luberon to Aix, and onto the autoroute toward Toulon. I found the Domaine, and as I drove up I could see that this was going to be an extraordinary place. I got out of

my car and found myself standing under an arbor in front of a hundred-fifty-year-old stucco farm house surrounded by terraced vineyards. In front of the massive wooden door a long table had been laid with white linen cloths and porcelain dishes. The receptionist told me that my hosts were at the *cave* and would be back shortly. I was happy to marvel at my surroundings while I waited for them.

Soon everybody appeared—Lulu and Lucien Peyraud, their sons Jean-Marie and François with their wives, Catherine and Paule; the food writer Richard Olney and his sister-in-law Judith, also a food writer; a wine merchant from Berkeley; and Nathalie.

Lulu served garlic croutons with *tapenade* and *anchoiade,* while Lucien poured chilled Domaine Tempier rosé. A small fire had been prepared on the ground outside, using wood and dried vines from the vineyard, and over it a huge copper caldron of fish and vegetable bouillon was heating. Lulu and her daughters-in-law came out of the kitchen with large cork trays holding about ten different kinds of fish and shellfish. When the bouillon began to simmer, she sprinkled in some saffron and added the fish. This was all very dramatic. After a few minutes, Lulu and Paule removed the fish from the bouillon and put it back on the trays, and ladled bouillon and vegetables into each bowl on the table.

Eating bouillabaisse at Domaine Tempier is a ritual. First you eat the bouillon and vegetables (leeks, potatoes, carrots), with croutons and *rouille,* a reddish-colored, spicy mayonnaise; then you eat more bouillon, *rouille,* and fish. There are so many different kinds of fish that you spend hours at the table, taking a little of one kind or another with each helping, washing each one down with vintage after vintage of the Peyrauds' wine. That day the bouillabaisse was followed by fresh goat cheese and figs, then Cavaillon melons filled with apricot puree and almonds.

I told the Peyrauds that this was my first bouillabaisse and that I'd been wanting to have the real thing for quite some time. "Your first bouillabaisse!" Lucien exclaimed. "This calls for Champagne!" And with that a plastic Champagne bucket in the shape of a top hat appeared, with two bottles of pale pink Champagne.

Small wonder that since that dreamy afternoon I've returned to the Domaine at least once a year, and I'm never without its wine. When I moved to Paris a year later, I immediately wrote to Lulu, asking if I could come for the *vendanges,* the grape harvest. Lulu wrote back at once, saying that my room would be waiting. I had been in Paris for barely two weeks when I got in my car and hurried down to Bandol. I had it in my mind to do a story on the harvest.

The first day I went to pick grapes in a spectacular hillside vineyard called La Tourtine. It was sunny as only a Provençal day can be, and I could see the shimmering Mediterranean. The mistral, which had sounded like the ocean the night before, had become a gentle, refreshing breeze, and the vineyard was fragrant with fennel, rosemary, thyme, and mint. The luscious, dark purple-blue grapes, which we were not barred from eating as we picked, also had a wonderful aroma.

The hours passed quickly. François Peyraud, who supervises the agriculture at the Domaine and directs the harvest, taught me how to use my *sicateur,* the small curved scissors used to clip off the grape clusters, and how to cut out the moldy and rotten grapes. I learned to reject the small clusters that grow off tertiary branches and aren't sweet enough, and the small white and pink bunches that aren't ripe. I had a bucket, called a *sceau,* and worked in a row by myself or with one other person. A crew of two men repeatedly provided empty buckets in exchange for our full ones, which they emptied into bins on a tractor. I was lulled by the constant sound of grapes falling into empty containers, the cries of *"Sceau!"* as the buckets filled up, and the tractor coming and going from the *cave,* where the wine is made.

I had done farm labor years ago in the United States. But this was very different. It wasn't just the surroundings; it was the mixture of tension and celebration everyone felt, workers and *patrons* alike. The *vendanges* is an extremely intense time. The year's labor and investment depend upon it entirely. No matter how good a winemaker is, the quality of his wine from

year to year will depend on timing, weather, and good luck. If the *vendanges* begin too early, the grapes won't be sweet enough; if they begin too late, there is a greater chance that foul weather will spoil the grapes. The sky that first day was as blue-violet as Wedgwood ceramic, bluer than I'd ever seen it. Yet Lucien, François, and Jean-Marie regarded it with suspicion. *"C'est trop beau,"* François remarked. *"Il faut avoir des nuages."* (It's too clear; there should be clouds.) Only rain could follow such clear weather, and rain would destroy the grapes. Luckily François was wrong, and the harvest proceeded under clement skies.

Lucien, François, and Jean-Marie Peyraud work with unbreakable concentration during this time. They maintain their good humor, but the strain of the *vendanges* shows in their faces. Lucien, like a new mother, gets up every two hours during the night to record the temperature of the fermenting wine, which must not rise higher than 26° C (about 80° F). François is in the vineyards at six every morning, checking the vines to determine which grapes are most ready for harvesting. Jean-Marie, who supervises the vinification, never takes his mind off the process going on in the *cave.* He is always late for lunch and eats little.

Yet all of the Peyrauds arrive with smiling faces, ready for conversation and fun, at the long outdoor lunch table where workers and family gather together daily. For despite the rigors of the *vendanges,* this is the most festive time of year, full of promise. During the rest of the year life goes on in a business-as-usual way; but during the harvest, with the influx of new workers and the mystery of this year's wine, there is always a feeling of novelty.

Nowhere is that more apparent than at Lulu's table. She above all adores *la fête,* and her meals reflect it. When I sat down to that delicious lunch after my first morning in the vineyards (marinated sardines, pasta with a garlicky tomato sauce, salad, bread, and fresh fruit), I realized at once that it was Lulu I wanted to write about. I went back to grape picking in the mythic afternoon light after lunch, but the following day I put down my *sicateur* and spent the next three weeks in the kitchen and at the markets with Lulu.

Lulu's *vendanges* meals are filling, Provençal country fare, fragrant with garlic and olive oil, washed down with ice-cold well water and the Domaine's table wine. I have learned much about fish cookery from Lulu, because she always respects my vegetarian preference and prepares fish dishes for me. She serves lunch to between fifteen and twenty-five people every day during the *vendanges,* and I don't know how she does it so effortlessly. Like all great hostesses, she is very organized, and it was a joy to go with her to the market every day and watch her find the best products and check off her lists. After the market we would go home to her beautiful kitchen, which still looks like the kitchen her grandmother built because all of the appliances are hidden behind closet doors, and prepare the lunch in two hours. Paule, Francois's wife, would always be there to help, along with whatever other daughters or daughters-in-law were around. It was a joy to work with Lulu in this lovely old-fashioned kitchen, with its stone hearth inside and another outside grill. She knew exactly what she wanted and was very direct. Every day I would be inspired by a new dish, and I left the Domaine with several additions to my repertoire. My palate, like Lulu's, is Mediterranean in spirit; we both love garlic, olive oil, fresh fish, herbs, and tomatoes.

At the end of the harvest, after the last grapes have been picked, there is a big bouillabaisse lunch. Like my first bouillabaisse at Domaine Tempier, it is always a party. It begins with rosé and a nice hors d'oeuvre like *tapenade* or *brandade;* then all of the workers, their spouses, several neighbors and family members, and guests like me sit down at a long, long table under the arbor for hours of bouillabaisse and wine tasting. Jean-Marie and the head *caviste* continually disappear and reappear with different vintages. There are guessing games as to the years. After the soup comes fruit or sherbet, then marc, the eau de vie made from the seeds and stems after the harvest. Lucien conducts a *dégustation,* or a tasting, after lunch at the *cave,* and François sets up the still for making marc.

The afternoon before this lunch, Lulu goes down to the port, either at Bandol or nearby Sanary or Toulon, wherever

she knows that the fishermen will be arriving with a good catch. She comes back with kilos of fish, and she and her helpers begin work on the soup. Lulu cleans all the fish at her soapstone kitchen sink. In her opinion it is essential to clean your own fish, because only then will you know if it is truly fresh. She saves the livers for the *rouille,* the spicy mayonnaise used to garnish the soup. The fish are for the most part Mediterranean species like *rascasse,* a succulent, white-fleshed member of the gurnard family that is unique to the Mediterranean, sea bass *(loup),* several Mediterranean varieties of bream *(sar, daurade, pageot),* John Dory, another member of the gurnard family called *galinette,* and red mullet *(rouget).* There are usually one or two varieties of crab, and mussels as well. While Lulu cleans and scales the fish her assistants make scores of garlic croutons, toasting rounds of French bread in the oven and rubbing them with garlic; they also peel dozens of cloves of garlic for the *rouille.*

In addition to the beautiful fish that will be cooked at the last minute in the bouillon, Lulu buys several pounds of tiny rockfish (called *soupe de poisson* or *bouillabaisse*) which she uses for the fish fumet. She sautés these fish with garlic and onion in olive oil, then adds water, tomatoes, and herbs and brings the mixture to a boil. After carefully skimming off all the foam, she simmers this fumet for about half an hour and presses it through a strainer. Later she will use it for her bouillon. It is Lulu's bouillon, with its many chunks of leeks, carrots, and potatoes, that makes her bouillabaisse taste so good. She says that it is the vegetables that make this a *bouillabaisse à la marseillaise.* I've eaten bouillabaisse in a few restaurants in the south of France, but I've never had one that tastes as good as Lulu's.

I don't think I could ever make one like Lulu's, at least in Paris or in the United States. You really need the Mediterranean fish for a real *bouillabaisse à la marseillaise,* both the tiny fish for the fumet and the larger fish for the soup. I thought about including a bouillabaisse recipe in this chapter, and even planned to go and work side by side with Lulu to make one. But if I put the recipe in, you would only be frustrated because you wouldn't be able to find the right fish. Instead, you can find a marvelous fish soup, my *"Chowder" à la Provençale* (Provençal-style Fish Soup) on page 141; it's not bouillabaisse but it sure is good, and much less trouble to make. At any rate, there is enough here to make you very happy, and Lulu will be pleased that you are enjoying her recipes.

SALT COD MOUSSE
Brandade de Morue

This creamy combination of salt cod, milk, olive oil, and garlic was a revelation to me the first time I tasted it, when Lulu served it as a first course at one of her *vendanges* lunches. When I tasted it a second time at a *dégustation/*luncheon she and Lucien gave for me, I resolved to learn to make the dish myself. Unfortunately, it wasn't as easy as it looked. If you cook the salt cod a minute too long it becomes as dry as cotton, and no matter how much milk and olive oil you add, you won't get the smooth texture necessary for a really elegant *brandade* (my first attempt went straight into the wastebasket). Lulu also insists that you must use salt cod with the skin still on, because it's the fat right underneath the skin that emulsifies the mixture. (Almost every recipe I've seen in a book tells you to remove the skin, but Lulu doesn't agree.) Do look for thick, white salt cod with its skin. Don't buy fish that is yellowing, because the texture will be dry and hard.

The measures I give below for milk and olive oil are approximate. You must use your eye and taste to judge exactly how much liquid to add. The puree should be smooth but not liquidy; the consistency should be somewhat similar to that of my Hummus (page 219), though it will be much lighter. Friends from Boston who ate this with me at the Peyrauds the day I learned to make it said it was much like the mixture used in New England cod cakes. They agreed, though, that it was much more refined than the fried cakes.

Besides serving it as described below, you can also fill tomato halves with the *brandade.*

DESALTING THE FISH, THE DAY BEFORE: Place the salt cod in a colander and set the colander in a large bowl. The salt cod must be suspended in the water, which should be changed continuously. The easiest way to ensure this is to place the bowl with the colander in it in the sink under the faucet, and run cold water over it continuously for 24 hours. If this isn't possible, use the same collander-bowl apparatus and soak the fish in cold water, changing the water at least 5 times over 24 hours.

Making the court bouillon: While the cod is soaking, combine all the ingredients for the court bouillon in a saucepan or fish poacher and bring to a simmer. Cover and simmer 30 minutes. Strain into a bowl. Add 2 quarts of cold water to the strained liquid and cool. (This can be done a day in advance.)

COOKING THE SALT COD AND MIXING UP THE BRAN-DADE: Place the cooled court bouillon in a large casserole or fish poacher, and add the desalted cod. Bring very slowly to a simmer over medium-low heat. As soon as the surface of the bouillon begins to tremble, turn off the heat and leave the fish in it for 10 minutes. *Don't let the liquid boil.* Drain the fish, place it on a board, and remove all the bones. Break up the fish into small flakes and discard any pieces that seem hard and dry, wrinkled, or like cardboard. The thickest pieces of the fish should be somewhat slippery. Place half the flakes in the processor, or all of them if your processor is large.

Puree the garlic along with a little salt in a mortar and pestle. Add to the flaked cod in the food processor and process the fish until it is a dry puree. The fish has to be pureed before you add the liquids. This can also be done in smaller batches in a blender or with a mortar and pestle.

Meanwhile, heat the milk and the olive oil in separate pans, removing from the heat just before they reach the simmering point. Turn on the food processor and add the milk and olive oil alternately, a little at a time (use about half if you are processing only half the fish), until you have a smooth puree. It should be smooth and satiny, although you will probably see tiny flakes of fish, and it should absorb all the liquid. Repeat with the remaining fish, milk, and oil, if necessary. Now combine both batches in a bowl and add pepper and lemon juice to taste. If the mixture seems dry and doesn't stick

FOR THE BRANDADE

2 pounds (1 kg) salt cod; the pieces should be thick, white, and contain the skin if possible
2 to 4 large cloves garlic, to taste
Salt
¾ to 1 cup (225 ml) milk
¾ cup (180 ml) olive oil
Lots of freshly ground pepper
Fresh lemon juice to taste (optional)
Parsley for garnish
Garlic Croutons (page 46)

FOR THE COURT BOUILLON

2 quarts (2 L) water
1 onion, quartered
1 leek, white part only, cleaned and sliced
1 stalk celery, coarsely sliced
1 carrot, coarsely sliced
Bouquet garni made with 2 bay leaves, several sprigs each of fresh parsley, fennel, and thyme
6 black peppercorns

together but breaks apart in clumps, work in more milk. Adjust the seasonings; you may want to add salt, but it probably won't be necessary.

Mound in a bowl and garnish with parsley. Serve on the garlic croutons.

SERVES 8 TO 10

SARDINES MARINATED IN VINEGAR
Sardines en Escabeche

6 to 8 small fresh sardines per person (about 1 ½ to 2 pounds, 750 g to 1 kg)
4 tablespoons olive oil
6 tablespoons red wine vinegar
3 medium-size yellow onions, chopped
2 cloves garlic, minced or put through a press
Salt and freshly ground pepper to taste

FOR GARNISH
2 lemons, cut in wedges
Chopped fresh parsley

This refreshing dish was served at the first of my *vendanges* lunches, when I was still picking grapes, and not long afterwards I moved from the vineyards to Lulu's kitchen. It's an easy, cold preparation that has good staying power. The sardines are pan-fried, then marinated in vinegar with onions and chilled. If fresh sardines aren't available, use small fresh herrings.

Scale the sardines, remove the heads, and clean. Rinse and pat dry with paper towels.

Heat 2 tablespoons of the olive oil in a large, heavy-bottomed skillet and sauté the sardines over medium heat until the flesh is white and flakes easily, about 5 minutes. Remove from the pan, drain on paper towels, and place in a casserole or serving dish. Toss with 3 tablespoons of the vinegar and set aside.

Rinse the pan, dry, and heat the remaining 2 tablespoons olive oil. Add the onions and garlic and sauté over medium heat, stirring often, until the onions are soft and golden. Add the remaining 3 tablespoons vinegar and continue to cook over medium-low heat for 10 minutes. Season to taste with salt and freshly ground pepper and remove from the heat.

Spread the onion mixture over the sardines, cover the

casserole, and refrigerate for at least 1 hour, tossing occasionally. Serve topped with chopped fresh parsley and garnished with lemon wedges.

This will keep for 2 days in the refrigerator.

SERVES 6 TO 8

TUNA (OR SWORDFISH) WITH TOMATO-CAPER SAUCE
Thon à la Marseillaise

I think the *sauce marseillaise,* the heady mixture of tomatoes, garlic, and capers that I learned from Lulu and serve at Supper Club with steamed fish fillets (page 178) and baked whiting (page 182), is best with grilled tuna or swordfish. Unfortunately I don't have a grill big enough for twenty-five people, nor would this be a convenient dish for me to make for Supper Club. Lulu, however, managed to pull it off for fifteen *vendangeurs.*

First make the sauce. This will hold for a day or two in the refrigerator.

Brush the fish steaks with olive oil and grill over aromatic wood for approximately 8 minutes, or 4 minutes per ½ inch (1.5 cm) of thickness, turning halfway through the cooking. Watch closely, because tuna and swordfish will become cotton-dry if you overcook them. The steaks should remain pink in the middle.

Remove from the heat and serve immediately, topped with the sauce.

SERVES 4 TO 6

Tomato-caper sauce (see page 178)

4 to 6 tuna or swordfish steaks, about 1 inch (2.5 cm) thick

1 tablespoon olive oil

GRILLED SARDINES
Sardines Grillées

There is nothing simpler or more satisfying than very fresh sardines grilled over aromatic wood. I first had them at the Domaine during the month of February. I was there with my then-young nephew, David, and we were invited to François and Paule's house on a cold, rainy day for lunch.

When I arrived, François had started a fire in their stone hearth. We feasted on the grilled sardines, pulling the skins off and eating them with our fingers, and washing it all down with Domaine Tempier rosé. For dessert we had raisins made from the Domaine's grapes, great big ones with the seeds still in them. It was a lunch my nephew and I will never forget.

A few years later, friends and I rented a house on an idyllic island off the coast of Yugoslavia called Korĉula. Our neighbors would often go to the docks early in the morning and come back with kilos of sardines as fresh as the ones I'd had in Bandol. They would grill them on the large open hearth in our kitchen, in the same way as the Peyrauds, with nothing but a little olive oil to oil the grill, and we would have marvelous lunches of sardines, Yugoslav salads (tomatoes, cucumbers, and onion), and my *pain de campagne,* all washed down with the thick red wine made on the island.

6 to 12 sardines per person, depending on the size, cleaned if large (the tiny ones are usually already cleaned)
Olive oil for the grill
Salt to taste

Prepare a fire in your grill, and oil the grill rack with olive oil. Place the sardines on it; grill small sardines for 1 minute on each side, large sardines for 2 ½ minutes on each side. The fish should fall apart easily but not be dry. Season to taste with salt.

Eat with your fingers, removing the skins, which are not very digestible.

Accompany with country bread and a big salad. You could drink a dry white wine like muscadet or Sancerre, or rosé wine from the south of France (such as Domaine Tempier), or a light red wine, such as a Chinon or a red Sancerre, chilled.

SERVES 4

LULU'S GRILLED FISH
Poisson Grillé

Lulu has a large grill outside her kitchen. She prefers cooking her fish outside, over vine branches, so that her kitchen won't smell like fish. I was always astounded by her knack for grilling twenty-five fish at a time without cooking one of them too long. Lulu insists that you should clean the fish yourself, especially since you use the liver and roe in this sauce. If you prefer to have your fishmonger clean the fish, make sure he saves the liver for you.

PREPARING THE FISH FOR GRILLING: Clean the fish but save the liver and roe for the sauce. Do not scale.

Prepare a grill with aromatic wood, such as mesquite (Lulu uses branches from the grapevines).

Rub the inside of the fish with a little oil, salt, and freshly ground pepper. Fill the cavity or cavities with sprigs of the fresh herbs: fennel, fresh savory, thyme, basil, or rosemary, and the bay leaf.

MAKING THE SAUCE: Pound together the fish liver, garlic, salt, pepper and dried savory in a mortar and pestle. Add the olive oil, a tablespoon at a time, incorporating each spoonful into the sauce with the pestle. Adjust seasonings. Add the chopped fresh basil or parsley and continue to mash and mix together until you have a thick, fragrant sauce.

FOR THE FISH

4 whole individual-serving-size fish (weighing about ¾ to 1 pound each), such as sea bass, red snapper, porgy, brill, John Dory, or bream, or 2 larger fish, weighing 1½ pounds (750 g) each, or 1 very large fish, weighing about 3 pounds (1.5 kg)
Olive oil
Salt and freshly ground pepper
3 or 4 branches either herb fennel or rosemary (or a combination)
Several sprigs of fresh savory, thyme, or basil
1 bay leaf, broken into pieces if using more than one fish

FOR THE SAUCE

The liver and roe from the fish
2 small or 1 large clove garlic
Salt and freshly ground pepper
½ teaspoon dried savory
¼ cup (60 ml) olive oil
2 tablespoons finely chopped fresh basil or parsley (or more, to taste)

SPECIAL PEOPLE

269

GRILLING THE FISH: Grill the fish for about 8 to 10 minutes, or longer if necessary (4 to 5 minutes for each ½ inch, 1.5 cm, of thickness), turning it halfway through. A 1-pound (500 g) fish takes about 4 minutes on each side if the fire is hot, a 1 ½ pound (750 g) fish will take 6, and a 2-pound (1 kg) fish takes 8 minutes on each side. Serve, and pass the sauce separately.

SERVES 4

SQUID RAGOUT
Ragoût de Calmars

When I spent the harvest at the Domaine, Lulu made this dish with octopus. Four years later I returned and had the same dish with small squid. I never have been much of an octopus fan, but I love the more delicate squid, which become extremely tender when cooked in the wine. You can add cooked rice to this ragout, which makes it like a squid jambalaya and stretches it to serve 8 people. You can also serve it with steamed potatoes or fresh pasta on the side. The ragout will hold for a day in the refrigerator and can be gently reheated on top of the stove.

Rinse the squid and pat it dry with paper towels.

In a large, heavy-bottomed casserole heat 1 tablespoon butter and 1 tablespoon of the olive oil and sauté the onion and garlic over medium heat until the onion is soft and golden, about 10 minutes. Add the tomatoes and sauté, stirring, another 5 minutes. Transfer to a bowl and wipe the pan with a paper towel.

In the same casserole, heat the remaining 3 tablespoons olive oil and sauté the squid pieces over medium heat until they begin to color (the edges will brown and the surface will turn pinkish), about 10 minutes. Add the Cognac, heat for a minute, and light it with a match. When the flames die down, add the wine, the sautéed onions, garlic and tomatoes, the hot pepper or cayenne, and a pinch of salt. Add enough water to cover by 1 inch (2.5 cm). Bring to a simmer, cover, and simmer 45 minutes, or until the squid is tender, stirring from time to time. Correct seasonings, adding more garlic if you desire, and salt and pepper to taste. Remove the hot pepper.

Mix together the remaining 1 tablespoon butter, which should be at room temperature, and flour, and whisk it into the stew in bits. Simmer, stirring, until the mixture thickens like gravy.

Sprinkle with chopped fresh parsley and serve hot over rice, if you wish. Or stir the cooked rice into the ragout and serve.

TO PREPARE AHEAD OF TIME: The entire ragout, up to the addition of the final butter and flour, can be made a day in advance, covered, and held overnight in the refrigerator. If you are using rice, do not add it until the day you are serving or the rice will absorb too much sauce. Bring the ragout to a simmer and whisk in the butter and flour mixture; cook until it reaches the desired thickness. Correct seasonings. Stir in the cooked rice and garnish with parsley.

SERVES 4 TO 6

2 1/2 pounds (1.25 kilos) squid, cleaned and cut in 1-inch (2.5-cm) pieces

2 tablespoons unsalted butter

4 tablespoons olive oil

2 onions, chopped

4 cloves garlic, minced or put through a press

4 medium-size or large tomatoes, seeded and chopped

1/4 cup (60 ml) Cognac

2 cups (450 ml) red wine

1 dried hot chili pepper or a pinch of cayenne

Salt to taste

2 teaspoons flour

Chopped fresh parsley for garnish

1 cup (200 g) rice, cooked (optional)

LULU'S HUGE VEGETABLE AND FISH PLATTER WITH GARLIC MAYONNAISE

Aïoli Monstre

FOR THE AÏOLI

2 egg yolks, at room
*   temperature*
½ teaspoon salt
¾ cup (180 ml) olive oil
¾ cup (180 ml) safflower oil
5 cloves garlic, peeled
Juice of 1 large lemon
Freshly ground pepper or a
*   pinch of cayenne*

FOR THE COURT
BOUILLON

1 quart (1 L) water
1 onion, sliced
2 leeks, cleaned and sliced
1 carrot, sliced
1 stalk celery, sliced
2 whole cloves garlic, peeled
1 sprig fresh parsley
1 sprig fresh thyme
1 bay leaf
1 teaspoon salt (more or less,
*   to taste)*
2 cups (450 ml) dry white
*   wine*
6 peppercorns

*A*ïoli monstre is one of the more festive *vendanges* meals, and sometimes Lulu serves it instead of the bouillabaisse at the end-of-the-harvest luncheon. It's a wise idea to wait until the grape picking is over, because *aïoli* is a garlic mayonnaise, and garlic is a known somniferant. A siesta is often required afterwards.

The *aïoli* is served on a large platter with a colorful assortment of vegetables and fish. I was intrigued by some of Lulu's vegetable choices, in particular sweet potatoes and beets. They all work, though, and they are simply prepared and delicious.

MAKING THE AÏOLI: Place the egg yolks and salt in a food processor bowl or blender jar. Turn on the machine and very slowly drizzle in the oils in a very thin, steady stream while blending. If you use a blender, you will have to stop it from time to time to stir down the mixture. Squeeze in the garlic through a press or pound it to a paste in a mortar and pestle and mix in thoroughly. Add the lemon juice and pepper and mix well. Adjust the salt. Refrigerate until ready to serve.

MAKING THE COURT BOUILLON: Combine all the ingredients for the court bouillon except the wine and peppercorns in a large saucepan or soup pot. Bring to a boil, reduce the heat, cover, and simmer 15 minutes. Add the wine and peppercorns and simmer another 15 minutes. Strain and retain the broth. Cool.

POACHING THE FISH FILLETS: Slap with the flat side of a knife to break down the fibers, and score a few times on the diagonal. Butter a pan or casserole wide enough to accommodate the fillets and lay them in the pan. Cover with cold or tepid court bouillon and bring to a bare simmer. Do not boil. Cover and cook 5 minutes for each ½ inch (1.5 cm) of thickness. The fish should be opaque and flake easily with a fork. Remove from the liquid with a slotted spatula.

ASSEMBLING THE DISH: After preparing the vegetables, place on a large platter along with the fish, interspersed with mounds of the *aïoli.* Pass the platter and allow guests to take portions of each vegetable and fish, with a mound of *aïoli* for dipping.

TO PREPARE AHEAD OF TIME: Everything for this—the mayonnaise, court bouillon, vegetables, and the poached fish—will hold for a day in the refrigerator. Bring the vegetables to room temperature before serving, or serve warm.

SERVES AT LEAST 10 PEOPLE

FOR THE FISH AND VEGETABLES

1 ½ pounds (750 g) fresh cod fillets or salt cod, desalted (see page 264)

1 cauliflower, broken into florets and blanched

12 small artichokes, steamed until tender and cut in half lengthwise, chokes removed

½ pound (250 g) green beans, blanched

1 pound (500 g) carrots, peeled, halved or quartered, and blanched

1 pound (500 g) fennel bulbs, trimmed, quartered and steamed 20 minutes

1 pound (500 g) beets, peeled, quartered, and steamed until tender

6 small sweet potatoes, baked in their skins and halved

6 hard-boiled eggs, halved

6 tomatoes, cut in half

ORANGE AND OLIVE SALAD WITH CUMIN
Salade d'Oranges et d'Olives au Cumin

8 navel oranges, peeled and
white pith removed, sliced

¾ cup (85 g) imported black
olives, cut in half and
pitted

1 red onion, sliced very thin

Juice of 1 medium-size lemon

½ to 1 teaspoon ground
cumin, to taste

Salt and freshly ground
pepper

1 tablespoon olive oil

The second time I went to Domaine Tempier during the harvest Lulu served this at lunch, followed by her *ragoût de calmars,* the Squid Ragout on page 270.

Toss together the oranges, olives, and onion.

Mix together the lemon juice, cumin, salt and pepper, then whisk in the olive oil. Toss with the salad and serve.

SERVES 6

LULU'S POTATO GRATIN
Gratin Dauphinois

1 clove garlic, peeled and cut
in half

2½ tablespoons unsalted
butter

1 thick slice of onion

Salt and freshly ground
pepper to taste

2½ pounds (1.25 kg) Idaho
russet potatoes, peeled and
sliced very thin

2 cups (450 ml) crème fraîche

6 ounces (170 g) grated
Emmenthaler or Gruyère
cheese (1½ cups)

Preheat the oven to 425° F (220° C, gas mark 7). Rub a 2-quart (2-L) earthenware gratin dish with the cut clove of garlic, then with some of the butter.

Bring a large pot of water to a boil, add the onion slice and some salt, and blanch the sliced potatoes for 5 minutes. Drain.

Spread half the potato slices in the buttered gratin dish. Add salt and freshly ground pepper, then top with half the crème fraîche and half the cheese. Repeat the layers, and dot the top with the remaining butter.

SUPPER CLUB
CHEZ MARTHA ROSE

Bake in the preheated oven for 35 to 45 minutes, or until the top browns. Serve bubbling hot.

SERVES 6 TO 8

My Lower-Fat Gratin Dauphinois

Substitute 1 ½ cups (340 ml) skim milk and ½ cup (120 ml) crème fraîche for the 2 cups crème fraîche. Reduce the cheese to 1 cup (4 ounces, 115 g), or reduce to 1 ounce (30 g), which you will sprinkle over the top. Use safflower oil for the baking dish and omit the butter.

Lulu's Potato Gratin with Sorrel

The ingredients for the Potato Gratin, prepared as above, plus:

1 bunch fresh sorrel
2 additional tablespoons
  unsalted butter

½ cup (120 ml) additional
  crème fraîche

Wash the sorrel and remove the stems. Dry and chop. Heat the butter over medium heat in a skillet and sauté the sorrel for about 3 minutes. Remove from the heat and mix with the additional crème fraîche. Divide into two portions.

Proceed with the Potato Gratin recipe, but before topping the potatoes with the crème fraîche and cheese, add a layer of the sorrel mixture. The acidity of the sorrel goes nicely with the potatoes.

Part IV:
Favorite Dishes from
Small Dinner Parties

MUSSELS STEAMED IN WHITE WINE
Moules à la Marinière

ITALIAN-STYLE MUSSEL SOUP
Soupe aux Moules à l'Italienne

FILLETS OF TURBOT WITH MUSSELS AND CURRY
Filets de Turbot et Moules au Curry

CAULIFLOWER GRATIN WITH GOAT CHEESE
Choufleur Gratiné au Chèvre

SALAD WITH CAULIFLOWER AND GOAT CHEESE GRATIN
Choufleur Gratiné en Salade

RAVIOLI WITH CHEESE AND WILD MUSHROOMS
Raviolis au Fromage et Champignons Sauvages

FRESH HOMEMADE PASTA WITH PESTO
Pâtés Maison au Pistou

GREEN MUSCAT GRAPES MARINATED IN MUSCAT WINE
Muscats au Muscat de Beaumes de Venise

COFFEE BAVARIAN CREAM WITH KAHLÚA
Crème Bavarois au Kahlúa

HONEY MOUSSE
Mousse au Miel

CRÊPES FILLED WITH LEMON SOUFFLÉ, WITH STRAWBERRY PUREE
Crêpes Soufflées au Citron, Coulis de Fraises

There are certain dishes that are too time consuming for me to consider making for twenty-five people. They're fine for four, six, or even eight people, but would be a nightmare if you had to multiply the recipes by three or four. So they don't occur in any of my Supper Club menus. But they're dishes I love, and I can't bear to leave them out of this collection.

The first three recipes are time consuming because of the mussels. Cleaning mussels can be tedious, but if you love them as much as I do, it's worth it. Until I moved here, I didn't know how delicious these mollusks could be, whether prepared simply, steamed *à la marinière* in white wine, or cooked in a more complicated soup or fish dish. In winter I sometimes get cravings for them and will invite a few friends over just for "moules" and a salad.

The cauliflower and goat cheese gratin is included because I often serve it with the Fillets of Turbot with Mussels and Curry on page 285.

Fresh pasta is difficult for me to serve at a Supper Club, unless it's a baked dish like the cannelloni on page 150 or the lasagne on page 105, or unless it's used in a salad (pages 166 and 188). By the time I get it out to all twenty-five people it has cooled too much, and there is always the danger of over-cooking it. But for my *small* at-home dinners, pasta, in fact, is what I most often serve, either as a main dish or on the side. I love making ravioli for six to eight people, though I would never attempt it for twenty-five.

And of course I'd never serve a soufflé, whether savory or dessert, for twenty-five people. Soufflés fall too quickly, and it's too important for everybody to see them.

I serve these smaller meals in my breakfast dining room, which opens onto the kitchen. It's a little, cozy, square room with French doors, on the courtyard side of the apartment. The walls are covered with burgundy fabric, and the round table will seat seven people comfortably. At Supper Club and big parties this is the room we use for prepping food and arranging plates and serving platters; it is part of the bustling inner sanctum of the kitchen. Many of my guests don't even see this part of the house, because it's separated from the living room by a long, narrow hallway. At my smaller dinners my friends watch me cook and sometimes help me with last-minute details. I love the intimacy and relaxed atmosphere of these candlelit events as much as the excitement and fanfare of Supper Club.

MUSSELS STEAMED IN WHITE WINE
Moules à la Marinière

Nothing could be as simple and satisfying as a big bowl of *moules à la marinière,* a few slices of crusty bread, a crisp green salad, and a glass of Muscadet or Sancerre.

Clean the mussels according to the directions on page 204.

Combine the onion or shallots, garlic, wine, parsley sprigs, bay leaf, peppercorns, and thyme in a very large lidded pot or wok and bring to a boil. Boil a minute or two, then add the mussels. Cover the pot tightly and cook over high heat for 5 minutes. Shake the pot firmly several times during the cooking to distribute the mussels evenly and ensure even cooking. If the pot is too heavy to do this effectively, stir a couple of times with a long-handled spoon. The mussels are ready when their shells have opened; this takes about 5 minutes.

Spoon the mussels into wide soup bowls, discarding any that haven't opened. Add the lemon juice and optional butter to the broth, bring to a boil again, and pour over the mussels. Sprinkle with chopped parsley and serve. Provide bowls for the empty shells, and fingerbowls, as the mussels are eaten by pulling them from the shells with the fingers, an empty shell or a small fork.

SERVES 4 TO 6

4 quarts (4 L) mussels, cleaned
1 onion or 4 shallots, minced
2 to 3 cloves garlic, minced or put through a press
2 cups (450 ml) dry white wine
4 sprigs fresh parsley
1/2 bay leaf
6 peppercorns
1/4 to 1/2 teaspoon dried thyme, to taste
3 tablespoons fresh lemon juice
2 to 3 tablespoons unsalted butter (optional)
1/4 cup (10 g) chopped fresh parsley

ITALIAN-STYLE MUSSEL SOUP
Soupe aux Moules à l'Italienne

4 quarts (4 L) mussels,
cleaned

2 tablespoons olive oil

4 large or 8 small shallots,
chopped

4 cloves garlic, minced or put
through a press

4 pounds (2 kg) tomatoes,
chopped

¼ teaspoon dried thyme, to
taste

¼ to ½ teaspoon dried
oregano, to taste

2 cups (750 ml) dry white
wine

Pinch of cayenne

Generous pinch of saffron
threads

Freshly ground pepper to taste

Salt, if necessary (the mussels
release their own salt)

¼ cup (10 g) chopped fresh
parsley

Here mussels are cooked in a gutsy tomato broth, slightly *picante* because of the cayenne. Serve this dish as a meal, like the previous recipe for *moules à la marinière*, with crusty bread and a salad, along with a southern French wine, like Côtes du Rhone, or Bandol, or a Chianti Classico.

Clean the mussels according to the instructions on page 204.

Heat the olive oil in a large flameproof casserole or soup pot big enough to eventually accommodate all the mussels. Add the shallots and garlic and cook over low heat until the shallots are tender. Add the tomatoes and stir together well. Add the thyme and oregano, bring to a simmer, cover, and cook 30 minutes. Add the white wine, cayenne, saffron, and pepper and bring to a boil. Add the mussels, cover and cook 5 minutes, shaking the pot or stirring the mussels, whichever is easiest, at least once to ensure even cooking. After 5 minutes the mussels should be opened; if not, cook a little longer, until they are all open. Immediately remove from the heat. Discarding any that refuse to open, spoon the mussels into wide soup bowls. Taste the broth and add salt only if necessary, then spoon over the mussels, sprinkle with parsley, and serve.

SERVES 6 TO 8

FILLETS OF TURBOT WITH MUSSELS AND CURRY

Filets de Turbot et Moules au Curry

I've used whiting fillets and sole as well as turbot for this elegant dish. Whiting is less expensive, but the flavor is not as distinguished as turbot. You could also use John Dory or plaice. I first made the dish for a fancy dinner party at Niki de Saint-Phalle's, and everybody was impressed by how rich tasting yet delicate it was, and how pretty it was to look at. Mussels are steamed in white wine, removed from their shells and set aside (this can be done a day in advance). Their cooking liquor is then subtly seasoned with curry and saffron and serves as a sauce for the fish fillets. The fish fillets are studded with a *mirepoix* of sautéed carrots and onions, and crowned at the end with the mussels, the saffron-colored sauce, and fresh coriander leaves.

This is one of those dishes that I will do for twenty-four or twenty-five people only when I know I will have assistance. For smaller dinner parties, count on an hour total for preparation. Since everything up to the baking of the fish can be done hours in advance, this is really a convenient dish for entertaining.

It is excellent with homemade green pasta or steamed potatoes, moistened with a spoonful of the sauce, served on the side. You might precede it with either of the cauliflower recipes that follow on pages 288 and 289, and serve Green Muscat Grapes Marinated in Muscat Wine (page 295) for dessert. As for wine, try a Cassis blanc or Châteauneuf-du-Pape blanc.

PREPARING AND COOKING THE MUSSELS: Clean the mussels according to the instructions on page 204.

Combine the wine, shallots, garlic, and parsley in a large, lidded pot or wok and bring to a boil. Add the mussels, cover,

FOR THE MUSSELS

1 ½ quarts (1 ½ L) mussels
1 ½ cups (340 ml) dry white
   wine
2 shallots, sliced
2 cloves garlic, crushed
Few sprigs fresh parsley

FOR THE FISH

3 to 4 tablespoons olive oil
2 medium-size onions, minced
½ pound (250 g) carrots,
   minced
1 ½ pounds (750 g) fillets of
   turbot
Salt and freshly ground
   pepper to taste
Juice of 1 lemon
2 bay leaves
¼ teaspoon saffron threads
1 ½ teaspoons curry powder
1 tablespoon unsalted butter
2 to 3 tablespoons chopped
   fresh coriander leaves for
   garnish

and cook 5 minutes, or until their shells open. Shake the pan once or stir the mussels with a long-handled spoon to distribute them evenly. Remove from the heat, drain, and retain the cooking liquid. Allow the mussels to cool, and when cool enough to handle, remove them from their shells. Discard any that have not opened. Place the shelled mussels in a bowl, cover, and refrigerate until ready to use. Refrigerate the cooking liquid as well.

PREPARING THE FISH: Heat 2 tablespoons olive oil in a heavy-bottomed skillet and sauté the onions and carrots over medium heat for 15 minutes, stirring from time to time. The onions should be golden but not browned. Add more oil, if necessary. Set aside.

Rinse the fish fillets and pat them dry with paper towels. Sprinkle lightly with salt and pepper on both sides. Oil a large baking dish. Spread half the onion and carrot mixture over the bottom of the baking dish and layer the fillets on top. Drizzle with the remaining olive oil and the lemon juice, top with the remaining carrots and onions, and the bay leaves. Cover tightly with foil. At this point you may refrigerate until ready to cook.

ASSEMBLING THE DISH AND FINAL COOKING: About 30 minutes before you wish to serve, preheat the oven to 425° F (220° C, gas mark 7) and remove the fish from the refrigerator. Add ½ cup (120 ml) of the mussel cooking liquid to the fish. Set the fish aside. Place the remaining cooking liquid in a saucepan and bring to a simmer. Add the saffron, curry powder, and butter and simmer 10 minutes, uncovered. Taste and adjust seasonings. Add the reserved mussels, turn off the heat, cover, and set aside.

Place the fish in the oven and bake 10 minutes. Remove from the oven when it is white and flaky, pour on the mussels and their liquid, sprinkle generously with fresh coriander, and serve.

TO PREPARE AHEAD OF TIME: The mussels can be cooked and shelled up to a day in advance, and held in a covered bowl in the refrigerator. Make sure to store their cooking liquor in a jar in the refrigerator.

You can chop the vegetables a day in advance and hold them in the refrigerator.

The whole dish, including the preparation of the fish fillets and assembling of the baking dish, can be held for several hours in the refrigerator.

SERVES 6

CAULIFLOWER GRATIN WITH GOAT CHEESE
Choufleur Gratiné au Chèvre

1 large cauliflower, about 2 pounds (1 kg), or two small ones, broken into florets

3 tablespoons olive oil or safflower oil (or less, to taste)

3/4 pound (340 g) fresh goat cheese, preferably not too salty (such as St. Christophe, Ste. Maure, or fresh local goat cheese, if available)

1 clove garlic

1/4 cup (60 ml) low-fat milk or plain low-fat yogurt

1 teaspoon fresh thyme leaves or 1/2 teaspoon dried

Freshly ground pepper to taste

6 tablespoons dry, fine breadcrumbs

This dish was inspired by Alice Waters' recipe for artichoke bottoms with a similar sauce. I had intended to make the artichoke dish for a dinner, but when I got to the market there were great big cauliflowers on sale, and my mouth began to water as I envisioned them prepared the same way.

This extremely easy dish can be assembled several hours in advance and popped into the oven 10 to 15 minutes before serving. I have used it as an entree, as I do here, as a side dish, and as the main attraction at a light dinner or lunch.

Preheat the oven to 450° F (230° C, gas mark 8). Oil a gratin or baking dish large enough to accommodate all the cauliflower.

Steam the cauliflower 10 minutes, drain, and toss with 2 tablespoons of the oil in the prepared baking dish.

In a food processor fitted with the steel blade, or in a bowl using a wooden spoon, mash the goat cheese and blend it with the garlic and milk or yogurt, the thyme, and freshly ground pepper until you have a smooth mixture.

Spread the goat cheese mixture over the cauliflower. Sprinkle on the breadcrumbs. At this point the dish can be set aside or refrigerated until ready to bake.

Just before baking, drizzle on the remaining tablespoon of oil. Place in the oven and bake 10 to 15 minutes, until the breadcrumbs are browned and the dish is sizzling. Serve at once.

TO PREPARE AHEAD OF TIME: The entire dish can be prepared several hours in advance, up to the drizzling on of the last tablespoon of oil and the baking. Hold, covered, in or out of the refrigerator.

SERVES 6

Choufleur Gratiné en Salade

Toss ½ pound (250 g) baby lamb's lettuce (mâche), red chicory, or curly endive with a mild vinaigrette. Serve the gratin surrounded by the salad, or serve them side by side.

RAVIOLI WITH CHEESE AND WILD MUSHROOMS
Raviolis au Fromage et Champignons Sauvages

R avioli, in a way, was the first thing I ever "cooked"—that is to say, the first time I was ever creative with food. I was fifteen; and before you begin envisioning me as a young girl rolling out the pasta and shaping the little squares while my friends were out cheerleading and chasing boys, let me tell you that it was canned ravioli, I was on a co-ed camping trip in Europe, and my friends and I embellished this dinner with slices of canned Vienna sausage. For some reason, seeing that you could take one dish and change the face of it by adding something to it made a great impression on me. One of the first things I told my parents, after my brother and I arrived home at the end of the summer and I'd announced that I was "really very European," was that I'd learned to make ravioli. My stepmother, who had spent two years in Rome, was beside herself with pride, and asked me what kind of ravioli I'd made. I carefully described the dish; it was, perhaps, my first recipe. My stepmother never

FOR THE PASTA

3-egg pasta dough, made with part whole-wheat pastry flour, part unbleached white, or all unbleached white flour (page 36)
Salt

FOR THE FILLING

1 1/2 ounces (45 g) dried mushrooms, such as porcini
Boiling water to cover
1 tablespoon unsalted butter or olive oil
2 cloves garlic, minced or put through a press
1 teaspoon fresh thyme leaves or 1/2 teaspoon dried
1 teaspoon chopped fresh rosemary or 1/2 teaspoon dried, crumbled
3/4 pound (340 g) ricotta cheese
4 ounces (115 g) Parmesan cheese, freshly grated (1 cup)
2 ounces (55 g) Romano pecorino cheese, freshly grated (1/2 cup)
Freshly ground pepper to taste

SUPPER CLUB
CHEZ MARTHA ROSE
290

forgot it. Years later, in Austin, I did make handmade ravioli for my parents—and served it from a can.

I know somebody else whose first culinary experiment was with ravioli. A friend brought him and his roommate some fresh ravioli from a local pasta shop. The two young men, right out of college, didn't know what to do with it; then they remembered eating baked ravioli at school. So they put the uncooked ravioli on baking sheets and baked them in a moderate oven until they were rock hard.

There *is* something very special about homemade ravioli. Perhaps it has to do with all those individual morsels, each filled and cut by loving hands. It is definitely a labor-of-love dish, one that you need time for. These cheese and wild mushroom ravioli are inspired by some tortellini I tasted in Verona, at the end of a five-day ski trip in the Dolomites. You could also fill them with the chard, herb, and cheese mixture used in the cannelloni on page 150 (omitting the eggs, or the filling will be too wet), and toss them with the same tomato sauce used for the cannelloni.

Serve with a Chianti Classico or a northern Italian wine such as a Barolo.

Make the pasta dough and allow it to rest while you make the filling.

MAKING THE FILLING: Place the mushrooms in a bowl and pour on boiling water to cover. Let steep 15 to 30 minutes, until softened. Drain, retaining the soaking liquid, and rinse thoroughly. Squeeze dry and chop fine. Strain the soaking liquid through a fine strainer and reserve it.

Heat the tablespoon of butter or olive oil in a small skillet and sauté the mushrooms, along with the garlic, thyme, and rosemary, for about 3 minutes, stirring. Remove from the heat.

Blend together the cheeses and stir in the mushrooms. Add freshly ground pepper to taste.

FILLING AND CUTTING THE RAVIOLI: Roll out the pasta

dough in strips about 5 inches wide and 12 to 18 inches (30 to 45 cm) long. Roll and fill one strip at a time; otherwise the dough will become too dry. Place the strips on a lightly floured table or board, and fold in half lengthwise, then unfold so you have a crease down the middle. Measuring every 2 inches (5 cm), place heaping teaspoons of the filling to one side of the crease, all the way down the length of the pasta. Using a pastry brush, lightly moisten the dough around each mound of filling and fold the top half over. Carefully squeeze out any air pockets around the filling, then press down gently between each mound of filling and along the bottom.

Lightly flour the strip of ravioli. Using a special crimper-cutter for pasta, a pasta cutting wheel, or a sharp knife, trim the bottom edge of the strip, then cut down between each ravioli. Place the ravioli on lightly floured baking sheets or on lightly floured parchment on top of baking sheets. Cover with plastic wrap and refrigerate until ready to cook.

COOKING THE RAVIOLI: Preheat the oven to 300° F (160° C, gas mark 2). Oil a baking dish. Cook only partially in salted, simmering water to which you have added the reserved mushroom soaking liquid. The water should not be boiling rapidly, as this could cause the pockets to open up. After 2 minutes, remove them with a slotted spoon and drain in a colander. The ravioli will finish cooking in the oven. Place in the oiled baking dish and keep warm in the medium-low oven until ready to serve.

FINAL HEATING AND SERVING: Melt the butter and olive oil together in a saucepan, add the sage leaves, and stir together over low heat for about 3 minutes. Toss with the ravioli and serve at once, passing the freshly grated Parmesan.

TO PREPARE AHEAD OF TIME: The filling and the pasta dough can be made up a day in advance. Wrap the pasta in plastic, place the filling in a covered bowl, and refrigerate.

Unlike cannelloni, ravioli are filled before they are cooked. You can hold them in the refrigerator overnight, but

FOR THE FINISHED RAVIOLI

4 tablespoons unsalted butter
1 tablespoon olive oil
2 tablespoons fresh sage leaves
½ cup (55 g) Parmesan cheese, freshly grated

do not cook them first. Place the assembled ravioli on lightly floured pieces of parchment, dust the tops so that they won't stick, and cover with plastic. The ravioli can also be frozen. In this case don't roll the dough quite as thin, because it becomes very brittle when it's frozen and tends to break when you handle it. Place on lightly floured pieces of parchment, flour the top, cover with plastic or parchment, then wrap in foil. Transfer frozen ravioli directly from the freezer to simmering water.

The ravioli can be cooked a couple of hours ahead of serving time and held in an oiled baking dish. Warm in the oven as indicated in the recipe.

SERVES 6 (ABOUT 80 TO 85 RAVIOLI)

NOTE: You may end up with more pasta than filling. But that's better than having more filling than pasta. Freeze the remaining pasta dough, or roll out, cut, and dry. You could also serve these ravioli in a chicken or mushroom broth, with a little parsley and freshly grated Parmesan.

If using the chard filling on page 150, heat the tomato sauce and toss with the ravioli just before serving, or place the ravioli in individual bowls or plates and spoon the tomato sauce over the top. Serve, passing additional freshly grated Parmesan.

FRESH HOMEMADE PASTA WITH PESTO
Pâtés Maison au Pistou

Pesto has become so popular in the United States that in many cities fancy delis and charcuteries sell it year round. But it's easy to make yourself.

Toward the end of August, I begin to make large batches of pesto to freeze for small dinner parties. I try to make enough to get me through the winter. The women in the St.-Germain market who sell the best, most opulent basil, know me very well, as I rarely go by their stand without purchasing at least four generous bunches, enough for a double batch of pesto.

I began giving pesto dinners one summer when a number of friends and friends of friends were in from the States. I would make up the pasta dough in the morning and roll it out right before I cooked it. Sometimes I'd make the pesto in the morning, other times my guests would join in, picking leaves off the stems. These were rather impromptu dinners—I was determined not to devote much time to them during the day —and everybody pitched in.

Sometimes I cook all the pasta at once and toss it with the sauce. I find, though, that when I have more than six people the pasta stays hotter if I cook each batch separately (it only takes seconds), transfer the noodles to a warm plate, spoon on the pesto and run it out to the table. I tell everyone to begin eating as soon as they get their plate so it won't get cold. I've served it this way for up to ten people.

Accompany with a big green or mixed salad and a hearty red wine from southern France or Italy, such as a Gigondas, Bandol, Barolo or Chianti.

MAKING THE PESTO FOR IMMEDIATE USE: Place the basil, pine nuts or walnuts, garlic, and salt in the bowl of a food

FOR THE PESTO

2 cups (2 ounces, 60 grams), tightly packed fresh basil leaves

2 tablespoons pine nuts or broken walnuts

2 large cloves garlic

1/4 teaspoon salt (or more, to taste)

1/2 cup (120 ml) fruity olive oil

2 ounces Parmesan cheese, freshly grated (1/2 cup)

2 tablespoons freshly grated Romano pecorino cheese

Freshly ground pepper

FAVORITE DISHES FROM
SMALL DINNER PARTIES

293

processor, a blender jar, or a mortar and pestle. Process or pound until finely chopped or pureed. Slowly add the olive oil and continue to process until the mixture is smooth and uniform. Stir in the cheeses and freshly ground pepper.

Making pesto for the freezer: Omit the cheeses. Stir in when you thaw the pesto, and correct seasonings.

FOR THE PASTA AND SERVING

Fresh pasta, either whole-wheat, spinach or herb, for 4 to 6 people (see page 36), cut into fettuccine, tagliarini (thinner than fettuccine), or spaghetti noodles

Salt

2 tablespoons butter, at room temperature

COOKING THE PASTA, SERVING: The pasta dough can be made before or after you make the pesto. Just before you serve the pesto, bring a large pot of salted water to a rolling boil. Have plates warming in the oven. Cook the pasta for just a few seconds, al dente. You can cook it all at once, or cook individual servings. Remove from the boiling water with a large deep-fry skimmer, place on a warm plate, and top with a generous spoonful of pesto (about 2 tablespoons) and a little bit of butter. The water on the pasta will thin out the pesto. Or drain the pasta in a collander, return it to the hot cooking pot and toss with butter and the pesto. Serve at once.

TO PREPARE AHEAD OF TIME: Pesto will hold for several days in the refrigerator, and can be frozen. Of course it is most fragrant when the basil is at its freshest.

The pasta dough will hold in the refrigerator for a day, and you can roll out the pasta and hold the noodles, dusting them well, in the refrigerator, or dry or freeze them.

SERVES 4 TO 6

GREEN MUSCAT GRAPES MARINATED IN MUSCAT WINE

Muscats au Muscat de Beaumes de Venise

Green Muscat grapes, with their distinctive sweet flavor, are my favorite European grapes. I have seen them in markets in New York and California, imported from Italy. The wine made from the Muscat grape is sweet and fruity, and tastes exactly like the grape. The most famous comes from a little town in the Vaucluse, along the "Route des Vins," called Beaumes de Venise. You could as easily use a good Muscat from another town, or a Corsican Muscat.

Remove the grapes from their stems, cut them in half, and remove the seeds. Toss in the wine and refrigerate several hours before serving. Serve in bowls, with some of the wine spooned over the grapes.

SERVES 4 TO 6

2 pounds (1 kg) Muscat
  grapes
2 cups (750 ml) Muscat wine

COFFEE BAVARIAN CREAM
WITH KAHLÚA
Crème Bavarois au Kahlúa

6 large eggs plus 2 egg yolks,
   at room temperature

2 envelopes unflavored gelatin

½ cup (120 ml) strongly
   brewed coffee, such as
   espresso

⅔ cup (140 ml) mild-flavored
   honey

1½ cups (340 ml) milk

½ teaspoon peppermint
   extract

¼ cup (60 ml) Kahlúa
   liqueur, plus 1 to 2
   tablespoons additional for
   the whipped cream

1 teaspoon vanilla

2 teaspoons brandy

¼ teaspoon cream of tartar

⅛ teaspoon salt

1 cup (220 ml) heavy cream,
   chilled

This recipe is in my first cookbook, *The Vegetarian Feast.* It's such a good dessert, with that subtle coffee taste and the drop of mint that surprises the palate, that I often serve it at small dinner parties. Since coming up with the original recipe I've reduced the quantity of honey a bit and increased the egg whites by one, but I haven't made any other changes.

The dish involves several steps, so if you can, you should probably make it the day before you wish to serve it. It will hold in the refrigerator for a couple of days and needs at least 5 hours to set.

MAKING THE CUSTARD: Separate the eggs, placing the whites in a large, very clean bowl and the yolks, plus the two extra, in a second bowl (keep the extra egg whites in a bowl in the refrigerator, or freeze them).

Dissolve the gelatin in the coffee in a small, heavy-bottomed pan. Set it aside on the stove.

Beat the egg yolks and the honey together, using an electric mixer, until thick and lemon colored.

Meanwhile, heat the milk in a heavy-bottomed saucepan over medium heat until you see the surface begin to tremble. Making sure it is not boiling, slowly pour the scalded milk into the egg-honey mixture, beating all the while.

Transfer the milk and eggs back into the saucepan and place over a very low flame, or on a flame tamer over a low flame. Heat through, stirring, being careful not to let the mixture come to a boil, or the eggs will curdle. When the mixture reaches 168° F (75° C) small wisps of steam will appear and it will begin to thicken. It should coat both sides of a wooden spoon like cream. This usually takes a while if you are as paranoid about having the heat too high as I am. As soon as the mixture thickens, remove it from the heat and stir for a minute or so to cool.

Heat the coffee-gelatin mixture, stirring over very low heat to dissolve the crystals completely, then whisk it into the custard, being careful to scrape every last bit of it out of the bowl with a rubber spatula. Strain this mixture into a 3-quart bowl and stir in the peppermint extract, Kahlúa, brandy, and the vanilla. Set aside.

BEATING THE EGG WHITES: Begin beating the egg whites. When they begin to foam, add the cream of tartar and the salt. Beat until they form stiff, shiny (but not dry) peaks, then stir one-fourth into the custard, and gently fold in the rest.

BEATING THE CREAM: Leaving ½ cup (120 ml) of the cream in the refrigerator to chill further, beat the remainder in a chilled 1-quart bowl, circulating your beater or whisk to incorporate as much air as possible. Beat the cream until doubled in volume and until it adheres softly to a spoon when lifted, but not until it is stiff.

Stir the custard so it begins to set evenly. If you don't do this, the gelatin will settle at the bottom. Allow it to cool for about 10 minutes, stirring every minute or so, then gently fold in the whipped cream. Pour the Bavarian cream into a soufflé dish or a mold of your choice or into individual ramekins. Cover well and refrigerate for at least 5 hours, or overnight. Keep chilled until ready to serve.

Just before serving time, whip the remaining cream and flavor it with the remaining 1 to 2 tablespoons (to taste) Kahlúa. Serve from the soufflé dish or in ramekins, or unmold by dipping the mold in hot water for a few seconds and reversing it onto a serving plate. Refrigerate for a few minutes again to set. Top with the Kahlúa-flavored whipped cream.

SERVES 6 TO 8

HONEY MOUSSE
Mousse au Miel

This was inspired by a recipe in *Chez Panisse Desserts* by Lindsey Remolif Shere, which is delicious but very rich because of all the cream. I replaced half the cream with beaten egg whites, and have come up with a mousse that is very light in comparison, with the same lovely flavor. Make sure you use a very light honey for this—clover or acacia—or it will be cloying. Also, be sure to fold the gelatin mixture into the cream and egg whites thoroughly, or it will settle.

Serve with marinated fruit, or topped with crème de cassis liqueur.

1 teaspoon unflavored gelatin
1 tablespoon water
2/3 cup (140 ml) heavy cream
1/2 teaspoon vanilla
3 large egg whites
1/4 cup (60 ml) mild-flavored honey
2 to 3 teaspoons Grand Marnier, to taste

Sprinkle the gelatin into the water in a heavy-bottomed saucepan. Let stand to soften.

Beat the cream until it forms a soft shape when dropped from the beaters. Beat in the vanilla.

Beat the egg whites to soft peaks with clean beaters in a separate bowl.

Stir the gelatin mixture over very low heat. Stir constantly, and when the gelatin is thoroughly dissolved, stir in the honey. Continue to stir over low heat until you have a smooth, uniform mixture. Remove from the heat and stir until the mixture begins to thicken (placing the bowl or pan in a bowl of ice water will hasten the process).

Quickly beat the honey mixture into the whipped cream. Add the Grand Marnier and fold in the egg whites. Place the bowl in a larger bowl of cold water and continue to fold gently for about 5 minutes. Transfer to a soufflé dish, or a serving bowl, cover, and refrigerate several hours. Scoop out with a soup spoon and place rounded side up on plates to serve.

This will keep for a couple of days in the refrigerator.

SERVES 4 TO 6

CRÊPES FILLED WITH LEMON SOUFFLÉ, WITH STRAWBERRY PUREE

Crêpes Soufflées au Citron, Coulis de Fraises

I was introduced to this showy dessert when I ordered it at a Paris restaurant called Le Petit Montmorency. It makes a grand and unforgettable finale. Dessert crêpes are filled with a very light lemon soufflé, baked in a hot oven for 7 minutes, and served on a bright red strawberry puree (you could also use a raspberry puree). It's not the kind of dessert I'd make for Supper Club, but for a small dinner party it's dramatic, served hot and puffed from the oven.

MAKING THE CRÊPES: Break the eggs into the bowl of a food processor fitted with the steel blade, or into a blender, and add the water, milk, Grand Marnier, sugar, and salt. Turn on the blender and slowly add the flour and melted butter or oil. Blend thoroughly for 1 to 2 minutes. Let sit, in or out of the refrigerator, for at least 30 minutes before making the crêpes.

Make the crêpes in a heavy steel or nonstick crêpe pan. Heat the pan over a medium-high flame and brush with butter. It should sizzle and be just short of smoking. Lift up the pan with one hand, and with the other pour in a scant 1/4 cup (55 ml, or about 3 1/2 tablespoons or a little less) crêpe batter. Swirl the pan to distribute the batter evenly and place over the heat. Cook for 1 to 2 minutes, until the edges brown and come away easily from the pan. Using a wooden spatula or a knife, turn the crêpe over and cook 30 seconds or less on the other side. Turn onto a plate. Brush the pan and continue to make the crêpes, stacking them as they are done, until you have used up all the batter.

If you are going to hold the crêpes for more than a few hours in the refrigerator, stack them between pieces of wax

FOR THE CRÊPES

3 large eggs
1/2 cup (120 ml) water
1/2 cup (120 ml) low-fat milk
1/4 cup (60 ml) Grand Marnier
2 tablespoons raw light brown sugar
Pinch of salt
7/8 cup (1 cup less 2 tablespoons, 100 g) unbleached white flour
2 tablespoons unsalted butter, melted, or safflower oil
Unsalted butter for the crêpe pan

paper or parchment. Freeze extra crêpes and use for another purpose.

FOR THE STRAWBERRY PUREE

1 ½ pounds (750 g, 2 pints)
fresh strawberries, hulled
Juice of ½ lemon
1 tablespoon mild-flavored
honey or sugar

FOR THE SOUFFLÉ

6 tablespoons raw light brown
sugar
1 tablespoon mild-flavored
honey
⅓ cup (90 ml) plus 1
tablespoon fresh lemon juice
5 large egg whites
¼ teaspoon cream of tartar
Pinch of salt
Finely chopped zest of 2
lemons
1 teaspoon cornstarch
2 tablespoons unsalted butter
for the dish

MAKING THE STRAWBERRY PUREE: Hull the strawberries and puree in a blender or food processor until smooth. Add the lemon juice and honey or sugar, and set aside.

MAKING THE SOUFFLÉ BATTER: Preheat the oven to 425° F (220° C, gas mark 7). Generously butter one large or two medium-size gratin dishes, using about 1 tablespoon butter.

Dissolve the sugar and honey in the lemon juice in a saucepan double the volume of the lemon juice (1 pint or 1 quart).

Beat the egg whites at low speed until they begin to foam. Add the cream of tartar and salt and continue to beat at high speed until stiff, shiny peaks form. Turn off the mixer.

Heat the lemon juice mixture over high heat until it comes to a boil (you need the large saucepan because the honey will bubble up dramatically and overflow in a small saucepan). Cover, with the lid not quite tight, and boil hard for a minute or two, until the mixture reaches the soft-ball stage, 238° F (120° C).

Start beating the egg whites again at moderate speed and slowly dribble in the lemon juice syrup. When it has all been added, turn up the speed to high and continue to beat until the egg whites are tepid and glossy, and form stiff peaks when lifted with a spatula. Beat in the lemon zest and cornstarch, and remove the beaters.

FILLING, BAKING AND SERVING THE CRÊPES: Place a crêpe in the buttered gratin dish or dishes and spoon on 2 heaping tablespoons of the soufflé mixture. Gently fold the crêpe in half over the mixture and push it to one end of the dish. Fill all the crêpes like this, and dot the tops with the remaining butter, or they will stiffen in the oven.

Place the baking dishes in the preheated oven and bake

7 minutes, until the soufflé is puffed and just beginning to color on the edges.

Meanwhile spoon the strawberry puree onto individual dessert plates.

When the crêpes are ready, place two on each plate, on top of the puree, and serve at once.

TO PREPARE AHEAD OF TIME: The crêpes can be prepared a day ahead of time and held in the refrigerator. They also freeze very well.

The strawberry puree can be made hours before you wish to serve it and held in the refrigerator. It can be served cold or at room temperature with the crêpes.

The soufflé batter will hold for 30 minutes at room temperature. If it falls a little, beat again before using. The crêpes must be assembled and baked right before serving, and served immediately.

SERVES 4 TO 6 (16 TO 18 CRÊPES)

Index

Aïoli monstre (Lulu's huge
vegetable and fish platter
with garlic mayonnaise),
272–273
Almond
and cornmeal shortbread,
110
cookies, crisp, 88–89
piecrust, 41
Alsatian apple cake, 251
Apple
cake, 251
endive, apple, and walnut
salad, 213
pumpkin, sweet potato, and
apple puree, 86
Apricot
and peach salad with currants,
252
and plum tart, 193–194
Artichauts à la barigoule
(artichokes with
tomatoes, garlic, and
Provençal herbs),
243–244
Artichokes with tomatoes, garlic,
and Provençal herbs,
243–244
Avocado(s)
and sweet and sour red
peppers, salad of, 241
guacamole nachos, 115
tomato halves stuffed with
guacamole, 55

Baguettes, sourdough, 29–30
Baguettes de campagne (sourdough
baguettes), 29–30
Baked
fish fillets with salsa, 56
fresh figs with crème anglaise,
72–73
tomatoes, 192
whiting with tomato-caper
sauce, 182–183
Banana-pineapple-orange mint
sherbet, 122–123
Bavarian cream, coffee, with
Kahlúa, 296–297
Bean(s)
black bean frijoles refritos,
54
black bean nachos, 52–53
green, vinaigrette, 148–149
salad, Mexican, 214–215
salad, with warm green beans
and walnuts, 104
with rice salad, 80–82
Beaujolais
Beaujolais nouveau day, 79
pears poached in, 90
Beet garnish, 149
Berries, mangos, and peaches in
sweet white wine, 208
Biscotti di prato (crisp almond
cookies), 88–89
Black bean
frijoles refritos, 54
nachos, 52–53

Black-eyed pea salad à la
mexicaine, 215–216
*Blini au saumon, fromage blanc,
oeufs, et caviar* (blini with
salmon and fromage blanc,
egg, and caviar filling),
218
Blini(s), 45
with salmon and fromage
blanc, egg, and caviar filling,
218
Blue corn masa crêpes, 120–
121
Bouillon, vinegar court, 170
Bran, sourdough country bread
with, 21
Brandade de morue (salt cod
mousse), 264–266
Bread
cornmeal and millet, 26–27
country, with olives, 32–33
country rye, with raisins,
22–24
cumin and cornmeal, 28
freezing, 18
herbed whole-wheat, 30–31
millet and cornmeal, 26–27
mixed grains, 24–26
pesto, 34–35
sourdough baguettes, 29–30
sourdough country, 18–20
sourdough country, with
cornmeal and oats or bran,
21

Bread *(continued)*
  sourdough country, with
    raisins, 22
  Texas cornbread, 35
Broccoli
  and ravioli salad, 128–129
  puree, 83
Broth, garlic, 117
Buckwheat pasta, 37
  with Oriental salad, 166–167
Buffet, Tex-Mex, 200

Cabillaud en escabeche (marinated
    cod in escabeche), 118–119
Cake(s)
  Alsatian apple, 251
  Texas tea, 121
Cannelloni with chard, herb, and
    ricotta filling, 150–152
Cannellonis printanières
    (cannelloni with chard,
    herb, and ricotta filling),
    150–152
Cauliflower gratin with goat
    cheese, 288–289
Cerise aigres-douces (sweet and
    sour cherry pickles), 96
Ceviche, 158–159
Chalupa(s)
  crisps, 44
  extraordinaires, 160–161
Champagne and grapefruit juice
    punch, 166
Champignons poêlés (pan-fried
    mushrooms), 153
Chard, herb, and ricotta filling,
    with cannelloni, 150–152
Cheese
  cauliflower gratin with goat
    cheese, 288–289
  crudités with goat cheese and
    herb dip, 203

endive salad with baked goat
    cheese, 139–140
  pasta primavera with roasted
    red peppers and goat
    cheese, 188–189
  ravioli with cheese and wild
    mushrooms, 289–292
Cherry
  clafouti, 250
  pickles, sweet and sour, 96
Chick-peas
  hummus, 219
Chips, tortilla, 44
Choufleur gratiné au chèvre
    (cauliflower gratin with goat
    cheese), 288–289
Choufleur gratiné en salade
    (cauliflower gratin with
    salad), 289
"Chowder" à la provençale
    (Provençal-style fish soup),
    141–142
Christine's creamy cucumber
    salad, 242
Citrus and date gratin, 133–134
Clafouti, cherry, 250
Clafouti aux cerises (cherry
    clafouti), 250
Cod, marinated in escabeche,
    118–119
Coffee Bavarian cream with
    Kahlúa, 296–297
Cointreau, strawberries and
    oranges with, 154
Concombres poêlés (pan-fried
    cucumbers), 58
Cookies
  cornmeal and almond
    shortbread, 110
  crisp almond, 88–89
  honey-lemon refrigerator,
    60
  Texas tea cakes, 121
Corn

blue corn masa crêpes,
    120–121
Cornbread
  stuffing, 97
  Texas, 35
Cornmeal
  and almond shortbread, 110
  and cumin bread, 28
  and millet bread, 26–27
  and oats in sourdough country
    bread, 21
Coucou à l'iranienne (Iranian
    omelet with parsley and
    mint), 249–250
*Courgettes et poivrons rouges poêlés
    dans ses barquettes de poivrons*
    (sauteed zucchini and red
    peppers in bell pepper
    boats), 206
Courgettes poêlées (pan-fried
    zucchini with parsley
    butter), 161
Court bouillon, vinegar, 170
Cranberry relish, 87
Crème anglaise
  ginger, with pear crisp,
    143–144
  with baked fresh figs, 72–73
Crème bavarois au Kahlúa (coffee
    Bavarian cream with
    Kahlúa), 296–297
Crème de concombres (Christine's
    creamy cucumber salad),
    242
Crêpes
  blue corn masa, 120–121
  filled with lemon soufflé, with
    strawberry puree, 299–301
*Crêpes soufflés au citron, coulis de
    fraises* (crêpes filled with
    lemon soufflé, with
    strawberry puree), 299–301
Crisp almond cookies, 88–89
Croutons, garlic, 46

Croutons à l'ail (garlic croutons), 46
Crudités aux chèvre (crudités with goat cheese and herb dip), 203
Crudités with goat cheese and herb dip, 203
Cucumber(s)
  pan-fried, 58
  salad, creamy, 242
Cumin
  and cornmeal bread, 28
  with orange and olive salad, 274
Curly endive salad with baked goat cheese, 139–140
Currants, peach and apricot salad with, 252
Curry, fillets of turbot with, 285–287

Date and citrus gratin, 133–134
Deep-dish eggplant torte, 129–132
Délices d'airelles (pucker-up cranberry relish), 87
Délices de poires avec crème anglaise au gingembre (pear crisp with ginger crème anglaise), 143–144
Dessert piecrust, 42
Desserts
  Alsatian apple cake, 251
  baked fresh figs with crème anglaise, 72–73
  cherry clafouti, 250
  citrus and date gratin, 133–134
  coffee Bavarian cream with Kahlúa, 296–297
  crêpes filled with lemon

soufflé, with strawberry puree, 299–301
  fig tart with green grapes, 74–75
  green muscat grapes marinated in muscat wine, 295
  honey mousse, 298
  mangos, peaches, and berries in sweet white wine, 208
  peach and apricot salad with currants, 252
  peach sherbet with peach garnish, 58–59
  peach tart, 180
  peaches in red wine, with honey and cinnamon, 252
  pear crisp with ginger crème anglaise, 143–144
  pears poached in Beaujolais, 90
  pecan pie, 99
  pineapple-orange-banana mint sherbet, 122–123
  plum and apricot tart, 193–194
  pumpkin pie, 100
  strawberries and oranges with Cointreau, 154
  strawberry sherbet, 162
  tangerine sherbet, 109
  watermelon fruit basket, 207–208
Dinner parties, small, 277–301
Domaine Tempier, 255–263
Drinks
  champagne and grapefruit juice punch, 166
  margaritas, 51

Egg-lemon sauce with cold poached fillets of fish, 190–191

Eggplant
  ratatouille, 227–228
  torte, deep-dish, 129–132
Eggs and vegetables with olive paste, 68
En papillote
  new potatoes, 179
  salmon trout, 244–245
Endive, apple, and walnut salad, 213
Entertaining on a small or grand scale, 6–8

Farce au pain de mais (cornbread stuffing), 97
Fennel
  lemon, fennel, and mushroom salad, 217
  sautéed, and red peppers, 108
Fenouil et poivrons poêlés (sautéed fennel and red peppers), 108
Fig(s)
  baked, with crème anglaise, 72–73
  tart with green grapes, 74–75
Figues au four à la crème anglaise (baked fresh figs with crème anglaise), 72–73
Filets de poisson à la marseillaise (cold steamed fish fillets with tomato-caper sauce), 178–179
Filets de poisson à la salsa (baked fish fillets with salsa), 56
Filets de sole pochés à la sauce vierge (poached fillets of sole with pureed tomato sauce), 168–170
Filets de turbot et moules au curry (fillets of turbot with mussels and curry), 285–287

Fish and seafood
  baked fish fillets with salsa, 56
  baked whiting with
    tomato-caper sauce,
    182–183
  ceviche, 158–159
  cold poached fillets, with
    egg-lemon sauce, 190–191
  cold steamed fillets with
    tomato-caper sauce,
    178–179
  crazy salad with tuna tartare,
    176–177
  fillets of turbot with mussels
    and curry, 285–287
  grilled sardines, 268–269
  Iranian rice with monkfish
    ragout, 246–248
  Lulu's grilled fish, 269–270
  Lulu's vegetable and fish
    platter with garlic
    mayonnaise, 272–273
  marinated cod in escabeche,
    118–119
  Mexican-style mussels on the
    half shell, 203–204
  mussels steamed in white
    wine, 283
  poached fillets of sole with
    pureed tomato sauce,
    168–170
  Provençal-style fish soup,
    141–142
  salmon, with blini, 218
  salmon trout en papillote,
    244–245
  salt cod mousse, 264–266
  sardines marinated in vinegar,
    266–267
  squid ragout, 270–271
  tuna (or swordfish) with
    tomato-caper sauce, 267
Frijoles refritos, black bean, 54
Fromage blanc, egg, and caviar
  filling, with blini, 218

Fruit basket, watermelon,
  207–208
Fruit dishes
  Alsatian apple cake, 251
  baked fresh figs with crème
    anglaise, 72–73
  cherry clafouti, 250
  citrus and date gratin,
    133–134
  fig tart with green grapes,
    74–75
  green muscat grapes marinated
    in muscat wine, 295
  mangos, peaches, and berries
    in sweet white wine, 208
  peach sherbet with peach
    garnish, 58–59
  peach tart, 180
  peaches and apricot salad with
    currants, 252
  peaches in red wine, with
    honey and cinnamon, 252
  pear crisp with ginger crème
    anglaise, 143–144
  pears poached in Beaujolais,
    90
  pineapple-orange-banana mint
    sherbet, 122–123
  plum and apricot tart,
    193–194
  strawberries and oranges with
    Cointreau, 154
  strawberry sherbet, 162
  tangerine sherbet, 109
  watermelon fruit basket,
    207–208
  See also names of individual fruits

Galettes au mais bleu (blue corn
  masa crêpes), 120–121
Galettes au miel et au citron
  (honey-lemon refrigerator
  cookies), 60

Galettes texanes (Texas tea cakes),
  121
Garlic
  broth, 117
  croutons, 46
  mayonnaise, 272–273
Garnish
  beet, 149
  peach, 59
  tangerine, 109
Gâteau alsacien aux pommes
  (Alsatian apple cake), 251
Ginger crème anglaise with pear
  crisp, 143–144
Goat cheese
  and herb dip with crudités,
    203
  and roasted red peppers with
    pasta primavera, 188–189
  baked, with endive salad,
    139–140
  with cauliflower gratin,
    288–289
  with crudités, 203
Grapefruit juice and champagne
  punch, 166
Grapes
  green, with fig tart, 74–75
  green muscat, marinated in
    muscat wine, 295
Gratin
  cauliflower, with goat cheese,
    288–289
  citrus and date, 133–134
  low-fat, 275
  potato, 274–275
  potato with sorrel, 275
Gratin dauphinois (Lulu's potato
  gratin), 274–275
Gratin de fruits d'hiver (citrus and
  date gratin), 133–134
Gravy, mushroom ragout, 98–
  99
Green bean(s)
  and walnuts with salad, 104

vinaigrette with beet garnish, 148–149
with rice salad, 80–82
Green grapes
marinated in muscat wine, 295
with fig tart, 74–75
Green lasagne with spinach filling, 105–107
Grilled sardines, 268–269
Guacamole
nachos, 115
tomato halves stuffed with, 55

Haricots verts en vinaigrette (green beans vinaigrette), 148–149
Herb, chard, and ricotta filling, with cannelloni, 150–152
Herb butter, and sweet peas, with pasta, 183
Herb pasta, 36–37
Herbed whole-wheat bread, 30–31
Homemade pasta, 36–39
with pesto, 293–294
Homemade tortillas, 43–44
Honey
-lemon refrigerator cookies, 60
mousse, 298
note on, 11
Hors d'oeuvres
black bean nachos, 52
guacamole nachos, 115
Mexican-style mussels on the half shell, 203–204
mixed Provençal, 64
salt cod mousse, 164
stuffed jalapeños, 201
sweet and sour cherry pickles, 96
sweet and sour red peppers, 241
tapenade, 67

tomato halves stuffed with guacamole, 55
vegetables and eggs with olive paste, 68
Hummus, 219

Increasing recipes for large groups, 8
Iranian
omelet with parsley and mint, 249–250
rice with monkfish ragout, 246–248
Italian-style mussel soup, 284

Jalapeños, stuffed, 201

Kahlúa, coffee Bavarian cream with, 296–297

Lamb's lettuce salad, 69
Lasagne, green, with spinach filling, 105–107
Lasagne aux epinards (green lasagne with spinach filling), 105–107
Légumes à la grecque (vegetables à la grecque), 181–182
Lemon
-egg sauce with cold poached fillets of fish, 190–191
fennel, lemon, and mushroom salad, 217
-honey refrigerator cookies, 60
soufflé, crêpes filled with, 299–301
Lettuce, lamb's, salad, 69

Low-fat *gratin dauphinois* (potato gratin), 275
Lulu's recipes, 255–275
grilled fish, 269–270
huge vegetable and fish platter with garlic mayonnaise, 272–273
potato gratin, 274–275
potato gratin with sorrel, 275

Mangos, peaches, and berries in sweet white wine, 208
Mangues, pêches, et fruits rouges au vin doux (mangos, peaches, and berries in sweet white wine), 208
Margaritas, 51
Marinated cod in escabeche, 118–119
Mayonnaise, garlic, 272
Menus
chez Christine, 233–234
for a cool summer evening, 174
for a hot evening, 173
for Beaujolais nouveau day, 77
for small dinner parties, 279–280
from Domaine Tempier, 253
Mexican, 47, 111
migathon, 199
New Year's Eve, 209–210
picnic, 221
Provençal dinner, 61
spring, 135, 145
summer, 163
Tex-Mex, 155
Tex-Mex buffet, 200
Thanksgiving delights, 91–92
winter, 125
winter holiday, 101

Merlans à la marseillaise (baked whiting with tomato-caper sauce), 182–183

Metric equivalents, 11

Mexican
bean salad, 214–215
food, 49–57, 111–121
rice, 57
rice salad, 205
-style mussels on the half shell, 203–204

Migas, Steve's, 202

Millet and cornmeal bread, 26–27

Mixed grains bread, 24–26

Moules à la marinière (mussels steamed in white wine), 283

Moules à la mexicaine (Mexican-style mussels on the half shell), 203–204

Mousse
honey, 298
salt cod, 264–266

Mousse au miel (honey mousse), 298

Muscats au muscat de Beaumes de venise (green muscat grapes marinated in muscat wine), 295

Mushroom(s)
fennel, mushroom, and lemon salad, 217
pan-fried, 153
ragout gravy, 98–99
tart, 84–85
wild, and cheese, with ravioli, 289–292

Mussel(s)
and curry, with fillets of turbot, 285–287
on the half shell, Mexican-style, 203–204
soup, Italian-style, 284
steamed in white wine, 283

Nachos
black bean, 52–53
guacamole, 115

Nachos aux avocats (guacamole nachos), 115

Nachos aux haricots noirs (black bean nachos), 52–53

New potatoes en papillote, 179

Niçoise salad hero sandwiches, 226

Nuts. *See* Almond(s); Pecan(s); Walnut(s)

Oats and cornmeal in sourdough country bread, 21

Olive
and orange salad, with cumin, 274
bread, 32–33
paste, 67
paste, vegetables and eggs with, 68

Omelet, Iranian, with parsley and mint, 249–250

Onion pizza, Provençal, 228–229

Orange(s)
and olive salad with cumin, 274
and strawberries, with Cointreau, 154
-mint garnish, 122
-pineapple-banana mint sherbet, 122–123

Oriental salad with homemade buckwheat pasta, 166–167

Pain au basilic (pesto bread), 34–35

Pain au cumin (cumin and cornmeal bread), 28

Pain au millet et au mais (millet and cornmeal bread), 26–27

Pain aux cereales (mixed grains bread), 24–26

Pain aux herbes (herbed whole-wheat bread), 30–31

Pain aux raisins (sourdough country bread with raisins), 22

Pain bagnat (Niçoise salad hero sandwiches), 226

Pain de campagne (sourdough country bread), 18–20

Pain de campagne au mais et à l'avoine (sourdough country bread with cornmeal and oats or bran), 21

Pain de campagne au seigle et aux raisins secs (country rye bread with raisins), 22–24

Pain de campagne aux olives (country bread with olives), 32–33

Pain de mais à l'américaine (Texas cornbread), 35

Pan-fried
cucumbers, 58
mushrooms, 153
zucchini with parsley butter, 161

Panier de pastegues aux fruits (watermelon fruit basket), 207–208

Parsley butter with pan-fried zucchini, 161

Pasta
buckwheat, 37
cannelloni with chard, herb, and ricotta filling, 150–152
green lasagne with spinach filling, 105–107
herb, 36–37
homemade, 36–39

homemade, with pesto, 293–294

homemade buckwheat, with Oriental salad, 166–167

primavera with roasted red peppers and goat cheese, 188–189

ravioli and broccoli salad, 128–129

ravioli with cheese and wild mushrooms, 289–292

regular, 36

spinach, 37

whole-wheat, 37

with sweet peas and herb butter, 183

Pâtés brisées complètes (whole-wheat piecrusts), 39–42

Pâtés fraiches maison (homemade pasta), 36–39

Pâtés maison au pistou (fresh homemade pasta with pesto), 293–294

Pâtés printanières aux poivrons rôtis et au chèvre (pasta primavera with roasted red peppers and goat cheese), 188–189

Peach(es)

and apricot salad with currants, 252

garnish, 59

in red wine with honey and cinnamon, 252

mangos, peaches, and berries in sweet white wine, 208

sherbet with peach garnish, 58–59

tart, 180

Pear(s)

crisp with ginger crème anglaise, 143–144

poached in Beaujolais, 90

Peas

and herb butter with pasta, 183

black-eyed pea salad, 215–216

Pecan pie, 99

Pêches au vin rouge (peaches in red wine with honey and cinnamon), 252

Peppers

red, and sautéed fennel, 108

red, and sautéed zucchini, 206

red, sweet and sour, 241

roasted, sweet red, 66

roasted, with pasta primavera, 188–189

sautéed, red and yellow, 132

Pesto, 293–294

bread, 34–35

Provençal vegetable soup with, 70–71

with tomatoes, 225

Petits gâteaux aux amandes et au mais (cornmeal and almond shortbread), 110

Peyraud, Lulu, xiii, 63, 227, 255–263; recipes, 264–275

Picasso, Christine Ruiz, 235–240; recipes, 241–251

Pickles, sweet and sour cherry, 96

Picnic, 223–224

menu, 221

Pie

pecan, 99

pumpkin, 100

Piecrust

almond, 41

dessert, 42

general technique, 40–41

savory whole-wheat, 42

whole-wheat, 39–42

Piments farcis (stuffed jalapeños), 201

Pineapple-orange-banana mint sherbet, 122–123

Pissaladière (Provençal onion pizza), 228–229

Pistou. *See* Pesto

Pizza, Provençal onion, 228–229

Plum and apricot tart, 193–194

Poached

cold fillets of fish with egg-lemon sauce, 190–191

fillets of sole with pureed tomato sauce, 168–170

pears, 90

Poires pochées au Beaujolais (pears poached in Beaujolais), 90

Poisson grillé (Lulu's grilled fish), 269–270

Poivrons aigres-doux (sweet and sour red peppers), 241

Poivrons rôtis (roasted sweet red peppers), 66

Poivrons rouges et jaunes poêlés (sautéed red and yellow peppers), 132

Pommes de terres nouvelles en papillote (new potatoes en papillote), 179

Potato(es)

gratin, 274–275

new, en papillote, 179

Provençal food, 61–75

fish soup, 141–142

hors d'oeuvres, 64

onion pizza, 228–229

vegetable soup with pesto, 70–71

Pumpkin

pie, 100

sweet potato, and apple puree, 86

Punch

champagne and grapefruit juice, 166

Punch au champagne, pamplemousse, et cassis (champagne and grapefruit juice punch), 166

Puree
  broccoli, 83
  pumpkin, sweet potato, and
    apple, 86
Purée de brocolis (broccoli puree),
  83
Purée de potiron, patates, et pommes
  (pumpkin, sweet potato, and
  apple puree), 86

Ragout
  monkfish, with Iranian rice,
    246–248
  mushroom, 98–99
  squid, 270–271
Ragoût de calmars (squid ragout),
  270–271
Raisin bread
  country rye, 22–24
  sourdough country, 22
Ratatouille, 227–228
Ravioli
  and broccoli salad, 128–129
  with cheese and wild
    mushrooms, 289–292
*Raviolis au fromage et champignons
  sauvages* (ravioli with cheese
  and wild mushrooms),
  289–292
Recipes for large groups, 8
Red peppers. *See* Peppers
Refrigerator cookies,
  honey-lemon, 60
Relish, cranberry, 87
Rice
  and zucchini mold, 65
  Iranian, with monkfish ragout,
    246–248
  Mexican, 57
  salad, Mexican, 205
  salad with green beans, 80–
    82

Ricotta, chard, and herb filling,
  with cannelloni, 150–152
Riz à la mexicaine (Mexican rice),
  57
Riz à l'iranienne au ragoût de lotte
  (Iranian rice with monkfish
  ragout), 246–248

Salad(s)
  black-eyed pea, à la mexicaine,
    215–216
  creamy cucumber, 242
  curly endive, with baked goat
    cheese, 139–140
  endive, apple and walnut, 213
  fennel, lemon, and mushroom,
    217
  lamb's lettuce, 69
  Mexican bean salad, 214–215
  Mexican rice, 205
  Niçoise, hero sandwiches,
    226
  orange and olive salad with
    cumin, 274
  Oriental, with homemade
    buckwheat pasta, 166–167
  peach and apricot, with
    currants, 252
  ravioli and broccoli, 128–129
  sweet and sour peppers and
    avocado, 241
  wild and Italian rice with
    green beans, 80–82
  with tuna tartare, 176–177
  with warm green beans and
    walnuts, 104
Salad dressing, 104, 129, 177,
  213, 217. *See also* Vinaigrette
*Salade aux deux riz et aux haricots
  verts* (salad of wild and
  Italian rice with green
  beans), 80–82

*Salade de fenouil, citron, et
  champignons* (fennel, lemon,
  and mushroom salad), 217
Salade de frisée au chèvre rôti
  (curly endive salad with
  baked goat cheese),
  139–140
Salade de haricots à la mexicaine
  (Mexican bean salad),
  214–215
Salade de mâche (salad of lamb's
  lettuce), 69
*Salade de pêches et abricots aux
  raisins de corinthe* (peach and
  apricot salad with currants),
  252
Salade de raviolis et de brocolis
  (ravioli and broccoli salad),
  128–129
Salade de riz à la mexicaine
  (Mexican rice salad), 205
*Salade d'endives et de pommes aux
  noix* (endive, apple, and
  walnut salad), 213
*Salade d'oranges et de fraises au
  Cointreau* (strawberries and
  oranges with Cointreau),
  154
*Salade d'oranges et d'olives au
  cumin* (orange and olive
  salad with cumin), 274
Salade folle (crazy salad with tuna
  tartare), 176–177
Salade orientale aux pâtés maison
  (Oriental salad with
  homemade buckwheat
  pasta), 166–167
*Salade tiède aux haricots verts et
  aux noix* (salad with warm
  green beans and walnuts),
  104
Salmon, with blini, 218
Salmon trout en papillote,
  244–245

Salsa
   baked fish fillets with, 56
   fresca, 53
Salt cod mousse, 264–266
Sandwiches
   hero, Niçoise salad, 226
Sardines
   grilled, 268–269
   marinated in vinegar, 266–267
Sardines en escabeche (sardines
      marinated in vinegar),
      266–267
Sardines grillées (grilled sardines),
      268–269
Sauce ragoût de champignons
      (mushroom ragout gravy),
      98–99
Sauces
   egg-lemon, for fish, 191
   mushroom, ragout gravy,
      98–99
   salsa fresca, 53, 56
   tomato, 130, 151
   tomato, pureed, 169
   tomato-caper, 178, 182, 267
Sautéed
   fennel and red peppers, 108
   red and yellow peppers, 132
   zucchini and red peppers, 206
Seating plans, 8–10
Sherbet
   peach, with peach garnish,
      58–59
   pineapple-orange-banana mint,
      122–123
   strawberry, 162
   tangerine, 109
Shortbread, almond and
      cornmeal, 110
Small dinner parties, 277–301
Sole, poached fillets of, with
      pureed tomato sauce,
      168–170
Sopa de tortilla, 116–117

Sorbet aux clémentines (tangerine
      sherbet), 109
Sorbet aux fraises (strawberry
      sherbet), 162
*Sorbet aux pêches avec son garniture
      de pêches* (peach sherbet with
      peach garnish), 58–59
Sorbet aux trois fruits à la menthe
      (pineapple-orange-banana
      mint sherbet), 122–123
Sorrel, with potato gratin, 275
Soup(s)
   garlic broth, 117
   Italian-style mussel, 284
   Provençal vegetable, with
      pesto, 70–71
   Provençal-style fish, 141–142
   sopa de tortilla, 116–117
   strawberry, 171
Soupe au pistou (Provençal
      vegetable soup with pesto),
      70–71
Soupe aux fraises (strawberry
      soup), 171
Soupe aux moules à l'italienne
      (Italian-style mussel soup),
      284
Soupe aux tortillas (tortilla soup),
      116–117
Sourdough
   baguettes, 29–30
   country bread, 18–20
   country bread with cornmeal
      and oats or bran, 21
   country bread with raisins, 22
Spinach
   filling, with green lasagne,
      105–107
   pasta, 37
Squid ragout, 270–271
Steve's migas, 202
Strawberry(ies)
   and oranges with Cointreau,
      154

mangos, peaches, and berries
      in sweet white wine, 208
   puree, with crêpes, 299–301
   sherbet, 162
   soup, 171
Stuffed jalapeños, 201
Stuffing, cornbread, 97
Supper Club Chez Martha, 1–5
Sweet and sour
   cherry pickles, 96
   red peppers, 241
   red peppers and avocado,
      salad of, 241
Sweet potato, pumpkin, and
      apple puree, 86
Swordfish with tomato-caper
      sauce, 267

Tangerine sherbet, 109
Tapenade, 67
Tapenade en barquettes (vegetables
      and eggs with olive paste),
      68
Tart
   fig, with green grapes, 74–75
   mushroom, 84–85
   peach, 180
   plum and apricot, 193–194
Tarte au potiron (pumpkin pie),
      100
Tarte aux champignons
      (mushroom tart), 84–85
Tarte aux figues et aux raisins (fig
      tart with green grapes),
      74–75
Tarte aux pecans (pecan pie), 99
Tarte aux pêches (peach tart),
      180
*Tarte aux quetsches, reines-claudes et
      abricots* (mixed plum and
      apricot tart), 193–194
Tea cakes, Texas, 121

Texas
  cornbread, 35
  tea cakes, 121
Tex-Mex food
  buffet, 200
  in Paris, 197–198
Thanksgiving food, 91–100
Thon à la marseillaise (tuna or
  swordfish with tomato-caper
  sauce), 267
Tian de courgettes (zucchini and
  rice mold), 65
Tomates à la purée d'avocat
  (tomato halves stuffed with
  guacamole), 55
Tomates au four (baked
  tomatoes), 192
Tomates au pistou (tomatoes with
  pesto), 225
Tomato(es)
  and garlic, with artichokes,
    243–244
  baked, 192
  -caper sauce, with baked
    whiting, 182–183
  -caper sauce, with cold
    steamed fish fillets, 178–179
  -caper sauce, with tuna (or
    swordfish), 267
  halves stuffed with guacamole,
    55
  sauce, 130, 151
  sauce, pureed, poached fillets
    of sole with, 168–170
  with pesto, 225
Torte, deep-dish eggplant,
  129–132
Torte aux aubergines (deep-dish
  eggplant torte), 129–132
Tortilla(s)
  chips, 44
  homemade, 43–44
  soup, 116–117
Tortillas maison (homemade
  tortillas), 43–44

Trout, salmon, en papillote,
  244–245
Truite saumonée en papillote
  (salmon trout en papillote),
  244–245
Tuna
  tartare with crazy salad,
    176–177
  with tomato-caper sauce, 267
Turbot
  cold poached fillets of, with
    egg-lemon sauce, 190–191
  fillets of, with mussels and
    curry, 285–287
*Turbot ou barbue froid à la sauce
  avgolimone* (cold poached
  fillets of fish with egg-lemon
  sauce), 190–191

Vegetable(s)
  à la grecque, 181–182
  and eggs with olive paste, 68
  and fish platter with garlic
    mayonnaise, 272–273
  artichokes with tomatoes,
    garlic, and Provençal herbs,
    243–244
  baked tomatoes, 192
  black bean frijoles refritos, 54
  black bean nachos, 52–53
  broccoli puree, 83
  cauliflower gratin with goat
    cheese, 288–289
  crudités with goat cheese and
    herb dip, 203
  deep-dish eggplant torte,
    129–132
  green beans vinaigrette,
    148–149
  hummus, 219
  Lulu's vegetable and fish
    platter with garlic
    mayonnaise, 272–273

  mushroom tart, 84–85
  new potatoes en papillote, 179
  pan-fried cucumbers, 58
  pan-fried mushrooms, 153
  pan-fried zucchini with parsley
    butter, 161
  Provençal soup with pesto,
    70–71
  pumpkin, sweet potato, and
    apple puree, 86
  ratatouille, 227–228
  roasted sweet red peppers, 66
  sautéed fennel and red
    peppers, 108
  sautéed red and yellow
    peppers, 132
  sautéed zucchini and red
    peppers, 206
  sweet and sour red peppers,
    241
  tomato halves stuffed with
    guacamole, 55
  tomatoes with pesto, 225
  zucchini and rice mold, 65
Vinaigrette, 81, 148, 215, 216,
  226. *See also* Salad dressing
Vinegar court bouillon, 170

Walnut(s)
  and green beans with salad,
    104
  endive, and apple salad, 213
Watermelon fruit basket,
  207–208
Whiting, baked, with
  tomato-caper sauce,
  182–183
Whole-wheat
  bread, herbed, 30–31
  pasta, 37
  piecrusts, 39–42
Wine
  red, peaches in, 252

suggestions, 11
sweet white, mangoes,
    peaches, and berries in, 208
white, mussels steamed in, 283

Zucchini
    and red peppers, sautéed, in
        bell pepper boats, 206
    and rice mold, 65

pan-fried, with parsley butter,
    161